# Engage!

# Engage!
## Having Conversations About God

Carmen Mayell

FOREWORD BY
Pastor Bob Coy

All proceeds from the sale of this book go to help underwrite the initiatives of The YLDP, Inc. in its mission of supporting committed, Christian university students as they change the world.

Published by The Youth Leadership Development Project, Inc.
25 Seabreeze Avenue, Suite 300
Delray Beach, FL 33483

ISBN: 978-0-578-00371-9

Design and layout by Jonathan Gullery, SelfPublishing.com

Printed in the United States of America

# Contents

Carmen invites you to join him at his blog.
There he will share with you new conversations,
and the insights he gains, as he continues
to engage others concerning a relationship with God.

www.ready2engage.com

Wonder who the author is? Why not become a friend of his on
Facebook? There you can connect with Carmen and ask questions that
may have arisen from your reading. Or share with him how reading
Engage! has helped you! You will find a link to Carmen's Facebook
profile at his blog.

*This book is dedicated to my wife, Betsy;*
*unquestionably one of God's finest gifts to me.*

# Acknowledgments

So many have contributed to the writing of this book that I feel a bit imperiled to begin listing the few my memory will recall, given the two years encompassing this project. I trust my ability to remember the few will not diminish the depth of my gratitude for the many.

My mother and father, who raised and nourished me in the faith from childhood, surely are due inestimable credit and appreciation. Though neither lives today, both are responsible for introducing me to a life lived in relationship with God; eternity will record my gratitude.

I am also deeply indebted to the friendship of Dr. and Mrs. William R. Bright. The spiritual influence they have exerted in my life is a gift from God.

Were it not for the board of The Youth Leadership Development Project, which encouraged and supported my efforts to write, this project would have never been undertaken. Blaine Strickland—chief motivator and critic—is largely responsible for its inspiration. Chuck Wenger, Jim Miller and Bill Stewart kept me "on task" as they encouraged me each step of the way.

The ministry partners of the Youth Leadership Development Project, Inc.—those who so generously give of their prayers and financial resources—have made it possible for this project to become a reality. They have believed in the mission of this organization ("*to support committed Christian students as they change the world*"), even through difficult times. The appreciation I feel for their encouragement is difficult to fully quantify by words alone.

Furthermore, I must express a special word of gratitude to the following individuals who provided substantive input at strategic points in the manuscript's development: Dr. Craig Hazen, Dr. David Kawasaki, and Dr. Charles Ryrie. Apart from their invaluable insights, that which I have written would have proven itself far less beneficial to the ready.

Moreover, my good friend, Les Stobbe—an author in his own right—offered wise counsel at the outset that helped me frame my writing for greatest readability. Karen Myers provided editorial assistance throughout the span of this project; her excellent suggestions greatly influenced the final result. And for the very special investment they made in Engage!, Jerry and Jery Kaufman will never fully know the encouragement they brought Betsy and me.

Also, given the fact that I targeted university students in my writing, it was important to have representatives of that generation evalutate the manuscrpit for relevance and readibility. The following surely know the gratitude I feel for their contribution to this work: Miguel Benitez, Jamie Gardner, Isha Girisgen, Dustin Godwin, Robbie Kleinberg and Jimmy Prehn.

Above all, I am eternally grateful to God, who has revealed Himself through His Son, Jesus, and in an infallible written record, the Bible. The foundation for a faith worthy of confident assent is a pathway to life for the many who are searching for purpose in today's turbulent times.

# Foreword

You can't get away from the fact that we're becoming a society of people who are increasingly isolated and cut off from one another. Look at your own life, and you'll come to the conclusion that personal interaction doesn't happen like it once did.

Just a few years ago, you had to leave the house and rub shoulders with other people if you wanted to do some shopping at the mall, rent a movie, add the latest CD to your collection, or even take a quick trip to the bank.

Now, you can accomplish these and a whole host of other tasks without ever leaving your bedroom. And this trend doesn't show any signs of stopping, as the virtual world continues to seep into every aspect of our lives, even to the point of offering us virtual lives.

Don't get me wrong; I appreciate and utilize technology just as much as the next person. But I also believe that we're losing something in the process of becoming such a cyber-centric society. We're losing the art of engaging other people in conversation, especially conversation that concerns Jesus Christ.

That's why I so appreciate the book you're holding and reading right now. Its purpose is to encourage and equip those who have had their hearts changed by God to engage others in a manner that is effective and perhaps even eternal. This book isn't about "cold calling" people for Christ; it's about initiating conversations that lead to relationships that can develop into friendships.

When you think about it, that's the same way God works. He reached out relationally by sending His Son, and calls us to know Him as our friend. And it's in the context of this friendship that our understanding of truth and love approach their apex.

But none of this happens apart from the act of engagement, without starting the conversation to begin with. The author of this volume has turned that act into an art form that can be practiced and applied in any setting, with anyone, at any time.

When we consider the fact that Jesus engaged people from every strata of society, from an ostracized Samaritan woman to a wealthy man named Zacchaeus, the importance of a book like this becomes all the more obvious, particularly in light of the tendency (and temptation) to be less and less involved with other people.

God engaged us, because He has a heart to help those who are hurting and in need of the healing that can only come from Him. If we're rightly connected to His heart … so will we.

Until the whole world hears,

Bob Coy, Senior Pastor
Calvary Chapel Ft. Lauderdale
Ft. Lauderdale, Florida

# Preface

## Why You May *Not* Want to Buy This Book

If you have decided to pick up this volume, wanting to have those "silver bullet" answers for your friends' many questions about the Christian faith, you will undoubtedly be disappointed. This book is not about how to spar with others as much as it is how to enjoy conversing with those for whom you care on the most important matter of life—having a relationship with the eternal God.

This is not a book for those wanting to nail that skeptical person to the wall. But it may help free you up a bit to really get to know that person and, in the process, challenge him or her to consider why belief in God and His Son, Jesus, may actually be quite a rational decision.

It has been my experience that so many of those who seemingly oppose the Christian faith do so for reasons that have little to do with the things Jesus said and did. More often than not, they have been disenfranchised by organized religion, disenchanted with particular Christian viewpoints (whether political or otherwise), or completely disgusted by the simplistic answers we, as Christians, sometimes so casually lay out for life's toughest questions.

For some, the choice of a worldview has more to do with the affirmation of a particular lifestyle than anything else. They want to live a certain way; thus, they choose to hold to an accommodating belief system.

And for others, the worldview they affirm is, quite simply, the only one they have ever known.

The purpose of this book is to help you engage with—rather than react to—people who so often know nothing of the hope and acceptance offered in a relationship with God through His Son. It is to serve as a guide, particularly for the Christian student, to help navigate the often tricky waters of having conversations about God in the context of a meaningful friendship.

If you are willing to *engage*, then I encourage you to read on!

## How to Read This Book

This book has been designed to help encourage the reader to take the first step in sharing his or her faith in Christ. Rather than telling, however, the approach begins by asking. By asking pertinent questions in a straightforward manner, it is the author's experience that conversations about God and His Son, Jesus Christ, can be engaged in virtually any setting and with anyone who is willing to think seriously about life and its meaning.

The conversations you read at the beginning of the book are real. The people are real. The circumstances presented are real. And the responses given are real and have been conveyed as accurately as the author's memory permits.

During the conversations (including the *faux* conversation between Ryan and Lisa) various key questions are asked and illustrations given. To get the most out of *Engage!*, it is suggested that the reader use two highlighter markers of different colors. One color should be used to highlight the questions the author uses to initiate and continue discussion; the other to highlight the illustrations he gives. Though some of the illustrations the author uses may be of a more personal nature, and thus not as easily adapted to conversations that the reader may have, even they can help the reader consider similar illustrations from his or her own experience.

The final major section of *Engage!* essentially deals with the basis of belief. Though not by any means exhaustive, the footnoting is purposefully quite extensive so the reader can explore additional resources in particular areas of interest. It is the author's conviction that one will not engage others in conversations about God and/or Christ unless he or she is convinced that Christianity is unique among world religions and uniquely defensible.

# SECTION I

## Conversations About God

CHAPTER 1

# Engaging the Discussion:
# Two Key Questions

I've never enjoyed offending a friend, and I assume you don't either. From all that I can tell, friendship is a gift from God to be highly valued.

Yet it seems that so many of the techniques suggested to help one share his or her faith in Christ seem awkward at best or downright confrontational at worst. Though many of the approaches suggested for sharing the Christian message may be used effectively at shopping malls and sidewalks, they just don't "play well" in situations involving people whose friendships we've come to enjoy and value. As a result, it seems better simply to keep a friendship by not sharing Christ than to share Christ and put a valued relationship at risk.

But is that the way it has to be?

For several years, this was my struggle. It was not that I was one of those who deferred to the "not going to risk a friendship by sharing my faith" mode. In fact, virtually all of my friends knew I was a Christian. But when it came to initiating conversations with others, I was at a loss to know what to do. And I observed that others—including young adults in high school and college— were challenged similarly.

Furthermore, though the majority of my friends knew I was a follower of Jesus Christ, surely some of them could not clearly convey what that really meant. To many, being a follower of Christ entailed going to church and choosing a particular lifestyle devoid of a lot of the things they really enjoyed.

So how can I engage both friend and acquaintance with meaningful conversation concerning the person of Jesus Christ?

Is there a way to do this without creating immediate offense?

Is there a way to initiate such conversation in a manner that creates discussion rather than reaction?

Is there a way to engage people in order to present the claims of Christ while laying a credible foundation for the rationality of belief in God?

Several years ago, as I had been thinking and praying and wrestling about this very matter, it occurred to me that there were two basic and essential questions in life. Your answer to these fundamentally important questions will virtually govern how you view life and how you live it. Indeed, your answer to these two questions will address not only what you think about God but set the foundation for your understanding of life, as well as the ethics and morals by which you live it.

These two questions are:


1.   "Is there a God?"

2.   "If there is a God, can He be known?"


Though these two questions are composed of fewer than 15 words, total, history records humanity's attempt to provide answers to them from the earliest of times. A society and the people within that society are, in large part, defined by the answers they provide to these questions.

I have asked these questions for the past three years of acquaintances, waiters and waitresses, business professionals, and high school and university students. What I have discovered is that people actually enjoy answering the questions! Their answers provide the perfect opportunity for me to explore with them what it means to know God personally through His Son, Jesus Christ.

Now, don't let me mislead you. The questions do not always eventuate into a full-blown Gospel presentation. Yes, I always hope and pray for that. But that just isn't the way it works. Sometimes God has other plans, and more often than not, those plans include using other believers—in other places at other times— to complete the conversation.

I like to consider myself one piece in a multidimensional puzzle. Sometimes I am the last piece—the one that completes the picture (thus experiencing the joy of seeing someone place his or her trust in Christ)—and sometimes I am the first piece (or a very early piece). And sometimes I may contribute a few pieces along the path. The part I play in the life of a person is a mystery that God often chooses not to reveal.

It is my role to simply be faithful and available.

And that is *your* role, too!

Yes, it is my role and yours to develop relationships with those who do not yet believe. Who can read the Gospels and not discover a Jesus who engaged individuals and befriended the multitudes? How can one escape notice of the criticism leveled by the religious leaders of Jesus's day of His "too close association" with those less than religious (e.g., tax collectors, prostitutes, you name it!)? Indeed, Jesus chose to associate with the very ones for whom He came to give His life.

And that is what this book is about. It is about living this life for Christ and for others. It is about being intentional in our relationships with people as we search for opportunity to engage them on the most critical issue of life. Indeed, it is about helping you to have the privilege of, someday, leading a friend into the most significant of all relationships—a relationship with the eternal God.

# CHAPTER 2

# Engaging the Atheist: "I Don't Believe in God."

Yesterday I was eating lunch at one of my favorite restaurants. One of the highlights of any day is engaging students in faith-related discussions. Although I still enjoy learning, my age betrays the fact my "official" years as a student have long since passed. Thus, I have to work at finding places where students congregate. One of those places is the local restaurant scene. The wait staff are typically young men and women in their teens and twenties. Some are in school, some are not, but they are all looking to make the most of life.

Joe is a twenty-something whose accent easily gives away his New Jersey roots. I had been meaning to talk to Joe for some time, and yesterday I had the opportunity. At the end of lunch, and after we had conversed a bit about his family background, I queried, "Joe, I would like to ask you a couple of questions. I would like to suggest that they are two of life's most fundamentally-important questions: Is there a God? and, if so, Is He able to be known? What do you think?"

Almost immediately, he responded, "I'm really not very big on religion. Though my mom raised me to go to church, my dad didn't have much to do with it. I've also seen some things in life that have pretty much caused me to question God's existence outright."

Now, let me pause for a moment and tell you forthrightly that there was a time when even the thought of having to converse with one who did not believe in God—an atheist[1]—created an internal angst. It was not that I disliked such a person; it was that I was afraid they would want to debate me on the matter and I wasn't sure how I would fare.

Today, however, through thoughtful study and lots of prayer I'm much more confident in my faith and enjoy sharing it even with those who claim to be atheists. In fact, when one claims to be an atheist (or suggests that position as did Joe), I simply comment, "Thanks for your honesty." Why? I want a person to know that his or her disbelief does not end my desire to continue discussing the matter. Today, I even have a few friends who claim not to believe…praying that, someday, they will not only come to believe there is a God but also affirm faith in the person of Jesus Christ as a result of the illuminating work of God's Spirit.

There is something I have come to realize that has helped me gain a bit of perspective on this matter—particularly as it relates to students who profess an atheistic philosophy of life—and which may prove to be helpful to you as well. Many students hold an atheistic philosophy of life more by *default*, due to the philosophical climate of the university, rather than deep-seated convictions. The consensus of many universities seems to be that only those things verifiable through scientific inquiry can be known as assuredly true or real. Interestingly, on the other hand, the growing postmodern movement within the university would suggest that even the results of scientific inquiry are tainted by the "cultural lenses" we all wear; in effect few things, if any, can be known with absolute certainty.

What I really want to communicate to you, even at this very early point, is the vital importance of understanding *why* a person believes what they do—*whatever* that belief may be. By understanding the "why" you are in a better position to understand the "who." And when you understand who a person is, you have a greater ability to engage that individual in more substantive and potentially life-transforming conversation. Regardless of the label one wears, I want to know *why* that person has arrived at the position he or she holds. Then, on that basis, conversation—*real* conversation—can ensue.

So, with an atheist, I continue by asking, "Tell me … what have you discovered that leads you to assert that God does not exist?" In Joe's case, however, I wasn't required to ask this question; he made it clear from the outset why he did not believe.

In fact, Joe's response is typical of those who have arrived at an atheistic worldview because of their interaction with the realities of life. Yet, what is a *worldview*? Christian philosopher Norman Geisler defines *worldview* as "a way of viewing or interpreting all of reality. It is an interpretive framework through which or by which one makes sense out of the data of life and the world."[2]

In Joe's case, personal experience had caused him to question the reality of God's existence. During our brief conversation that day, he went on to tell me about a very good friend of his who had recently committed suicide motivated by the tremendous suffering resulting from cancer. Furthermore, he shared with me a bit of his own background which contained ample evidence of social injustices and family issues that would cause most to question whether or not a God truly existed or, at the very least, indict Him for His seeming indifference.

The problem of pain and suffering—and the evil actions of others that often serve as the cause—are among the most difficult questions with which you will ever deal. There are many in our world, perhaps Joe being one, who are inclined to assert that because of such pervasive evil, God either must be less than sovereign (in absolute control), or He is not all-knowing and acts of evil occur without His prior knowledge. The atheist, for example, will often assert that the presence of horrific evil is one more proof to question the existence of God. "Since evil exists," he reasons, "and since God is presumed to be all-powerful and good, then either God is not good or He is not all-powerful or, quite possibly, there is no God at all."

Joe's approach to life, however, was more straightforward than philosophical. I knew his questioning was sincere and felt it important to engage him on this basis. "So, Joe, the big question in your mind is that if God really exists, then where was He when your friend needed Him? Does that sound right?"

"Exactly," Joe responded very thoughtfully.

Realizing that the basis for Joe's conclusion stemmed from the tragic death of one of his best friends, I had to proceed carefully.

"If I may, Joe, let me suggest something for your consideration. If all humans are a chance collection of atoms, then what is this thing we value called friendship? Why do we even bother? Death is a reality, regardless how it plays itself out, so what's the big deal? Yet we do value relationships, even as you valued your relationship with your friend who took his life. And all of us grieve such as a tremendous loss."

"Yeah, I see what you mean," he agreed. "Why *do we* value life and relationship so much if we owe nothing more to our existence than chance?"

Joe was beginning to resonate with my reasoning. Indeed, the depth to which we value the relationships in this life—relationships that transcend the human drive to fight, feed, flee, and reproduce in order to ensure the continuance of the species—suggests something deeper. Nothing in the human experience has been discovered to adequately replace meaningful, human relationship. When it is missing, people go to great extent to search for it … and some go to the grave early because they fail to have it satisfied.

In essence, Joe had asked himself the ever-present "Why?" questions: "Why *my* friend?," "Why *this* disease?," "Why *now*?," and had come up empty. Though I understood his questioning, I chose not to follow that particular path. Let's face it; any answer I would have proffered would have seemed hollow given the relationship involved between Joe and his best friend. Furthermore, how could I presume to know the answers to such questions?

Though Joe's questioning was honest and, therefore, required a response, it was equally as important that my answer took into consideration what he had recently experienced—the death of his closest friend. And that is why I pointed to the value of human relationship. It was the context of the particular conversation that elicited my particular response. It was the perfect opportunity to suggest that the very matter most troubling to him—the loss of his friend—was perhaps an indication that we, as humans, are somehow very different than all other species of animal life. Eventually, I would want to direct Joe to consider the plausibility of inferring from such a human quality that, rather than we having been created by blind, mindless chance, it would be even more rational to see the handiwork of a personal God.

I realized, however, that this would likely be my first conversation with Joe. I had laid the groundwork, and God would now have to provide additional opportunity.

Even at this very early stage of our conversation, however, I wanted Joe to realize that removing God from the equation of life because of evil, or pain and suffering, only makes the problem less understandable and even more difficult to explain. Though, with Joe, no actual or perceived evil act was at the root of his friend's suffering, evil and pain are often linked by a cause and effect relationship.

What *is* the result then if one chooses to remove God from life's equation because of pervasive evil? It is simply this: if there is no God, then how can one assert that something is evil? In other words, by whose standard do I determine something to be wrong?

Though some might contend that the standards of good and evil primarily find their root in our species' drive to survive (i.e., it is wrong to murder because it undermines the fundamental propensity of the species to ensure its continuance), this position fails to address the problem as to *why* such things occur in the first place. *Why* is it, for example, that some work to eliminate others of the *same* species? *Why* is it that even among peoples of the same race (such as in Sudan, Vietnam, China, and Cambodia), we see such pervasive, even genocidal, acts of evil perpetrated? Moreover, if the human species has this built-in drive to survive, then from where do these horrific and pervasive acts of destruction come?

But such a position also fails at another point. Why is it that the pain and suffering of *others* so often affect *me*—the one not suffering? To suggest that the human species has developed its habits and attitudes simply in response to the innate drive to survive fails to address the deep emotion we feel for those who become the objects of brutality or, as in Joe's case, the inner pain we experience when we see someone for whom we care suffer so needlessly.

No, when I hear of such things, I do not necessarily feel a sense of loss for the species as a whole; I experience a sense of grief for families who have lost loved ones, for fathers who have lost daughters, for children who have been robbed of their parents' love and, for friends who have lost their closest friends. Why did I, for example, bother to empathize with Joe?

It is for such reasons that the atheistic (or naturalistic[3]) worldview fails to adequately answer some of the fundamental questions we have just considered. Its response is really more descriptive than prescriptive. It observes that which is, and then tells us that it is without telling us why it is or why it should be any different. Given its fundamental premise that a species has the built-in drive to ensure its own survival, it cannot adequately explain why evil occurs with such great frequency in the human species—one of the most advanced of all. And, it definitely has difficulty suggesting a plausible response to the importance all place on meaningful relationship. Let's face it; all other species of animals carry on quite exquisitely without it—the procreation of progeny being the sole basis of "relationship."

Indeed, the presence and practice of evil affects us, as well as the people whose friendships we value so highly. And when it surfaces with such personal impact, we detest it vigorously. Indeed, *all* detest it.

Most of those with whom you speak about the problem of evil, pain, and suffering have, at some point, attempted to reconcile the belief in an all-powerful God, while living in a world where evil often seems to win. Indeed, could there be a bigger picture . . . even when it involves the death of one of our closest friends?

Thus in my conversations I've often asked the question, "Is it possible that evil, as well as the pain and suffering that so often result, have some *positive* benefit?" Though no one likes pain, most recognize pain does serve some kind of purpose ... and a positive one at that. Without pain, minor infections could turn into major infections, and a broken rib left unattended (because of the absence of pain) could puncture a lung, leading to death.

Could we infer from this illustration an analogy that would help us gain perspective as to why, perhaps, God allows evil and its results to persist? Let me provide an example very close to home:

My mom was a wonderful woman. In her early eighties, she developed dementia. In many ways the dementia kept her from constantly focusing on the aches and pains of growing old. For example, I might know that her knee was bothering her because she would emit a quiet groan as she walked. Then, almost as quickly as she recognized the pain, her mind was on to another matter! In this way, dementia was a friend.

Near the end of her life, my mom spent a few days in the hospital. We didn't realize, however, that she had contracted a serious internal infection during her stay. Since she did not have the mental capacity to tell us of her discomfort, the infection developed undetected until it had spread throughout her entire body. A few days later, she died.

So let me ask you: Could we not consider the importance of pain in warning of infection potentially analogous to the painful effects of evil in alerting us to a problem in the human experience? In other words, if not for the presence of evil, how would we know that something was seriously wrong with the human race?

You might counter, "Well, couldn't God have made the world so there was no evil with which to contend?" In fact, the Bible does tell us that God created the world *without* evil—that His creation was good. He did not, however, choose to create it without *the potential* for evil, in that He granted humanity the ability to act freely. Intrinsic within the concept of a relationship is the idea that both parties choose contact and communication with each other. Thus, it is difficult to understand how He might have removed the potential for evil without removing free will and, henceforth, the foundation for relationship which, according to the Bible, He values very highly.

But let's assume that God could have at least created a world in which the *effects* of evil were negligible; that the result of humanity's rebellion against Him was not as egregious as we observe in our experience. Perhaps He could have even designed the world so that there was covetousness but no stealing; pride that did not result in arrogance or prejudice; and hatred without anger or hostility. Indeed, He could have created the great "theme park" of life—not the real situation but surely something a bit more palatable.

Though the results would seem more pleasurable, the end would be disastrous. Given the fact of our rebellion and disobedience, we could not have contact and communication with Him—either currently or ultimately. The righteous character of God cannot be nullified or marginalized through His uncaring acceptance of those who disobey and rebel.

Let's face it: would you or I say that God is just if He allowed a Hitler, a serial killer, or even a greedy corporate executive who had stolen his employees' retirement funds to come into His presence with impunity? And where do you draw the line? Indeed, each of us would have his or her own standard of justice!

Consider this: *if man were free to be good without being just, then man would be free to be just without being good.*

The point is clear: it would not be a merciful thing for God to remove the effects of evil for our enjoyment now, only to be separated from Him for eternity; it would be an act of great injustice. And few would suggest that it would be better to be controlled by God in our every thought and action, rather than to be free and possess the ability to have a true relationship with Him.

Though the atheist says God does not exist, it is vitally important for you and me to help our friends realize that to eliminate a Creator from the equation of life—a Supreme Being to whom we will all give account—leaves some very important questions unanswered. By asking questions, our aim is to help them understand the inconsistencies in their particular position and, even more importantly, understand why belief in God is rational. And that's my desire for Joe.

# *Notes*

[1] It is one thing to say one is an agnostic—literally meaning "without knowledge" and generally applied to one who has assumed the position that God's existence lies outside the realm of factual inquiry. (Thomas Huxley, who coined the term, posited that scientific inquiry was the only way to know something with certitude.) It is quite another to affirm being an atheist—literally meaning "no God" and understood as one who believes, beyond doubt, that God does not exist. The one taking this label suggests that he or she has "inquired" and the evidence for God was sufficiently compelling to the contrary.

[2] Norman Geisler and William D. Watkins. *Perspectives: Understanding and Evaluating Today's World Views* (San Bernardino, CA: Here's Life Publishers, 1984), 11. For one of the classic texts on worldviews see *The Universe Next Door* by James W. Sire (Downers Grove, IL: InterVarsity Press, 4th ed, 2004).

[3] The naturalistic worldview is the "seedbed" of atheism. The naturalistic worldview assumes that nothing exists outside the world of matter. There is no spiritual realm, or if there is, it is ethereal and nonverifiable. The universe has always existed. Although science, today, generally accepts that the universe had a beginning, this worldview rejects any role of divine intelligence or initiative in that beginning.

CHAPTER 3

# Engaging the Agnostic: "I'm Not Sure if There Is a God."

I was attending a student evangelism and leadership development conference in Wichita, Kansas, and our team had decided to have lunch at a local sandwich shop. Two university-aged girls were taking the orders behind the counter, and one of them complimented me on the shirt I was wearing. This led to a brief conversation that ultimately led her to ask, "So what are you doing in Wichita?"

Now, there were people—*hungry* people—standing behind me in line, but the question obviously begged a response (even if my response *was* a little more than she might have expected).

"I'm here at a conference of Christian students," I answered. "We are helping them explore the viability of their faith—helping them think through answers to important questions, such as 'Why is Christianity unique among world religions?' and 'Is Jesus Christ really who He claimed to be?' The students also learn there are two key questions in life: 'Is there a God?' and if so, 'Is He knowable?'"

By this point I knew that I was going to have to ask these two young ladies behind the counter what they thought about the questions, but first I needed to get their names—I always like to address those I'm engaging by name. "So," I continued, "my name's Carmen. What are your names?"

"I'm Lisa," one responded; the other followed quickly with "And I'm Natalie."

By now I could almost feel those behind me pressing forward, but still, I continued. "So, what about those two questions? 'Is there a God?' And *if so,*

'Is He knowable? Is one able to have contact and communication with Him?' What do you think?"

I'll never forget their text-message-type responses. Lisa answered first: "Yes, and yes."

Natalie's response, however, was different: "Yes, and I'm not sure." She went on to explain, "I'm a biology major," implying that her doubt had to do with the scientific aspect—if evolution were true, then perhaps God was unnecessary in life's equation.

Rather than engage her in the evolution versus creation debate, I took a step back. "The big question is," I said, "from where did living matter come? Even if you assume the Big Bang, you must answer the question: From where did that infinitesimally small singularity of time, space, matter, and energy originate? Did it just happen?"

She paused, looked at me, and said simply, "I see what you mean."

Some people live life unsure of God's existence. In fact, many of them think they have legitimate reasons for not believing in God. We just need to inform them that there are *rational reasons* to believe God exists. And this process begins by asking good questions.

Something important can be garnered from my conversation with Natalie: You do not have to be an expert *in* a particular field of study to ask a good question *about* that field. I am not a biologist, astronomer, or scientist of any kind. But I do know that science has never been able to create something from nothing. Furthermore, is it rational to contend that living matter just arrived on the scene? Or that matter and energy, time, and space just appeared? This pursuit goes beyond the field of science, because science studies relationships between things that are, not things that are not.

Logical questions and/or observations about something are always in order. God can use logical questions and observations as a way to cause people to more carefully evaluate their belief systems. It has always amazed me how many people hold a particular belief but have never asked basic questions that are pertinent to that system of thought.

When asking questions of others, I encourage you to do so sincerely. Remember, you are attempting to help the person evaluate the merits of his or her worldview, so do so *gently*. Your goal is not to win a debate but to encourage that individual to explore the rationality of belief in God. Ultimately, it is to help him or her see that God has made provision to know Him through His Son, Jesus.

Talking with an agnostic is one of a Christian's great privileges. Essentially, if someone says "I don't know if there is a God," one of your first questions likely will be: "If I could give you evidence that God exists and that He is able to be known, would you be interested?"

Some agnostics will strongly defend their position of ignorance (remember, the word *agnostic* has its root in a Greek word, meaning "without knowledge"). Others, however, are sincere in the statement of who they are—they realize they do not know and will likely be interested in any input you might have. For the individual who indicates interest in evidence that God exists, I would then ask: "Have you ever considered the person of Jesus Christ and the claims He made about what role He plays in the equation of knowing God?"

I then simply share Christ, sometimes with a concise tract, other times writing out a few key points, with corresponding verses, on a napkin or piece of notebook paper. *There is no need to anticipate questions that have yet to be asked. Allow God to speak to the person's heart through the truth of the Gospel.*

And so it was in the lunch line at the sandwich shop in Wichita. The occasion did not allow further conversation with Lisa and Natalie, so I handed them both a small tract I often carry (*Connecting with God* by Campus Crusade for Christ) and left them with these final words: "This booklet is not about a particular church or religion. It is about a relationship with God. If what Jesus said is true—that He came to reveal God to us and how to know Him—then there is no other story like it in all of history."

Though that was my last contact with Lisa and Natalie, I am quite confident it was just one piece in the puzzle of God's working in their lives. What a great privilege God has allowed us to participate with Him in communicating His truth to the world in which we live. And you can have this privilege too.

CHAPTER 4

# Engaging the Skeptic: "I Don't Think So. There Seems to Be Little Evidence for God's Existence."

Atheists solidly affirm there is no God. The agnostic says, "I do not know if there is a God." The skeptic, however, is somewhere in between. It is the skeptic's assumption that evidence which suggests the existence of God is lacking or that (ala Hume) it is impossible to ascertain the existence of the supernatural via the natural.

As Christians, it is admittedly difficult for us to understand this perspective. We look around us and see a world of marvelous beauty and complexity and therein see God's hand. We contemplate the world in which we live, think about deep matters, and believe that the ability to reason is due to the fact we are created in God's image. We listen to news reports from around the world from virtually every culture, and we see the evil perpetrated by humanity and realize that evil is identifiable because there is a moral Law Giver.

But not everyone views the world as we do.

Remember, the fundamental assumption of individuals raised apart from Christ in our culture is that we are here by sheer chance (plus genetic mutation plus natural selection plus time). It is not that they are "against us" or oppose our beliefs; it's just that this assumption is oftentimes the only perspective they know. In many cases they have not considered the idea that another rational possibility exists.

We want to help them see differently. We need to challenge their current position through some good questions. Remember: questions are key! And it is through the use of excellent questions that God's Spirit can use your explanation of the facts to present the Gospel.

37

My method of question-asking was recently tested in a conversation I had with a leading business executive. His name is Jorge, and I had invited him and his wife to a luncheon for professional adults at which one of my favorite speakers, Dr. Craig Hazen, would be presenting a rational defense for faith in God through His Son, Jesus. Though gracious in his manner, Jorge said, "Quite honestly, [understanding more about God] is not something my wife or I consider that important right now."

A couple weeks later, at a friend's wedding, Jorge and I had a conversation that I recall most vividly. I really do try and resist having conversations that may become a bit "testy" on such occasions, but a good conversation with one who is not sure about the existence and / or relevance of God is difficult to resist, especially when God seems to set the stage.

And that's where three of our mutual friends (including the groom) played primary roles. One by one, these three friends approached Jorge and said something such as, "Jorge, you really need to listen to what Carmen says"—implying, of course, the whole "God thing." Now, that was the last kind of introduction I wanted. I prefer a low-key, nonconfrontational conversation over a "put the guy on the spot" kind, but it was with the latter that our talk began.

As I asked Jorge the two questions, he retorted that he had been turned off of the whole religion thing through architectural work he had conducted with churches. He couldn't understand how one could claim to follow God and then act no differently than those who didn't. (A church or two had evidently ripped him off financially.)

On any given day, I won't even respond to this "reason" for a lack of belief. Frankly, sometimes it seems the person with whom I am conversing is a bit disingenuous, offering the existence of hypocrites as the stellar reason for his unbelief. And, sometimes, I just silently wish for a few more faithful agnostics than some of the faithless Christians who cross my path—only adding more fuel to the fire of one, like Jorge, who is looking for reasons *not* to believe.

In this particular instance, I chose to move ahead after saying, "Yeah, I've known a few hypocrites myself." I wanted to get to the crux of the matter by suggesting several compelling reasons why one *should* consider God's existence.

So I proceeded: "Jorge, do you mind if I give you several reasons why I *do* believe it is at least rational to consider the existence of God?"

Seeking permission allows a conversation to be engaged on "equal terms."

It also sets the tone for it to be a *conversation*, not some kind of lead-in to a prepared presentation. If the person doesn't want to hear you out, then just stop. You've already accomplished something important by having that person hear the reasoning behind their own belief system.

You will be amazed by the number of people who have adopted an entire worldview or philosophy based on one or two life experiences, the input of a single professor, or even in reaction to their heritage or, as in Jorge's case, hypocritical church leaders (an important reminder for all Christians to *consistently* live as Christ). Many there are, too, who base their lives on a philosophy of life that remains unquestioned (and unevaluated) for the duration of their lives.

So often I have discovered that many of the skeptics whom you and I meet and know have never been personally presented rational evidences suggesting God's existence. Thus a brief but well-articulated overview of some of the evidence can be a good starting point. We simply want to adjust our friends' perspective a bit by helping them understand that the Christian faith is not a faith rooted in experience alone; it is based, firstly, on evidence, and the veracity of the conclusions deduced are validated in the realm of experience.

Though going into lengthy and extraneous detail would not (at least at this point in Jorge's and my relationship) further my objective of continuing conversation with Jorge, laying out some fundamental reasons as to why theism has validity does have its place and so was the case here. Jorge needed to be challenged in his assumption that belief in God was for those who did not think.

"Jorge," I continued, "the evidences I find for God lie in several areas. First, there is the area of cosmology—the beginning of the earth and its universe. From where did that infinitely dense concentration of time, space, matter and energy first originate? I just find it difficult to believe that something came from nothing; and that these fundamental constituents of the universe have come to possess such order by themselves and without any external influence or direction.

"Secondly, I think of the area of biology. There are so many facets of the body that consist of parts that have little or no significance apart from the whole. Take the eye for example. What significance do the rods and cones have apart from the eye's function of *seeing*? Why would natural selection have chosen such parts given the fact that those parts possess no known value apart from the role they play in the function of the eye as a whole? It is almost as though natural selection had the idea of seeing in order for it to choose.

"Thirdly, I find evidence in the area of psychology. Why is it we have this concept of self wherein we think thoughts about ourselves and in comparison to the 'selfness' of others? And why do we place such value on personal significance if, indeed, we assume that the sole purpose for our existence is the furtherance of the species on this planet?

"Fourthly, take the field of sociology, especially as it relates to morality. Why do we intrinsically know some things to be good or right and others to be bad or evil? From where does pervasive evil come? And from where does this inherent standard of good and evil arise?

"Finally, in the area of philosophy, why do we even waste our time talking about this? I find it strange to think that so many people discuss and argue and write—and have throughout the centuries—about that which makes little difference to whether we eat or sleep or live or die. There seems to be inherent within humanity this search for something deeper, something more in life. I would like to suggest that it is because God created us for greater purposes than simply to feed and breed, fight or flee.

"Do any of the reasons I've given resonate with you, Jorge?"

"I just want *tangible* evidence that God exists," came his solemn reply.

Realizing I obviously hadn't made the headway I'd hoped for, I decided to focus in on one particular point: the existence of evil. Though there are many who appeal to evil's existence as a basis for dismissing God's existence, I think it offers an excellent reason for the existence of a Supreme Being who, by His nature, is good. Otherwise, why should one assume that evil is a departure from the norm, rather than the norm itself? And could we not just as easily relegate acts of evil to the evolutionary category of "survival of the fittest?"

So I asked, "Jorge, don't you think that the existence of evil, and our abhorrence of it, at least *suggests* the existence of some kind of divine being who possesses ultimate goodness—an understanding of which allows to see evil for what it is?"

"No," Jorge responded, almost without emotion.

"So, it wouldn't really matter to you if someone ripped you off in another business deal?" I questioned, deciding to dig a bit more deeply.

Once again, he gave his expressionless answer: "No."

I thought I would go for the jugular. "What if I smacked you in the face right now?" "Not really."

I determined that Jorge was either not being honest in his responses or, as he'd previously mentioned, belief in God was just not that important to him.

Looking back on that conversation, I see that it might have been better to ask a very telling question up front: *"If I could offer some rational reasons suggestive of God's existence, would you be interested?"*

This would have been the better conversation starter with Jorge on that evening. Sometimes, though, God, or knowledge of Him, just isn't of much importance to the skeptic—either because of simply a lack of interest or because of a presupposition that disallows evidence in the natural realm to point to the supernatural. Though I do commend Jorge for his honesty, I fear for his destiny. My sincere prayer is that God will do His work of grace by helping Jorge understand why belief in the God is an issue deserving serious consideration.

But let's assume that Jorge had responded to what I had laid out by saying something like, "You know, I had never thought about it like that before." Then, if appropriate, I would have continued by asking a couple of final questions: "Don't you think it is a bit unusual that we should be having this conversation if we are all here simply by chance? I mean, if all we are is a random compilation of atoms, what leads humans to engage in these kinds of conversations? How do conversations about philosophy or beauty or love really advance the continuation of the species?"

What's the point of my question? Simply this: If we are products of the evolutionary process, then that process is a random process. It is purely a matter of incredible luck that we have developed. It is a process based on mutation, plus natural selection, plus time alone. So, if we are simply products of natural processes, why do we seek to understand things that lie outside the realm of the natural? Why, when we live in a world navigated by touch, taste, smell, hearing, and sight, do we seek anything more?

Isn't it really the other dimensions of life that make life so wonderful? Can you imagine a world without love, without hope, without anticipation, without trust? What about a world where we simply ate, slept, and worked? Every other species of animal does exactly that. Everything is related just to survival. The human species is far and beyond any other and in ways that are difficult to explain, if we buy the "here only by chance" explanation.

Recently, I was listening to a series of talks presented by Ravi Zacharias at Ohio State University. Dr. Zacharias is a brilliant defender of the faith. He summed up the important questions that must be answered by any philosophy.

Those questions are *origin*, *meaning*, *morality*, and *destiny*. Any philosophy of life must address those four essential points.

It occurs to me that the skeptic cannot answer even one of those points. He leaves the explanation for man's origin as unknowable. He cannot derive from his skepticism a reason for significant meaning in life or an answer to the question of the why of morality. And, by virtue of the fact that he likely buys the notion that life arose by chance, he must conclude, likewise, that his destiny is subject to the same arbiter.

Yet if we are simply the products of mindless chance, then why is it we hope for more in this life? Why do we spend so much time talking, writing, debating, and thinking about meaning and purpose in life? It seems that between the two bookends of nothingness, there is this "somethingness" that calls to us.

Indeed, life is far more. And you and I have, in Christ, the answer to each one of those categories above. Someday, I pray, it will be my privilege to share that message of ultimate meaning with Jorge, even as you will have the opportunity to do the same with whomever God brings into your life.

It was only one week following my conversation with Jorge that over 30 students and faculty were gunned down on the campus of Virginia Tech University. I have often wondered if Jorge's casual interest in the whole God question was not severely challenged by that horrific incident. If there is no God, then there cannot be an *ultimate* authority other than that created by the power-brokers of a society and "might makes right" will serve as sufficient justification in any human relationship.

# CHAPTER 5

# Engaging the Postmodernist: "Isn't It Just a Matter of What You Believe?"

Melissa was 15—and a very sharp fifteen-year-old at that. Her dad was of Caribbean island descent; her mom was Chinese. He was from a Catholic background; she was from a culture entrenched in Buddhist philosophy. When they eventually had Melissa, they mutually decided it would be best to raise her as a Catholic.

Our family first met Melissa and her family during a Thanksgiving weekend with some friends from upstate New York. Our conversation about spiritual matters really began on Thanksgiving evening, when I handed Melissa a copy of a new magazine our organization had just produced. One of the articles was titled "Jesus or Buddha? Who Cares?"

On the day following Thanksgiving, we all decided to take a trip into New York City to see the sights. As we walked from Chinatown on the way to the World Trade Center memorial area, we passed a Buddhist temple, and Melissa made the seemingly innocuous comment, "That's where my grandmother's funeral was held. I'll never do that again."

I have learned to listen "between the lines" in my conversations with others. So often, it is that which is left unsaid that opens the door to greater understanding and further conversation. It seemed clear from Melissa's comment that her grandmother's funeral was a very negative experience.

I asked, "Melissa, was your grandmother's funeral the first funeral you attended of a family member?"

She responded in the affirmative.

"That can be a pretty tough time," I told her. "My grandmother's funeral, though many years ago, was an occasion I'll never forget either." It now seemed

evident to me that this was an opportunity for a deeper conversation about spiritual matters. So, I proceeded: "Melissa, have you come to a point where you
have been able to reconcile the differences between your Catholic/Christian
background and your Buddhist background?"

"Isn't it just a matter of what you choose to believe?" she asked.

Her response didn't surprise me; students, in particular, consider one's religious belief simply a matter of choice. It has little to do with a consideration
of the merits of the belief system. It is a "You like a latte and I like café mocha"
kind of scenario. At the end of the day you both had coffee; just different variations of the same drink.

In order for my conversation with Melissa to continue to the next level, I
realized it would be essential for me to go deeper by comparing and contrasting
the fundamental differences between the worldviews of Buddhism and
Christianity. And so I continued accordingly.

"Melissa, as you know, in the Eastern worldview represented by Buddhism,
we are one with the universe. A personal God is not known, and inquiry into
such is deemed futile or unnecessary. Furthermore, that which one perceives
to be 'real' is a guise; true Reality exists beyond the realm of our senses or the
analysis of reason. That's why Buddhist monks seek to deny the physical desires
of life in their pursuit of 'enlightenment'—that is, awareness of the realization
of their unity with the Void which is the essence of all that is."

I then continued by distinguishing the particulars of the Christian
worldview.

"On the other hand, Melissa, you have the Christian worldview which
affirms the existence of a personal God who is *distinct* from the world He
created. Yet He is *personal* and desires to have contact and communication with
the people of this world—people like you and me. Furthermore, the world
in which we live is real. And the evil which impacts us is real as well. It is not
illusory. In fact, it is an indication of humanity's rebellion against God—a God
who is, by His very nature, holy and just. Yet this same God is also perfectly
good and loving. And, in order to provide for the potential of restored relationship, He responded by giving His Son, Jesus, as the payment for humanity's
debt and the basis of a renewed relationship with Him—a relationship gained
through *His* effort and not ours."

Melissa continued listening intently. It was obvious she had most likely
never considered the paradigm I was laying out for her on that beautiful fall

day in downtown New York City. The momentary pause in the conversation allowed me to think of an important follow-up question.

"So, Melissa, given the fact these worldviews are contradictory by their very nature, how do you think you can know which one is accurate; that is, which one most closely mirrors reality?"

Her response was telling: "Well, I guess you can't know, since you can't prove either one scientifically." Melissa's answer was textbook perfect for her generation. Let me explain ….

It was through reading Nancy Pearcey's book *Total Truth* that I more clearly understood the current scenario of our culture.[1] Essentially, we live in a society that views life in a two-storied manner. Using the analogy of a two-story house, let's imagine a line distinguishes the upstairs from the downstairs. The upper story relates to the spiritual realm; the lower story to the physical. In the upper story, we will find word concepts such as faith, values, experience—"truth" *subjectively* determined. The lower story, however, contains word concepts such as facts, verifiable data, scientific experimentation—Truth (at least according to our cultural understanding) *objectively* determined.

### SPIRITUAL REALM

| faith | values | experience | = | subjective "truth" |
|---|---|---|---|---|

### PHYSICAL REALM

| facts | verifiable data | scientific experimentation | = | objective Truth |
|---|---|---|---|---|

The diagram illustrates two important concepts. First, our culture views truth in the spiritual realm as relative. It is based on our experiences; how we perceive the world will directly affect how we define truth in this realm. Therefore, two opposing truths in the spiritual realm can be equally valid, though logically contradictory.

On the other hand, truth, as connoted in the upper-story realm, is not to be confused with the kind of truth denoted by the lower-story realm of the physical world. Our society considers this latter kind of truth to be the "capital-T-kind-of-truth" because it is based on the observation of our senses and subject to scientific analysis. Society asks, "How can you believe in something you cannot see?"

One of the essential questions one must ask when determining a philosophy of life is "How can I know that which is real or true?" In our culture, it is assumed that scientific inquiry is the primary basis of knowledge leading to truth. Most everything else (i.e., beliefs, morals, likes, dislikes, etc.) is conditioned by who we are and how our particular culture has shaped us. Postmodernism, interestingly, challenges even this lower-story concept of "Truth" by suggesting that one's cultural lenses are so colored that even the results in scientific inquiry are tainted by one's presuppositions and beliefs about life. So our society is quickly moving to the position that *nothing* can be known with absolute certainty.

Melissa, you remember, suggested that the only way to know something to be true is through scientific inquiry. Realizing it was important to challenge her culturally-conditioned response I asked, "Well, Melissa, if science is the only means of knowing something to be true, then how could we prove, 10 minutes from now, that we had this conversation? Given the basis of the scientific method, how could we repeat our conversation under the same set of circumstances?"

She thought for a moment. "I guess we couldn't."

It was obvious that Melissa was processing our discussion. My prayer was that God was using my simple words to open her heart and mind to a new understanding of truth as a foundation for understanding the Gospel message.

"There is a way," I countered. "Think about it for a minute. If you had to prove to someone that we had this conversation, on this particular day and in this particular location, how would you do it?"

She thought for a moment, her eyes lit up, and she exclaimed, "I would call the members of our group as witnesses!"

"Absolutely! There are other ways of knowing truth apart from scientific inquiry. One of those ways is through historical inquiry—you listen to the testimonies of eyewitnesses and examine the historical context through relics and writings of a particular era. And that is exactly one way you would explore the truthfulness of the claims of Christianity.

"You see, Melissa, the followers of Christ who wrote about His life and recorded His words were not content to leave belief in Christ in the 'upper story.' In fact, if you read the New Testament accounts of Christ's works and words, you will notice a particular attention to detail—specific places, people, and events are mentioned. And when those accounts were written and circu-lated, there were people still alive who would have been able to verify or falsify what was stated in those accounts. His closest followers—those who would have surely known whether or not that what they were teaching was true or false—literally traded their lives for what they said." As we were approaching our destination, I realized I needed to wrap up our conversation. "Melissa, do you like to read?"

"Yes, I enjoy reading a lot," Melissa responded.

"If I sent you a book about some of the things we have discussed, would you read it?" "Sure," she said.

I sent Melissa the book *Mere Christianity*, authored by the famed Oxford professor, C.S. Lewis. Lewis was an atheist who, through examination of the evidence, became a follower of Jesus Christ and went on to write *Mere Christianity* as a defense of theism and Christianity. Though that conversation with Melissa on the streets of New York City was my last with her, I am confi-dent that God is going to provide others in Melissa's life who will convey His message of truth and reconciliation. Perhaps that person might even be you!

## Notes

[1] Nancy Pearcey, *Total Truth* (Wheaton, IL: Crossway Books, 2004), 74–121.

# CHAPTER 6

# Engaging the One Who Is Not Sure

My wife and I were having lunch at one of my favorite places with my sister and brother-in-law, who were visiting from California. We were having one of those "catch-up" conversations that tend to block out much of anything else taking place.

I couldn't help but notice, however, the university-aged young person waiting our table. He was gracious and very helpful. I had been talking to my sister and brother-in-law about the "experiment" on which I was working—asking people the two questions—and thought this was as good as time as any to engage him in conversation.

"Hi, I'm Carmen Mayell. What's your name?" Thus, I threw out the line to see how he might respond.

"I'm Spencer," he replied.

"Thanks for your good service, Spencer. Are you a student?"

It's always a good idea to get the context of the person's life. Apart from communicating interest, it will allow you a certain level of understanding as you commence your dialogue.

"Yes, I'm in my first year at Florida Atlantic University. I am studying archaeology."

"How interesting!" I exclaimed. "That study has always interested me." Wanting to move beyond matters of introduction, however, I continued. "Hey, Spencer, we've been talking about a couple of questions that we think may be fundamental to life: 'Is there a God?' And if so, 'Is He knowable?' What do *you* think?"

Spencer looked intrigued. His answer was equally as intriguing. "I don't know. I'm Jewish. After I had my bar mitzvah at age 13, I went through my atheist stage. Now I'm thinking there may be a God of some kind. But whether

He is knowable or not, I'm not so sure; if God is close by, why is there so much injustice in the world?"

Spencer's comments were thoughtful. His obvious willingness to engage clearly opened the door for continued dialogue—a dialogue I knew I could not make too lengthy, given the current context. At the same time, another couple of comments were in order.

I confess that I have not spoken to many people who believe there is a God but who do not think He can be known. In my experience, once a person comes to the conviction that God exists, the attendant corollary of "knowability" is assumed. Philosophically, deism has historically had adherents, but it is not as common today. More often, once a person posits the existence of God, he or she is just as confident to posit their own version of "god," along with how that "god" can be known.[1]

Spencer had moved from atheism to, at least, belief in the supernatural. His reluctance to consider God as "knowable" had more to do with wondering how God (whom he presumed to be good) could be involved in this world with such pervasive injustice.

"Spencer, you are asking a very important question," I said. "The issue of good and evil, or justice and injustice, is a discussion that has intrigued great minds throughout the centuries. May I suggest an additional question for your consideration? How do you know that there is such a thing as injustice? In other words, would it be possible to say that someone is unjust if it were not for an accepted standard of justice? All of us could play the role of Robin Hood in our own Sherwood Forest. Even Hitler condoned his barbaric atrocities in the name of advancing the German people and culture."

Spencer nodded in agreement.

Often people are quick to point out the existence of evil as an indisputable "proof" for the non-existence of God. There is only one problem: to identify something as evil suggests that we have some kind of understanding of evil's counterpart, good.

Furthermore, by virtue of the fact that, throughout history, civilizations have recognized objective moral standards suggests the existence of a Moral Law Giver. And far from being some kind of impersonal being, the fact that moral law assumes and responds to the intrinsic worth of the individual suggests that this Moral Law Giver possesses selfhood as well.

Through their condemnation of evil, people are admitting that there is as pervasive an understanding of good as there is of evil. But from where is this internal standard of goodness derived? And why should goodness be considered the norm? I like to suggest that God has made Himself known, at least to some extent, through the inherent understanding of goodness that the majority of us possess.

But it is also the *obligation* which one feels to do the good, as opposed to the evil, which suggests that there is something involved here that is much larger than simply human awareness of some abstract principle of right and wrong. It was C.S. Lewis who wrote of this "oughtness" that governs the action of humans. It seems apparent that God has created us to act freely. We can, to some degree, choose to do good or bad things, noble or ignoble deeds. Lewis writes:

> The laws of nature, as applied to stones or trees, may only mean "what Nature, in fact does." But if you turn to the Law of Human Nature, the Law of Decent [Behavior], it is a different matter. That law certainly does not mean "what human beings in fact, do"; for as I said before, many of them do not obey this law at all, and none of them obey it completely. The law of gravity tells you what stones do if you drop them; but the Law of Human Nature tells you what humans *ought* [emphasis mine] to do and do not.[2]

This oughtness lies beyond any explanation offered by the naturalistic worldview. It defies animal-like responses due to hunger, tiredness, or the need to mate. And, at times, this oughtness leads us to help others at the expense of benefit to oneself.

If time had been on my side, I could have illustrated my point by commenting on the police and firefighters who rushed into the World Trade Center buildings on 9/11. At the risk of their own lives, they seemed compelled to help the people in those burning buildings. To my knowledge, there was no debate or discussion among those on the job that day as to the merits of going in or not going in. They just went in! I would suggest that every one of those police and firefighters were aware of the dangers of running into burning buildings, including that the structures risked compromise or collapse.

No, the we-are-here-by-chance-aided-by-natural-selection worldview does not have an explanation for the "oughtness" that compels people to do right things at particular moments. In fact, any act or practice of putting one's life in harm's way for the sake of another does little to advance the survival of a species or to pass on heritable traits.[3]

I continued the dialogue.

"Spencer, let me tell you where I am coming from. I am a follower of Jesus. I believe there is a God who created us to know Him. This God has established in each of us an understanding of good and evil, of justice and injustice. And it is because He is just and good that you and I consider such things as murder and child abuse as evil—not simply some corollary to the survival of the fittest principle. And I wonder, too, could it be that the very value of the individual inferred from objective moral law suggests a God who values us highly? If what the Bible says is true, then God has been pretty forthright in His desire to relate with us by sending His Son, Jesus, to communicate a message of ultimate sacrifice and love."

Realizing Spencer had other tables to attend I decided to move toward a conclusion. "Do you like to read?" I queried.

"I love to read," Spencer responded enthusiastically.

"Great. I'm going to bring you a book by a great British author, C.S. Lewis. Lewis deals with some of the same questions you are asking and explores who Jesus was—obviously an important question for you, being Jewish. Perhaps we can have a conversation about this at another time."

Spencer responded enthusiastically to my suggestion: "That would be great! I'm here throughout the week except for on Tuesdays and Thursdays. If you come for a late lunch, I'll have some time to talk."

Before continuing with Spencer's story, let me interject that, for many years, I would feel as though I had not taken advantage of an opportunity to share my faith if I did not give the person all the facts during my first conversation with them. Though my desire was right—to see a friend come to know Christ—I now realize my methodology was wrong. Though there are times I share the Gospel completely, I now realize that the content of the message we share, more often than not, may take time for an individual to process. The truths of Christianity—the nature of God, the sinfulness of the human nature, the means of salvation, the person and work of Christ, the historical reliability of the Scriptures—are rapidly becoming foreign, even to those within Western culture.

It's important to keep the following principle in mind: *be willing to walk with a person down the path leading to belief.* That means your conversation will likely span several talks, rather than just one point of interaction. I view my conversational relationship with an individual as a road that's partially paved, partially unfinished. As I travel down this road, I'm sensitive to travel only *the paved part of the road*—that's the extent to which God has worked in the life of the individual—and I'm willing to stop traveling when the pavement ends, until additional work has been completed, so that I can travel a bit farther.

It was a little over a week later that I returned to see Spencer, bringing a copy of *Mere Christianity*, as I had promised. When I handed him the book, he was elated.

I stayed for about 90 minutes; during that time I had the opportunity to speak with Spencer for at least 45 minutes. Much of it was spent in listening to Spencer process why he was even beginning to ask questions about God's existence.

As we spoke on that Friday afternoon, he revealed to me that both his sister and his closest friend had died during the past year. It was almost as though he had discovered, in that instant, why he had this renewed interest in the question of God's existence. He was attempting to process the pain and suffering he had experienced; life without God has no antidote for either. Given the compelling depth of human relationship, the loss we experience when separated from loved ones compels us to hope that there is a tomorrow, as well as wonder why we feel the way we do if we are only a species that has arrived here by chance.

Spencer assured me that he would read *Mere Christianity* and that he likely would encourage his girlfriend to read it as well. As always, I left him my name, cell number, and e-mail—just in case he had additional questions.

I look forward to my next meeting with Spencer. In the meantime, I will be praying that God continues to accomplish His work in Spencer's life and that I, in some small way, may be used by God to help Spencer become acquainted with a God who cares deeply for him and sent His Son to prove it.

# *Notes*

[1] I do realize there are those who affirm belief in some kind of deity yet assert that such is unknowable to us. My problem with this position is that one is asserting to know something about that which they say nothing can be known. To say, for example, "God exists but He is not able to be known" assumes at least some degree of understanding about God and thus makes that position a self-refuting one.

[2] C.S. Lewis, *Mere Christianity* (San Francisco: Harper San Francisco, 1980), 17.

[3] The assumption of the naturalistic worldview is that we live in a closed system and that one's every activity (thought or action) is determined by either chemical, biological or environmental causes. Logically, this assumption would seem to complicate the discussion of human ethics (e.g.—"oughtness") for, by its very nature, ethics must assume the existence of human self-consciousness and self-determination. Though most naturalists accept both as uniquely human qualities (this being an interesting discussion in itself), James Sire asks the telling question, "How does one get from the fact of self-consciousness and self-determination, the realm of is and can, to the realm of what ought to be or to be done?" (see James W. Sire, The Universe Next Door, 4th ed. [Downers Grove, IL: IVP Academic, 2004], 72-74).

CHAPTER 7

# Engaging the One Who Is Sure
# but Doesn't Know How

It was one of those "God appointments"—a beautiful day in South Florida, just perfect for taking a group of students to the beach with the intention of providing them an opportunity to share their faith.

The students attending the leadership and evangelism conference, sponsored by our ministry organization, were eager to take to the streets and practice that which they had learned. Of course, the usual anxiety was present—I still experience it to this day as I prepare to engage someone about eternal matters. So during the half-hour bus ride from our meeting location to the beach, I worked with the group to help them consider good opening remarks to initiate dialogue.

As we approached the beach area, people were everywhere—surfers, skaters, roller-bladers, and sunbathers; all types of people and every age category.

During our conference's evangelism practicum, it is the job of the staff to stay on the outlook for groups having difficulty taking the step toward that first conversation. So, on occasion, I will swoop in on a group of two or three students and try to embolden them to approach the first small group of teens or twenties they see.

I was enjoying the day, while playing my staff role, when I noticed a group of four or five of our students walking toward me. It was evident they needed some encouragement. "Hey, guys!" I greeted them. "Having a difficult time getting started?"

Matt, who had taken lead of the group, said they had spoken to a couple of people but with no real interest expressed. South Florida, with its strong New York City influence, is not the easiest place in the world to just strike up a conversation. Usually, though, you can find *someone* at the beach who is willing to talk for a few moments.

"Well, may I give you a couple of recommendations?" I queried.

"Sure!" came the eager response from all group members. They assumed that I must possess that "golden key" to successful witnessing.

"I always like the up-front approach," I told them. "People here in South Florida are used to that. You might say something like, 'Hi! We are a group of Christian students who are interested in your perspective on spiritual matters. Do you mind if we ask you a couple of questions?' Or you could also say something like, 'Do you mind if we take just five or six minutes of your time to get your opinion about two questions that we think are of ultimate importance?'"

As I looked at the students' faces, it was clear that they had attempted to put my suggestions into practice and nothing had worked. As I was thinking about what to recommend next, I looked up and saw a guy roller-blading down the sidewalk toward us. Without hesitation, I blurted out, "Follow me! Let me show you." As soon as the words were out of my mouth, I realized I had no real plan, but I walked quickly to meet the roller-blader who, because of the foot traffic on the sidewalk, had slowed his pace a bit. As the twenty-something guy approached, I spoke up. "Hi! I need to ask you a favor." He slowed up to listen, so I continued. "I'm here with a group of students who are learning how to talk to others about their faith in God. Would you mind helping me out?"

He stopped and nodded his head. "Sure," he murmured.

"My name is Carmen Mayell. We are with a conference designed to help Christian students know how to more clearly communicate their faith. May I get your response to a couple of questions? By the way, what's your name?"

"I'm Ryan. I'll be glad to answer your questions."

"Well, Ryan," I proceeded, "I would like to suggest there are two fundamental questions in life: 'Is there a God?' And, if so, "Is He knowable—can one have contact and communication with Him?' What do you think?"

"Yes, I do believe in God," he replied. "And I think He can be known. I'm a Catholic."

One thing I have found consistently to be very good advice is to never let someone's church background become the primary issue. You actually can tell very little about whether one has a personal relationship with Christ, based on church background alone.

"So, Ryan, if I were to ask you if you have a *personal* relationship with God, how would you respond? Is the idea of having a personal relationship with God something you are familiar with?"

Frankly, I am not sure why I posed this particular question. Sometimes, when someone suggests they are confident that God can be known and they are of a Christian background, I may ask a rhetorical question such as, "Do you believe that God can be known through His Son, Jesus Christ?" After an affirmative response, I will often share with them how revolutionary it was in my own Christian walk to learn of God's unconditional love for and acceptance of me. This, of course, allows me to gauge where that person is in his understanding of the Christian life, and may lead to exactly where I started off with Ryan.

In looking back on my contact with Ryan, it seemed to me that he lacked a sense of confidence that God could be known, especially in the personal sense, which is at the core of the Gospel message. Thus, I was prompted to ask him the question I did—focusing in on the operative phrase "personal relationship with God."

Sure enough, Ryan was not familiar with such a concept—this is common among those who consider church affiliation a sufficient explanation when asked if they believe in God.

It has always seemed, at least to me, that it is wise to be prepared to share one's faith just in case God might provide an opportunity. Thus I typically carry some kind of tract or written presentation that concisely explains the good news of Christ. Sometimes, if a tract presentation seems unnatural, I might write out the key points of the Gospel on a piece of paper, along with what it means to establish a relationship with Christ. Given the beach setting as above, however, I decided to go with the printed tract I had with me—Campus Crusade for Christ's *Connecting with God*. (The key point here is to find a tract that you like and use it.)

As I pulled the tract from my pocket, I explained, "Ryan, do you mind if I simply review with you some key points about how you can have a personal relationship with God? This booklet simply contains some statements made by Jesus as he explained His role in this very important equation. Again, this booklet isn't about a particular church or denomination; it is what the Bible says about knowing God."

Ryan responded positively to my suggestion, and so I proceeded. He listened intently as I moved from page to page; explaining that 1) there is a God who created him for a purpose, 2) everyone is separated from God because of sin, 3) Jesus Christ is God's payment for our sin, and 4) by placing our trust in Christ as that payment, we will receive God's gift of life in a relationship with Him.

The concept of substitutionary atonement is not easily understood by most people. Essentially, it speaks of Christ as our substitute, so that we are not held responsible for the payment—atonement—of our own sins. The phrase describes that which is at the foundation of our grace relationship with God. I decided to illustrate the concept through use of the following example, which I learned while a high school student.

"Ryan, it's like this," I said. "Let's say you enjoyed speeding in your vehicle, but finally, you exceeded the limit of tickets the law would allow. You must appear before the traffic court judge, who may not only fine you but also may take away your license. Your day in court finally arrives and, much to your surprise, the judge happens to be the father of one of your best friends. As he calls you to stand before him to review the charges and assess the fine you owe, he does something that shocks all those looking on. He comes around from behind the bench, removes his robe, and goes to the clerk of the court. He then takes out his wallet and pays the fine you deserved to pay."

Ryan was listening intently. It was evident he was deep in thought considering the significance of my illustration. (Or, perhaps, maybe he was on roller-blades for a reason!)

I continued: "Ryan, that is exactly what God has done for you and me. The only difference is that we were guilty of breaking God's law. Sometimes it was in thought, sometimes in action, sometimes in things we know we should have done but didn't do. But what was God to do? From a human perspective, God faced a dilemma. He had created us for relationship with Him. Yet He could not simply excuse us for our sin—our indifference and rebellion against God expressed in so many ways—without diminishing His just and holy character. How could a just God, for example, excuse the sins of a Hitler and still be just?

"Similar to the judge in my illustration, God chose to pay the penalty Himself. He chose to send His only Son, Jesus, to live a perfect life and to demonstrate to humanity His perfect nature. It was only as the perfect individual that Jesus could pay the penalty for our sins. And it is by accepting His payment toward our overdue account that God has made it possible for us to enjoy a relationship with Him."

Ryan said little during my presentation; his focus was on what I said, despite the many distractions around; it was clear God's Spirit was working in his life. I now wanted to give him the opportunity to experience the most significant relationship of his life.

"Ryan, would you like to establish that relationship with God today that He has made possible through His Son, Jesus Christ?"

"Yes." The simple, yet straightforward response seemed to typify of Ryan's quiet demeanor.

As I led Ryan in the prayer found in *Connecting with God*, I was mindful of the fact that God had brought Ryan across our path that day at the beach, both to change his eternal destiny and to challenge some committed students to take the initiative in sharing their faith. As Ryan and I parted ways, I turned around to discover the students had already left. They had obviously seen enough of God's handiwork in Ryan and wanted to see if God might have another "Ryan" waiting for them somewhere else along the beach.

CHAPTER 8

# Engaging the One Who Believes There Are Many Ways

I do love the outdoors, though the thought of wading in a stream for the better part of a day doesn't really appeal to me. That's why I was standing outside the fly-fishing shop on Crested Butte's main street, while my kids were inside getting all geared up for the adventure awaiting them. Our family was in Colorado on vacation, a gift from some very gracious friends.

Little did I realize that the surreal atmosphere of an absolutely beyond-believable day in the Rockies was to be soon interrupted by a pretty testy conversation with a particular young lady named Michelle. My wife and I were chatting with her, and it seemed benign enough at first—covering all the basics from weather, to background, to all the questions tourists typically get asked by the locals in such parts.

Somehow, our conversation moved from the mundane to the spiritual. It just seemed to happen, and I realized that I was involved in dialogue with someone who felt there was a God and that sincerity of belief was the primary bridge to awareness of and/or contact with that God.

Although I did not think to ask Michelle at the time, I generally like to know why someone feels she has sufficient insight into God that she can suggest the means by which to establish contact or awareness. There are, after all, innumerable paths suggested by others that perhaps are equally as sincere.

As we spoke, Michelle continued to assert her sincerity theory, so I decided to ask, "Have you ever considered the claims of Jesus Christ and what He said about the role He played in knowing God?"

"Yes. Jesus Christ said some pretty cool things." The casual, nonspecific nature of Michelle's reply indicated to me that if she had read Jesus's words, it was likely not from reading the Bible. Whatever she understood, she quite likely took His words no differently than the opinions of her college philosophy professor.

I decided to test her opinion by bringing up a claim of Jesus's that I assumed had undoubtedly escaped her notice. "Yes, Jesus did say some pretty cool things," I agreed, "like 'You should love your neighbor as yourself.' But He also said some very radical things like, 'I am the way, the truth, and the life. No man comes to the Father but by Me.' In other words, Jesus claimed that He was the *only* way through whom one could establish a meaningful and relational contact with God."

Michelle's response was almost explosive. "I really can't believe you would say that! To think that you really believe that Jesus is the only way to God seems elitist! What about those who sincerely believe their way to God is right?"

Though it had been a beautiful, sunny day, I was convinced a major rain cloud had just formed overhead. Yet, I had committed myself by this point and needed to move forward.

"Well, Michelle, it really doesn't matter what *I* think. It is what Jesus said. So, you have to deal with *His* claims." Still it was evident she not going to swallow this "only way" claim easily. And, though my explanation didn't do much to soothe her anger, I have always found it important to help the person realize that if they don't like what Jesus said then they really shouldn't be angry with *me* but with *Him*!

I will say, however, Michelle didn't insist that I was only reflecting what *I* understood Jesus to say, but you will inevitably run into those who do. We live in a world where a "your interpretation vs. my interpretation" mentality exists. Still, however, I have come to discover that words are still words, and the clearest meaning of the text is usually the preferred one—at least, to most people.

For those who *do* suggest the "that's only your interpretation" idea, I have found the following to be a good question to ask: "What do *you* think Jesus meant by what He said?" That's simply enough! And, if you have your New Testament handy, let them read the first few verses of John 14 for themselves.

Michelle, however, did not seem ready for a recitation of the Gospel. She was angered by Jesus's claim of exclusivity. Without question, she assumed that spiritual truth was a matter of personal taste. If she preferred Chinese food, and I preferred Italian, it was just a matter of personal taste. Both were food. One was not right and the other wrong. So it was, even with our religious preferences. Spiritual truth, from her perspective, was not objectively determined but subjectively derived from one's own experience.

It was important to challenge her reasoning at that very point.

Somewhere during our discussion, Michelle had mentioned that her dad was a cardiologist. It always amazes me how seemingly insignificant pieces of information can be used later in conversations for very personal analogies in helping illustrate spiritual truths. Just listen carefully, and God will create points of common reference for you. And such was the case here.

"Michelle," I began, "let's say your dad's best friend experiences recurring symptoms of tightness in his chest. He is convinced that it is nothing more than indigestion—he's been eating more and exercising less the past few weeks. His wife, however, is concerned and wants him to get a physical. Rather than go to the family doctor, he decides it is easiest to set up an appointment with his best friend—your dad, the cardiologist. And so he does. He just wants to satisfy his wife's demands for a checkup.

"Your dad examines his friend and, interestingly, requests an angiogram and stress test. He determines that his best friend has at least two or three significantly blocked arteries and, to save him from a life-threatening heart attack, must have bypass surgery immediately. But he is conflicted. Your dad, of all people, knows the risk involved in open-heart surgery. He realizes that you must break the sternum, pry open the chest, cut a blood vessel out of the leg or elsewhere to use for the heart bypasses, and so on. His friend will experience pain as his wounds heal, and rehab will be required, severely restricting his normal, everyday life. Furthermore, medications will be necessary for the duration of his life, and the rich foods he once enjoyed will have to be abandoned.

"Your dad has a couple of options. Not wanting his friend to experience the pain of the surgery and life-altering habits that will necessarily follow, he could simply send him on his way. Or he could tell his best friend that he is not to go home but that he is going immediately to the local hospital, where a cardiovascular surgical team is preparing to meet him and prep him for surgery. Otherwise, he might die from a massive heart attack. There is no other option if your dad's friend is to live." My illustration ended; now was the time for application. "So, Michelle, what do you think your dad would do?"

I thought Michelle would respond immediately by affirming that her dad would apprise his best friend of the need for the surgical procedure. Surely she knew that her dad would do the right thing—the responsible thing—even if it meant a very painful reality for his best friend. There was only one viable option in the scenario I presented. At least, that's the way *I* looked at it.

Yet Michelle, paused. And that pause revealed that my illustration had challenged her entire paradigm for evaluating spiritual reality. Indeed, if a God does exist, then would He, not unlike Michelle's father, have the prerogative to both diagnose the problem and prescribe a *particular* cure?

Perhaps for the first time, Michelle was being forced to realize that an "only way" claim does have merit in particular situations—at least in the physical realm. Could the same rationale, perhaps, be applied in the spiritual realm? If a cardiologist can say "You must do it this way or die," could not the Divine Cardiologist make the same pronouncement about one's spiritual well-being?

Michelle's response, after she thought for several seconds, finally came: "My dad would let his friend to do what he thought was best."

I don't remember much about what transpired past that point. It was clear Michelle couldn't face the implications of the illustration and that, very quickly afterward, she no longer wanted anything to do with my view of spiritual matters.

It continues to amaze me how people perceive a God who offers only one way of relationship with Him as unjust. The reality is that the same people who decry God as unjust for offering only one way really want God to accept them on their own, one way (e.g., *my* way) terms.

I am quite convinced that even if God had suggested 1000 ways for us to know Him, but those 1000 ways did not include Michelle's way, our conversation would have been much the same. Or perhaps the accusation would have been leveled against God that He had made the matter much too confusing and complicated by offering so many ways. It was clear to me that Michelle believed—and incorrectly so—that God owed *her*.

Though we never saw Michelle again during our stay in Crested Butte, I have no doubt that my conversation with her on that beautiful day was designed by the same God who had created the delights of that day. Sometimes I wonder why my wife and I were there to talk with Michelle. Did we serve as just one piece of a multi-faceted puzzle that ultimately led her to the truth? Or was my conversation with her a final piece in a series of previous dialogues that would render her, one day, inexcusable before God?

# CHAPTER 9

# Engaging the One
# Who is Jewish

I was on flight to Boston when I began a conversation with the woman sitting next to me. Her name: Sylvia. I had been reading my Bible, and she had taken note. After we began our discussion on spiritual matters, Sylvia mentioned her Jewish background.

I'd lived for over 20 years in an area boasting one of the nation's largest Jewish populations, so hearing the phrase "I'm Jewish" didn't unnerve me as it once would have—at one time I didn't know how to continue the discussion much beyond that point because I was pretty sure that many Jewish individuals just weren't that fond of Jesus.

Over the years, one of the things I most admire about so many of the Jewish people with whom I've become acquainted is their emphasis on education. In Southeast Florida, the favorite pastimes of many young people are surfing, skiing, wake-boarding, "skurfing," and a host of other water sports. Entertainment often becomes *the* purpose for life, not simply a welcome respite from hard study and work.

The primary exception to this rule is the Jewish community. Jewish kids study; talk about becoming doctors, lawyers, financiers, and company CEOs and CFOs; and plan on going to Harvard, Yale, and NYU. My only point here is that if you want to understand the Jewish culture, you must recognize this penchant for education and learning.

In line with their interest in learning, then, it is not difficult to engage those of Jewish heritage in substantive, if not *lively*, dialog. A monologue presentation of the Gospel will seldom work. Therefore, my conversation with most Jewish individuals begins with exploring who they are, what they believe and who they understand me—as a *Christian*—to be. And so it was with Sylvia.

Almost as soon as Sylvia had identified herself as being Jewish, I asked her the important question: "So, Sylvia, do you consider yourself Orthodox, Conservative, or Reformed?"

I have learned that not all Jewish people believe the same thing. In fact, there is great diversity among them. And that includes their beliefs about God and the Hebrew Scriptures as well. In the U.S., a very small minority, the Orthodox (about 15 percent of U.S. Jewish population), believe much the same as the Jewish people we read about in the Bible. Members of the Reformed and Conservative (which reacted against the liberal Reformed movement in the mid-1800s and sought to *conserve* Jewish tradition) branches of Judaism are all across the board as to what they believe about God's nature and His role in human affairs. A current-day movement known as Kabala (or Kabbalah) could be described as Jewish mysticism; it closely resembles New Age.

Unless you are speaking with one of the 15 percent of Orthodox Jews, you are talking with someone whose beliefs are not unlike most of your friends and acquaintances. At the same time, there are three convictions that most people of Jewish heritage have been raised to affirm, regardless of what they believe theologically. First, they are not to believe in Jesus. Second, the term "Christian" has some very negative connotations, being associated with acts of anti-Semitism throughout the centuries. And third, the Holocaust (and the possibility that such could occur again) is a unifier of their people.

Sylvia had come from a Conservative tradition. She did not quantify her current preference, which led me to believe that she most likely did not attend synagogue or temple services beyond those for the High Holy Days (Rosh Hashanah and Yom Kippur) and/or Passover.

Though I did not ask Sylvia, this would have been the opportune time to pose the questions: "What do *you* believe about God? Do you think God exists and, if so, is He able to be known?" Many Jewish people today are Jewish by birth, but not necessarily in their beliefs. Thus the two primary questions I ask are equally effective with those from a Jewish background and help me discover what the individual believes rather than what I *think* he or she may believe.

Furthermore, such questions help move the discussion from a "Jewish vs. Christian" framework to an exchange between two individuals who are sharing their beliefs with each other. As a result, it is quite likely you, too, will be granted the opportunity to share what you believe.

As I mentioned, one of the key unifiers of the Jewish people is the Holocaust. Trips to Germany and the concentration camps of World War II are common among Jewish high school and college students. The implicit message is clear: never forget! By extension, Jewish young people are reminded that what has been could occur again. The question of evil is, therefore, one of the important issues you must address as your discussion unfolds. If it is not raised by the Jewish individual, your reference to the Holocaust (and the questions implicit therein) will open a door to an even deeper level of discussion and understanding.

So how should one tread?

As in any discussion pertaining to the existence of evil in this world, you must begin by affirming it as a complex matter that involves many questions: If there is a good God who is sovereign, why does evil exist? Why do even very good people suffer? How can a good God allow innocent men, women, and children to suffer? (I would specifically raise these or similar questions in order to demonstrate I have considered such matters.)

In your discussion, you will not answer all of the questions, but you can provide input that will help the individual reconsider the assumption he or she may have drawn from an awareness of evil's existence—that if God does exist, He surely is not all powerful.

Often, as the problem of evil is raised, I have responded something like this: "Yes, evil is pervasive in this world. Without a doubt it can cause one to question the reality of God's existence. If God does exist and if this God is purportedly all good and all powerful, then why does He allow evil to exist at all, much less allow it to continue seemingly unchecked?"

At this point, the individual may not be sure which side of the debate I'm arguing. Thus I continue. "But even if we were to take God out of the equation, little would be solved. In fact, by removing God from the equation, we make matters worse. Without God, we really have *no* standard by which to judge evil in the first place."

I now make an appeal to the Hebrew Scriptures and the traditional understanding of the nature of God contained therein. "So, how *does* one reconcile the teaching of the Hebrew Scriptures, which posit God as just, loving and all powerful with the often grim realities of life? What do you think?" Then, I just stop and listen. Here's where I clearly discover the philosophical orientation of the person, for it is up to him or her to either reject the teachings of the Hebrew Scriptures or affirm them.

I love the phrase, "Could it be …?" That phrase sets up a question that invites continued discussion while giving input. It is a gentle yet effective way to have someone consider other options that may even challenge his or her stated position.

So, in this case, I would simply proceed by saying, "Could it be that God is not finished yet? In other words, it is easy to assume that because evil continues, God is either not powerful or not good. Yet, could it be that He is both all-powerful *as well as* good, but His plan for addressing evil is not complete? In fact, if the Hebrew Scriptures are accurate, God takes evil very seriously, so much so that the prophet Daniel speaks of a judgment for everyone at the end of time. According to the Scriptures, everyone will be judged for the evil they have committed."

At this juncture, I pause again and let the person respond. If he or she does not respond after a moment, I continue with another "Could it be …?" phrase: "Something that has always intrigued me is the ability of humanity to act freely. In fact, free will is something that surely sets us apart from the rest of the animal species. Could it be that God, in choosing to grant us free will, has allowed us to act as we wish? How could we truly be free if all our actions are predetermined? And how could God really end evil without ending our ability to be free, in that free-willed man is the perpetrator of evil?"

The point I'm making is simply this: God has chosen to allow man to act freely. Theologically, humans sin because they are sinners by nature, but the sinful acts they commit are done so as a matter of choice. Determinism—the belief that all human action results from mechanistic causes or by preceding events and not the free will of the individual—compels us to reject that which all of us know to be true. We live our lives as free agents, not as animals following some kind of migratory path composed of habits, without regard to the ulti-mate questions pertaining to significance and meaning.

Obviously, at this point, I have laid the groundwork for a presentation of the Gospel. And that is exactly where I was in my conversation with Sylvia. But how would I present the Gospel to someone who is confident the one thing she shouldn't be is a follower of Jesus? Though my entry point may be a bit different, the message remains the same.

"Sylvia," I said, "if I were to ask you to briefly quantify the message of the

Bible, how would you respond?" Most Jewish people, at least in our country, know little about the Bible (including the Hebrew Scriptures) and its message. Even if they do have a cursory understanding, few have considered its key themes sufficiently in order to be able to offer any kind of summary statement.

Sylvia was straightforward in her response: "I don't know." Her honesty was compelling.

"Would you object if I simply offered a brief overview of several of the key themes as I understand them?" I queried. My approach was to inform Sylvia. My prayer was that God would convince her in His time.

She agreed.

I continued. "Sylvia, the Bible's message comprises at least four overriding themes. First, the Bible begins with a declaration in the Torah [Law—the first five books of the Bible as we know them] that there is a God who created. As Moses declared in the very first part of the Law, 'In the beginning, God created …'" It is this God who designed men and women to relate to Him. And it was this God who set aside a particular people, the Jewish nation, to proclaim Him.

"Secondly, the Jewish prophet Isaiah warned his people that their sins had separated them from God [see Isaiah 59]. The same is true today for *all* of us. The result of this rejection and rebellion is clearly evidenced in the world in many ways—greed, prejudice, hatred, war, and the like. All are evidences of the fact we, as people, are separated from the God who created us to know Him."

Sylvia continued to listen intently. Both of us realized our flight was nearing its end. As a result, Sylvia allowed me to continue uninterrupted.

"But, Sylvia," I continued, "the Scriptures offer hope! If you recall, the need for atonement is clearly evidenced in the Law's provision of Yom Kippur [the Jewish Day of Atonement prescribed in Leviticus]. On that day a lamb was to be sacrificed as payment for the sins of the nation that God's displeasure might be averted. Later, however, the prophets foretold of a coming Deliverer, or Messiah, and the prophet Isaiah even spoke of God's servant who would take *our* sin on Himself and be 'pierced' and 'crushed' and 'disciplined' by God on our behalf [Isaiah 53: 1-12]. Thus, the Messiah was to provide final and complete deliverance based on atonement, in order to reconnect the Jewish people with their God.

"Finally, the Bible presents Jesus as the one who fulfilled the proclamations of the Hebrew prophets. Jesus claimed to be God's Son bearing the image of the eternal God in human flesh. He lived a life as an Orthodox Jew, fully obeying the Law of Moses. Yet His mission was far more than a perfect example to humanity. In fact, Jesus claimed to be God's final sacrifice for my sins and yours; for my rebellion and the rebellion of all. His death, rather than being a tragic event of history, was the payment God provided so that the people He created could, once again, enjoy a relationship with Him.

"Sylvia, I would like to give you something to take with you."

"Of course," she responded readily.

"This small booklet simply reiterates some of that which I have just shared with you. Perhaps it will allow you to consider at a more opportune time some of Jesus's claims and their relevance to you as a Jewish individual. If what Jesus said is true, then He has provided for your final atonement as well as a personal relationship with the God of your heritage."

The plane flight had ended and so concluded my conversation with Sylvia. I knew that chances were great I would never know the impact of my words, but I was fully assured that God had allowed me to converse with one of His people, through whom His Son had come and for whom His Son had died. In a strange sort of way I, too, had experienced God's using me, even as He did the prophets of old, to proclaim His way of salvation and deliverance to the people of my Savior.

# CHAPTER 10

# Engaging the One Who Is Spiritual

As I engage individuals in conversations about God, on occasion there will be those who will respond to my two questions by simply asserting, "I'm very spiritual." In many (if not most) cases, I could properly restate their remark through the following question: "So, you feel connected to the Spiritual Force of the universe?" To that question they would readily agree.

What always puzzles me, however, is that those who affirm such a position tend to have difficulty defining precisely "what" or "who" that Spiritual Force, or God, is. They consider that God is "within them" or, more accurately stated, they are a part of a Universal Soul that pervades everything. What is clear, however, is that the God they "know" is quite different from the God of whom you and I speak. Often, such individuals have been deeply influenced by a pantheistic worldview—the worldview underlying both the Hindu and Buddhist religions.

Let's begin by considering the following definition of pantheism:

In pantheism God is all in all. God pervades all things, contains all things, subsumes (includes) all things, and is found within all things. Nothing exists apart from God, and all things are in some way identified with God. In short, pantheism views the world as God and God as the world. Put more precisely, in pantheism all is God and God is all. Nothing exists that is not God.[1]

To be sure, Eastern religion, the seed bed for the pantheistic worldview, has permeated our society. Beginning in the 1960s with the Beatles, who were influenced by the Transcendental Meditation of Maharishi Mahesh Yogi, to the Hare Krishna (a branch of Hinduism) in the 1970s (who appeared at public locations wearing their floor-length orange robes), a great deal of exposure, and even acceptance, was afforded this worldview.[2] Today pantheism is expressed through the New Age movement and espoused by such popular authors as Deepak Chopra. And with the tremendous influx of immigrants from the East, those who follow the Hindu religion or the teachings of Gautama Buddha are no longer uncommon.

What makes addressing those holding to this worldview particularly challenging is that it is often difficult to know *exactly* what the individual pantheist may believe. In our country, even as throughout the world, Eastern pantheism has morphed itself into a multitude of variations often adapting nuances from the culture by which it is subsumed. Yet, perhaps the following brief synopsis of Hinduism and Buddhism will be helpful as a starting point.

The most popular form of Hinduism (the Advaita Vedanta system espoused by the Indian philosopher, Shankara) holds there is one Ultimate Reality (Brahman) behind all that we know.[3] This ultimate reality is manifested in one or several primary deities and their female counterparts. Beyond the primary deities are countless other deities (popularly said to be 330 million).[4] A fundamental premise of Hinduism is that meaning is <u>not</u> to be found in *separateness* (e.g., I in distinction to you, this tree as opposed to that tree, etc.) but in *oneness* with Brahman. James Sire explains as follows:

> In pantheism [Vedantic Hinduism] the chief thing about God is Oneness, a sheer abstract, undifferentiated, nondual unity. This puts God beyond personality. And since Atman [the soul or essence of each person] is Braham [the Soul of the cosmos], human beings are beyond personality too. For any of us to "realize" our being is to abandon our complex personhood and enter the undifferentiated One.[5]

Furthermore, Hinduism (as well as Buddhism) says that what is seen is illusory and not ultimately real (the state of illusion is referred to as *maya*)[6]. Indeed, that which we consider to be real (the material world) will ultimately be discovered to be illusory and, in fact, a barrier to one's enlightenment (e.g., the realization of our oneness with the All of the universe). Even matters that affect us deeply—good and evil, happiness and pain, fairness and injustice—are categories that are less-than-real, their significance only being understood in their unity with the universal All.

Unlike Hinduism, however, Buddhism[7] generally posits that true reality is nothingness.[8] To the Buddhist, discussion of God is irrelevant. There is really no God or identifiable deity behind what we know. The ultimate goal of the Buddhist is to come to the realization that one's identity is not to be found in his or her perceived existence as an individual but, rather, in unity with the All or Void—the Source of all that is. This realization is initiated through following a path to enlightenment (i.e., through denial of desires that keep one's attention focused on this illusory world), taught by an "enlightened one" (Buddha).

In both Hinduism and Buddhism, until enlightenment is attained one continues in a series of life cycles influenced by *karma* (the sum of both good and bad deeds and its effect on the individual in future life cycles). Release from the cycle of reincarnation and rebirth (referred to as *samsara*) will come only as one relinquishes all earthly desires (even relationships) and rejects all earthly categories of distinction (e.g., I versus you, this tree versus that tree, etc.) in light of the awareness of one's unity with Brahman or the Void.

Personally, I have always found it a bit frustrating to talk with someone who is of pantheistic persuasion. It is difficult to know exactly how they define that ultimate Reality. In part, I now realize that such is the nature of pantheism; logic and reason represent dualistic thinking and, as such, are considered as hindrances to enlightenment. Indeed, the nature of the pantheistic worldview does not lend itself to exact explanation. God is not to be explored, nor His nature explained (if, in fact, He is relevant to the pantheist with whom you are speaking).

Part of my mission in engaging a person, regardless of his or her worldview, is to be sure and ask questions that will help expose the inconsistencies of the particular worldview the person affirms. I do not do this to be caustic or disagreeable; I do it to challenge the person's thinking. Quite frankly, something greater is at stake than a person's feelings—it is one's eternal destiny.

But, let me caution you: though one's eternal destiny surely trumps the potential for hurt feelings, this does not grant you license for offense! The cultural background of the person with whom you are speaking, as well as the nature of the relationship you possess with them, should help you construct the proper parameters for your questions.

For example, just last night, my family and I were checking out a brand new sporting goods store that opened a few blocks from our home. Given the fact the store had opened ahead of schedule, few people were aware it was operational which meant we were virtually the only people in the store. That, of course, potentially presented a prime opportunity for conversation!

As I was exploring my favorite section—the tennis racquets—a young sales associate, named Eddie, came over and offered his assistance—which I gladly accepted (much has changed in the world of tennis racquets since I owned my first metal racquet in the early 1970s!). He was of Eastern descent and, I assessed, in his early twenties. And, by his conversation, I could tell he was undoubtedly a sharp student.

After a few minutes of explaining the various features of some of the newer racquets, our conversation began to shift onto other matters. Actually, I suppose it was I who took the initiative to change the conversation, wanting to move on to other, more important matters.

"So, Eddie, are you still a student?" I queried.

"Yes, I graduated last year from Boca High and have started pre-med studies at Florida Atlantic University." Eddie paused momentarily before continuing. "Actually, I should be at Columbia right now; my grandparents needed my help and so I decided to stay home."

As we continued to talk, Eddie explained that he had received a full ride to several of the country's best medical schools. In fact, he had chosen to give up those scholarships in the interest of his family—and not his parents, but his *grandparents*. I knew Eddie had to come from a cultural background that placed a high premium on family relationships. From *which* cultural background, however, I was not sure. And his name gave me absolutely no clue.

The opportunity to move the dialog onto spiritual matters seemed apropos; our conversation had moved to a deeper level than simply a discussion of surface matters. So I continued. "Eddie, I would like to suggest there are two key questions in life everyone deals with in one way or another. 'Is there a God?' And, if so, 'Is He knowable?' What do you think?"

"I am from a Hindu background and of Indian descent, Carmen." Eddie proceeded thoughtfully. "We believe there is one primary deity, though He has many manifestations."

At that point I thought it was important for me to demonstrate that I possessed at least some understanding of the Hindu religion. So, I interjected, "Yes, you mean Brahman. Am I correct?"

"Yes, that is right," Eddie affirmed.

Realizing the inextricable connection between a person of Indian background and the Hindu religion, I realized this was potentially the beginning of a new relationship and, perhaps, many future conversations. What I knew for certain, however, was that this was another God-given opportunity to begin the process of sharing the greatest message of history.

"Well, Eddie," I continued, "I am a Christian—that is, a follower of Jesus. Quite frankly, I seldom have the opportunity to talk with someone of a Hindu heritage, so I consider this a great privilege."

As we continued to talk, it became clear that Eddie was a young man who, though Hindu by background, was open to inquiry concerning my understanding of God from my Christian background. I, too, knew there would be questions I would eventually ask Eddie concerning his Hindu beliefs. And one of the primary questions I would want to explore with my new friend would be pertaining to his perception of reality of the world in which we live.

The question pertaining to reality is an important one. When you hold a pantheistic worldview, you hold that the world in which we live is less than real. Now, of course, there are variations of this common "theme." An absolute pantheist, for example, is one who believes there is only one ultimate Reality, or God, and that all that appears to exist is not real.[9] Others, however, consider the world and our existence to be real, yet still a distant reflection of that ultimate Reality. Either way, the pantheist has a problem with one thing: *reality*.

The problem is that few pantheists live-out the worldview they espouse. If they did, they would drive on the wrong side of the street whenever they desired; they would fail to show up to class or work; they would stop spending money on food; and Tibetan monks would stop protesting China's rule of their nation. Why? Because the physical world is ultimately not real and making distinction between one thing or another only hinders understanding of who one truly is: either one with Brahman (ala Hinduism) or one with that eternal (and indefinable) Source or Void of all that is (ala Buddhism). Quite frankly, pantheists should be in hot pursuit of doing anything and everything that would validate the worldview they affirm and that which causes them to live more consistently with that reality.

The timing was not right, however, to explore such pointed questions so early in my relationship with Eddie. I only share the previous assessment with you so that you might be more fully aware of the seeming inconsistencies in the worldview of your Eastern friends.

As we neared the conclusion of our conversation, I simply asked Eddie if he enjoyed reading (given his apparent scholastic ability, I already knew the answer). "Very much so," came the virtually-automated response.

"Very good," I continued—I definitely wanted to give him something to read or consider so that I might have the opportunity to pick up our conversation at another time. "One of my favorite authors is Ravi Zacharias. As you can tell from his name, he is of Indian heritage. Though Hindu by birth, Ravi now professes belief in the person of Jesus Christ. I think some of which he has written may be of interest to you. Would you be willing to read one of his books if I purchased a copy for you?"

Eddie forthrightly accepted my offer. With that, our conversation ended and I left.

Frankly, I would suspicion that many from Eastern religious backgrounds live with an inner angst; living in a world where "non-reality" seems far more compelling than the Reality to which they should aspire. In other words, why is one like Eddie pursuing a medical degree rather than seeking to remove himself from the distractions of such a materialistic culture? Why is he not choosing a life profession that would allow him to much more aggressively pursue a path to "enlightenment" (*moksha*)? And, assuming his desire to achieve is for all the right reasons (which I surely do not question)—to help those less fortunate— why should not disease and the suffering it brings be considered one alternate path to "enlightenment?" Surely, suffering of any kind increases one's desire to be removed from the constraints of this earthly "shell."

I remember watching a documentary several years ago on the young entrepreneurs of Silicon Valley. It was before the great tech crash of 2000, and all eyes were on the growing number of millionaires who were barely in their thirties. This particular documentary featured a young Japanese-American entrepreneur who had developed a software application that advanced the user-friendliness of e-mail.

As a young man who espoused Buddhist philosophy, even though he lived in the heart of Silicon Valley, he maintained a very modest lifestyle, living in a two-bedroom apartment that most would consider barely furnished. (Remember, the path to "enlightenment" involves self-denial.) He was the perfect model of the untainted pantheist!

Enter reality: his e-mail software application was purchased by Microsoft.

Perhaps a year later, I happened to catch a news clip that featured the same entrepreneur. He was now driving a brand new red Porsche and was in the process of building his new several-thousand-square-foot home overlooking San Francisco Bay.

It seemed that a greater reality had struck. And, from my viewpoint, that presents a significant problem for the pantheistic worldview: why is it that, if we are one with Brahman or the eternal "Void" we have strayed so far? And how is it that we, having our being or source in either, have become so deceived that it inevitably takes countless cycles of birth, death and rebirth to truly understand who we are and have been all along?

In addition, I am compelled to wonder from where does this illusion of reality come, if all is a reflection of Brahman or of that ultimate Reality. Or, as in the Buddhist worldview, why does this "somethingness" (which we call reality) seem so compelling in contrast to the "nothingness" or Void that is truly the essence and origin of all?

Because I want to continue my discussion with the one influenced by a pantheistic worldview, there is perhaps one question I can ask that will lead to a thoughtful, non-combative interchange: "Why is it that pain and suffering affect us so if our world is either not real or more ethereal than real?"

As you can attest, I've mentioned the themes of evil, pain and suffering at several points throughout this book. Why? They are ever-persistent themes you will confront when conversing with people about God.

I've been listening to a series of talks by Dallas Willard, professor of philosophy at the University of Southern California. Dr. Willard is both a brilliant philosopher and a believer in Christ. In speaking on the important questions of life, he suggests that the number-one question is on the nature of reality; that we all must answer the question, "What is real?" How you answer that question will govern how you live. Rather than giving a deep philosophical definition to "reality," he simply suggests: "Reality is what you run into when you are wrong. … It is what you have to deal with."[10]

I like that! And that is exactly the issue here. The person influenced by a pantheistic worldview either has to accept evil, pain and suffering as part of reality, or he must suggest that they are some kind of "lesser reality." If he dismisses them as less-than-real, then he should never need a Band-Aid, wear glasses, or require surgery. And he should ignore the evil acts of others—whether directed at him or someone else.

Furthermore, if this life is only a distant reflection of reality, the pantheist should ignore evil, pain and suffering as transitory and as indications of his or

her persistent ignorance—an indication of our continued need for enlightenment. For what is *personal* pain or *human* rights anyway if, in fact, we are to
find our identity in oneness with Brahman or our "nonbeing" in the eternal
Void? In fact, one would expect that the pantheist would view even the abuse of
others' human rights, and the pain which results, as having positive benefit—it
potentially creates the opportunity for greater self-denial and serves, ultimately,
as an aid to the enlightenment of others leading to nirvana.

And if he simply believes pain and suffering to be a lesser reality, he must
explain why he considers ultimate reality to be absolute goodness when evil,
pain and suffering are so pervasive in our experience. If "all is God and God is
all," then even evil, pain and suffering are reflections of that ultimate reality in
that nothing exists independently of it.

Eventually (as the relationship allows), an additional question could be
asked, "Since the experience of pain is so pervasive and real to so many people,
is it possible that ultimate Reality, or even Brahman, is more painful than
pleasant, more evil than good?" It is important that the pantheist deals with the
source of evil and of pain. Simply to suggest both are illusory sidesteps the issue
in a system that views all as of the One.

I happen to be named after an uncle on my father's side, who died at only
10 years of age. Though my father was eventually raised in a Christian home,
there was a period of time when his mother explored the claims of Christian
Science (a religious system which resembles pantheism in that it views God
as the essential Soul of the universe and considers evil, pain and suffering as
merely illusory).

My uncle had evidently contracted a gastrointestinal infection which
resulted in the blockage of his intestinal tract and, undoubtedly, led to a great
deal of pain. Desiring to be faithful to her Christian Science beliefs, my grandmother was instructed by her Christian Science practitioner that she should
ignore what the doctors were saying and feed her son a full course meal, because
the perception of her son's being sick was an incorrect perception. She did so,
and hours later my uncle died in convulsions.

It seems incredulous that, at such an early age, my uncle had strayed so far
from the awareness of his Source. Yet, even infants suffer and die! Those who
have never even spoken a word succumb to the grim "false reality" of this world.
Yet, *why* is this?

Even as you and I, the pantheist must wake up in the morning and look in the mirror. And, one day, he or she will have to face the all-important question, "Is the philosophy to which I ascribe consistent with what I know of the world in which I live and how I function within it?"

Regardless of the worldview they hold, your friends who have been influenced by pantheistic thought are still affected by the "realities" of this world—whether perceived to be real or less than real. They, as you and I, enjoy the morning sunshine as well as a home-cooked meal. They, as well as you and I, experience both emotional and physical pain resulting from evil words and deeds. And they, too, live life much the same way you and I do: they get up and attend classes at school, show up for work, and watch for cars when crossing a street. And they, even as you and I, mourn the death of a friend who has met death.

The more you deal with people, the more you will come face to face with the inconsistencies in the worldviews they hold. And you will more clearly understand why Jesus performed miracles, such as restoring the sight of the physically blind—these were object lessons pointing to the greater need of spiritual sight which He came to restore. His ability to change reality in the physical realm was in evidence of His ability to transform one's life in the spiritual. Jesus did not simply *dismiss* the dual realities of the physical and spiritual—He *transformed* them!

After I write the final words of this chapter, I will head over to the sporting goods store to see Eddie and deliver the book, *Jesus Among Other Gods*, by Ravi Zacharias. My prayer is that, though with a few additional words the chapter of this book will conclude, my conversation with Eddie tonight will comprise the beginning of a new chapter in my ongoing friendship with him.

We must remember that, even today, God desires to use us to communicate His transformational truth. He is the One who can leverage the often-difficult realities of this life to challenge the worldview of those aspiring to an enlightenment that ultimately erases the value of who we are—creations of God.

On his way to Damascus to persecute the Christian Church, Saul was stopped by the risen Christ and was given a new commission (and, eventually, a new name). In that roadside conversation, Jesus revealed to Saul his new mission: he was being sent to the Gentiles "to open their eyes, so that they may turn from darkness to light and from the power of Satan to God, that they may receive forgiveness of sins and a place among those who are sanctified by faith in me" (Acts 26: 17–18).

No greater message can you or I communicate to such a one, like Eddie, than that there is a God who has personally created us to know Him. Therein, he or she will discover an intrinsic value for life—previously unknown—having believed that ultimate reality is to be found in oneness with the universal Void or with the unknowable Brahman.

# *Notes*

[1] Norman L. Geisler and William Watkins. *Perspectives: Understanding and Evaluating Today's World Views* (San Bernardino: Here's Life Publishers, 1984), 70.

[2] The initial introduction of Eastern pantheism came decades earlier at the World's Parliament of Religions of 1893, held in conjunction with Chicago's Columbian Exposition of the same year. One of the most memorable speakers was an Indian Hindu sage by the name of Swami Vivekananda whose presentation was so well received that it provided him a broad national platform in the United States thus allowing him to spread the teachings of Vendantic Hindu philosophy specifically and Eastern pantheism in general.

[3] One must be careful not approach Hinduism as a monolithic belief system. It has taken on multiple forms during its approximately 3500-year development. As Corduan notes: "This religion (or, maybe better, religious culture) has moved back and forth through the various phases of monotheism, henotheism, polytheism and animism, with each phase retaining at least a vestigial presence in the ensuing one. There is no set of core beliefs that remain constant throughout. The name itself, actually a label devised by Westerners, simply means "religion of India" (Winfried Corduan, Neighboring Faiths [Downers Grove, IL: InterVarsity Press, 1998], 189). Today, however, Hinduism is accurately considered a pantheistic religion.

[4] Winfried Corduan, *Neighboring Faiths* (Downers Grove, IL: Intervarsity Press, 1998), 200–201.

[5] James Sire, *The Universe Next Door* (Downers Grove, IL: IVP Academic, 2004), 150.

[6] "The life that we experience day in and day out is simply magical play arising out of Brahman; it does not possess genuine reality. Subsequent Vedantic Hinduism thought of maya as illusion, though it is not completely necessary to say that maya has no reality whatsoever. It is sufficient to say that maya's reality is completely derived from Braham ... Everything that we experience or think about rationally belongs to maya. Maya encompasses all physical objects, including our bodies. Our feelings and emotions are maya; so are our thoughts. Even religion is part of maya..." (Corduan, 198).

Consider the following passage from the Upanishads:

"Thus Brahman is all in all. He is action, knowledge, goodness supreme. To know him, hidden in the lotus of the heart, is to untie the knot of ignorance. Self-luminous is Brahman, ever present in the hearts of all. He is the refuge of all, he is the supreme goal. In him exists all that moves and breathes. In him exists all that is. He is both that which is gross and that which is subtle. Adorable is he. Beyond the ken of the senses is he. Supreme is he. Attain thou him!" ("Mundaka," *The Upanishads: Breath of the Eternal,* trans. by Swami Prabhavananda and Frederick Manchester [New York: Mentor Books, 1957], 45).

[7] Buddhism developed in reaction to and rejection of Hinduism in that it does not accept the caste system and does not believe the Vedas to be authoritative (Ravi Zacharias, "Jesus Among other Gods." A compact disc available through Ravi Zacharias International Ministries, Atlanta, GA. www.rzim.org. Also see Corduan, 224).

[8] Technically, it is not correct to say that Buddhists consider the ultimate Essence of all to be "nothingness." Once again, note Sire:

"Zen Buddhist monism [arguably the most popular form of Buddhism in our country] holds that final reality is the Void [*sunyata*]. Final reality is nothing that can be named or grasped. To say it is nothing is incorrect, but to say it is something is equally incorrect. That would degrade its essence by reducing it to a thing among things. The Hindu One is still a thing among things, though it is the chief among things. The Void is not a thing at all. It is instead the origin of everything" (James W. Sire, *The Universe Next Door* [Downers Grove, IL: InterVarsity Press, 158]). In traditional Buddhism that "Void" could be characterized as "emptiness;" in the Mahayana branch of Buddhism, compassion (*karuna*). See also chapters seven and eight in Corduan from which I have attempted to summarize key points in view of the limited scope of this book.

[9] Geisler and Watkins, 71.

[10] Dallas Willard, "Knowledge of God Today: How it is Possible," in the compact disc series Knowledge of Christ in Today's World (available through Heart, Mind and Soul web site: http: //www.heartmindandsoul.com/ProductDetails.asp?ProductCode=Kno wledge+of+Christ+Today).

# CHAPTER 11

# Engaging the One Who Thinks Jesus Was Just Another Religious Leader

His name was Jose de Si´mon, and he was an exchange student from Spain. It was my senior year at Cajon High School in San Bernardino, California, and Jose and I had become friends.

It was an exciting year. Fifteen or 20 of the Christian students on Cajon's campus had determined to do all we could to reach our school for Christ. Apart from sponsoring school assemblies and after-school events, a significant part of the plan was simply to share the Good News of Christ with as many of our peers as possible, on an individual basis.

I knew that I had to share Christ with Jose. He was to return home to Spain, and it was quite likely our paths would never cross again.

Though I can clearly picture sitting across from Jose at lunch that day at an off-campus restaurant, I do not recall a significant portion of our conversation. What I do remember is that somewhere in my presentation of the Gospel, Jose indicated that he felt Jesus was a good man, perhaps even a great man. But at the same time, Jose believed Jesus to be just another religious leader.

It was the "God claim" that motivated Jose's response.

Jose was from a Catholic background. Of all the issues I might have anticipated in a conversation with Jose, Christ's claim to deity would not have one of them. Catholic theology is quite clear on this, and the majority of Catholics I have met hold to this unequivocally. But not Jose.

But where, in the New Testament, *did* Christ claim to be God? Though Jose did have questions about my assertion of Jesus's deity, he did *not* question the reliability of the Bible in accurately reflecting Jesus's words and works. It was just that he had never been presented with the direct claims of Christ and the words of the apostles with regard to Christ's divine nature.

The message of Christianity is fourfold: creation, separation, redemption, restoration. God creates, man rebels; God pays the penalty at His expense (Christ); man is now able to be restored in his relationship to God. For God to accept the sacrifice of Jesus, sinlessness was required. A man could surely not provide this. Yet a purely divine being could not provide a sacrifice for man.

Therefore, God chose to provide His Son, born a human yet still completely divine, in order to solve this divine dilemma. If Jesus had not been divine, He could not have been sinless. And if He were not sinless, He could never have provided a payment for the sins of others. Thus, Jesus would have become just another in the long list of religious leaders.

Jose did not simply need to understand the God claim of Christ as academic exercise; he needed to make the connection as to the "why" of its significance. Fundamentally, Jose needed to understand that Jesus's message was inextricably linked to *who* Jesus was. Thus clarification of the claim was the matter at hand.

Rather than overwhelm someone with numerous verses and passages, I have found it best to stick with one or two of the most succinct. For example, in John 10: 22–33, Jesus is conversing with some of the religious leaders of His day. They demanded to know whether or not He was the Christ.

In response to their questions, Jesus contended that His miracles should have been a sufficient indicator leading to belief. To those who did believe ("My sheep"), however, Jesus asserted that He would give them "eternal life" and that no one could take them away. He then emphasized the security of those believing by affirming that His Father would protect them as well for, indeed, "My Father, who has given them to me, is greater than all and no one is able to snatch them out of the Father's hand" (John 10: 29).

It is at this very point that Christ makes an extraordinary claim of deity— especially when you consider the strong monotheistic stance of the Jews. After proclaiming that His Father would protect those who believed in Him (Christ), He simply stated, "I and the Father are one" (John 10: 30).

Some might suggest that what Jesus meant was simply that He and God were agreed (i.e., "one in purpose"). The only problem with this position is that John records the response of the Jewish leaders, so that what Jesus meant and what was understood by the people is undeniable. If you accept John's record of what Jesus said, then you must accept the response of the people as John records it as well. If you don't, then you must not accept either. Either John provides us with an accurate historical record, or he does not.

And this is how John records the reaction of the Jewish leaders:

> The Jews picked up stones again to stone him. Jesus answered them, "I have shown you many good works from the Father; for which of them are you going to stone me?"

> The Jews answered him, "It is not for a good work that we are going to stone you but for blasphemy, because you, being a man, make yourself God." (John 8: 11-13)

If your friend requires further verification pertaining to the teaching of Jesus's deity, then why not go directly to the first chapter of John's Gospel and show him or her how the apostle, himself, viewed Jesus? John writes:

> In the beginning was the Word, and the Word was with God, and the Word was God. He was in the beginning with God (John 1: 1). [Jesus is identified as "the Word" later in the chapter.]

Jehovah's Witnesses tend to say that because the definite article ("the") does not precede "theos" (God) in the Greek, the verse should be translated *a god*, thus making Christ less than God. Though the role of the definite article in Greek is debated by scholars, one thing becomes clear as you read on—*the apostle attributes the creation of the world to the Word*: "All things were made through Him, and without Him was not any thing made that was made" (John 1: 3).

Surely John is not suggesting that the Word (Jesus) is some *lesser* god who carried out creation! How would such a declaration be in sync with the rest of Scriptures (i.e., Exodus 20: 3; Deuteronomy 32: 39; Isaiah 43: 10)? And can you really imagine that such a concept would be readily accepted by the initially, largely rabbinic readership of first century Christianity?

Furthermore, one cannot simply dismiss Christ as only God's agent (emphasizing the Greek preposition *dia*, translated as "through," at the beginning of verse three). Though that is accurate, the Scriptures make it clear that God created, and even if it was accomplished *through* Christ, the Word must share in the very nature of God.

The dynamic of John is found in his identification of Jesus as the only Son of God. The very concept of son assumes a father; the two sharing the same nature. A human father does not beget a less-than-human son. The analogy is clear: neither does a divine Father beget a less-than-divine Son. Jesus claimed to be God, and the religious leaders of His day understood that clearly. (See John 5: 16–18.)

God, in His infinite wisdom, has chosen to reveal Himself as three—not separate entities at separate times but as three co-equal and co-eternal Persons who, in relationship to one another, accomplish God's eternal plan with complete harmony, each working out His divine role. (See Ephesians 1 for a good illustration of this.)

To suggest that John is putting forth Jesus as some kind of lesser god (in contrast to Jehovah) is also contrary to the picture the apostle paints concerning Jesus's character. For example, John attributes qualities to Jesus attributed to God in the Old Testament (e.g., grace, mercy, truth); he asserts that Jesus is a reflection of God's glory or essence (John 1: 14 and 1: 18); and, the miracles of Jesus he cites place Him in close association with the Jehovah of the Old Testament.

Therefore, if Jesus were not God in human flesh, John would be advancing a polytheism absolutely foreign to the Jewish mind and contrary to the (Old Testament) Scriptures that the authors of the New Testament passionately and consistently affirmed in their writings. One must not forget that the apostles (being Jewish) were ardently *monotheistic* yet had come to the conviction that their hope of a Messiah—concerning which their Scriptures so clearly prophesied—had found fulfillment in the person of Jesus of Nazareth.

The biblical record is unmistakable. The claims Jesus made as to His deity are backed up by the authors of the New Testament. If one is ready to accept the Bible as an accurate record of Jesus's words and actions, as well as a reliable source of the writings of His followers, then it is virtually impossible to dismiss Jesus as simply "another great religious teacher."

As I sat across from Jose on that sunny California afternoon, I knew I had to challenge his misconception of the person and work of Jesus Christ. Otherwise, he would continue to view Christianity as simply another can on the shelf—one more choice among religious systems, equal in merit, having more to do with the cultural framework of the follower than the validity of the belief system itself.

Earlier that year, I had become acquainted with an illustration first used by C.S. Lewis in *Mere Christianity* and later popularized by Josh McDowell in his compendium of evidences for the Christian faith, *Evidence That Demands a Verdict*. The illustration was appropriately titled *The Trilemma: Lord, Liar, or Lunatic*. After I had pointed out to Jose a couple of key passages, like the ones cited above, I drew out the diagram (pictured below) on a napkin as I explained its significance. Our conversation went something like this:

"Jose, you have two choices as to the claims of Christ. They were either true, or they were false." At this point, I wrote down "False" on the right-hand side of the napkin and the word "True" on the left. I pointed my pen to "False" as I continued.

"If Jesus's claims were false, then two options exist; either he knew they were false or he did not." At this point, I drew the two arrows slanting downward, as illustrated. At the tip of one arrow I wrote "Knew claims were false" and at the tip of the other, "Didn't know claims were false." Then I said, "If Jesus knew His claims were false, then He was a great deceiver, for He asserted that one's faith in Him would result in that person's having a relationship with God." I now drew another arrow down from "Knew claims were false" and wrote the word "Liar."

"As is obvious, Jose, if Jesus *knew* His claims were false, he would not have been a good, moral teacher. In fact, I would suggest He might even have been one of the most evil of people who ever lived, for He went to death purporting His claims to be true, knowing fully that there would be those who would place confidence in all He had proclaimed. As a result they would spend an eternity separated from God. Perhaps someone of such evil character could have been even a demon from hell." I now drew another arrow down from "Liar" and put at its tip the word "Demon."

"On the other hand, perhaps Jesus was a good man, just severely deluded. Perhaps He really believed His claims to be true, but just didn't know it."

I now pointed my pen to the words, "Didn't know claims were false," and continued. "Of course," Jose, "given the fact that He didn't know his claims were false, and He went to the cross believing them to be true, one must assume He was a lunatic; that is, He was mentally imbalanced." I now drew an arrow down from "Didn't know claims were false" and wrote the word "Lunatic" at the tip of that arrow.

THE TRILEMMA: WAS JESUS LORD, LIAR OR LUNATIC? [2]

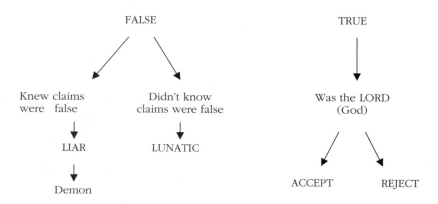

"Yet, given all that we know about the life and words of Jesus, it seems difficult to hold either of these two options. Could one who has influenced more people for good, whose words have brought hope and encouragement to people throughout the centuries, whose teachings have set the framework for just societies, truly have been evil? If so, we need more 'evil' people like Him!

"It seems incredible, at least to me, that one who spoke so clearly, who had followers as He, who argued with the religious leaders and intellects of His time really have been *crazy*? Indeed, there are few others throughout recorded history who have drawn people to themselves as Jesus did. Can you think of *any* historian or philosopher or psychologist who has suggested that Jesus was worthy of a mental institution?

"Jose, if Jesus was neither liar nor lunatic, then He must have been conveying the truth. His influence on those who knew him best—so that even they were willing to give their lives for what Jesus proclaimed—suggests that what He said and did was believed to be true. And if what Jesus said was true, then it means that He was God's Son and, as such, shared in the very nature of God. Indeed, Jesus claimed to speak and act with divine authority; in fact, He asserted that one's relationship with God would be based on one's response to the claims He made."

Though Jose had listened carefully, as I proceeded with my illustration point by point, it was evident by what little he said that much of what I presented was new to him. Jose had lived his life following a Jesus who was simply a very wise man, who offered good advice, rather than as the Son of God to whom he must, one day, give account. Though he was not willing to affirm Christ as God's Son during what would be the last of any significant spiritual conversation I would have with him, my prayer continues to be that God's Spirit will continue His work in Jose's life and even, perhaps, someday, remind him of the conversation we had on that sunny, California day, now so many years ago.

## *Notes*

[1] Affirmation of Jesus's deity is by no means confined to the authors of the Gospels. The following passages are in evidence of this:

"He is the image of the invisible God, the firstborn of all creation. For by him all things were created, in heaven and on earth, visible and invisible, whether thrones or dominions or rulers or authorities—all things were created through him and for him. And he is before all things, and in him all things hold together" (Colossians 1: 15-17).

"Long ago, at many times and in many ways, God spoke to our fathers by the prophets, but in these last days he has spoken to us by his Son, whom he appointed the heir of all things, through whom also he created the world. He is the radiance of the glory of God and the exact imprint of his nature, and he upholds the universe by the word of his power ..." (Hebrews 1: 1-3a).

[2] Adapted from *The New Evidence that Demands a Verdict* by Josh McDowell (Nashville: Thomas Nelson Publisher, 1999), 158.

# A Conversation Between Two Friends

# CHAPTER 12

# How *Not* to Begin

RYAN: Hey, Lisa! Que pasa?

Lisa: I'm fine. What's your day about?

Ryan: Not much. School's always the same. But right now I'm on the way to philosophy class.

Lisa: Philosophy class? When did you pick up that? Didn't know you were into philosophy.

Ryan: For sure! But I actually have been wanting to learn more about world beliefs and religions. I'm curious about all the issues in the Middle East, terrorism, and the motivations driving the craziness we see all around. By the way, speaking of religions, aren't you religious, or do you think of yourself as being spiritual?

Lisa: Yes. I'm a Christian. I go to Shoreline Chapel.

Ryan: Oh, that's interesting!

Lisa: What do you mean by "that's interesting"?

Ryan: Well, our teacher was talking about terrorism the other day and started on the subject of religious fundamentalism. He feels that religion—in all its forms—is just a way for people who feel disenfranchised to have a bigger purpose; you know, to help them gain a sense of belonging and power. He compared the people at Shoreline Chapel to the radical Shiites!

Lisa: That's crazy!

Ryan: I thought it was a stretch at first. But then he began to lay out his assertion rationally. Let's face it—radical Islam's agenda is to gain world attention through terrorism and some control over a world pretty much dominated by the West. It seems that Christianity has its own power bloc, and the Christians at a place like Shoreline Chapel seem to be pretty radical, trying to influence the politics of the area as well as get others to join in. So it seems somewhat logical to me, though I guess you guys haven't gone around killing people—yet!

Lisa: I thought we were friends. I can't believe you would fall for something so totally stupid! So, besides thinking I'm some terrorist in hiding, I suppose you don't believe in God or anything either! Am I correct?

Ryan: Well, it just depends *whose* God you are talking about. Right? I mean, your God is different from Islam's God, which is different from Hinduism's God or gods—and down the path we go. So if everyone is able to develop his own God, who's to say that belief in no God is all that bad? I mean, if everyone's belief in God is different, than who is to say one person's God is better than another's? Or that there is really any God at all?

Lisa: Well, *I* believe that there is a God, and that's all that matters.

Ryan: So, it really is OK for me to choose another God than yours? Is that what Shoreline Chapel would teach?

Lisa: All I know is that I have faith there is a God who really cares for me.

Ryan: And that's cool. But just remember that more than a billion Chinese have faith in the teachings of Buddha; hundreds of millions of Indians have faith in the teachings of Hinduism; millions of Middle Easterners have faith in the teaching of Mohammed. You really aren't suggesting that your particular belief about God is right and theirs is wrong, are you? If so, then maybe you are closer to the Shiites than I thought!

Lisa: This conversation is so totally not cool. You know, I think you should just go on to your totally stupid philosophy class and when you come back down to earth, we can talk again!

Ryan: OK. If that's the way you want it. I just thought you were a bit more tolerant than that.

Lisa: Oh, Mr. Tolerant plays the martyr. That's an interesting switch!

# CHAPTER 13

# How to Begin Again: Choosing to *Engage* and Not React

RYAN: (quietly reading a text message from Lisa) "Local terrorist wants to meet. Promise only to talk, not claw. Meet you at 3: 00 at Steinberg Hall Starbucks. OK? (Ryan quietly responds with a quick "OK.")

[Next scene: Starbucks. Both Lisa and Ryan enter simultaneously.]

Lisa: Que pasa, Ryan?

Ryan: Hey, Lisa. Thanks for the message. I didn't think you'd ever speak to me again after the other day. I guess I took it a bit far.

Lisa: Actually, Ryan, I think I took it a bit far. But before we talk about the other day, let me buy you a frappacino with double-shot of caffeine—if I remember correctly?

Ryan: Not bad, not bad at all! Guess I'll have to try that strategy again: insult girl, get free frap at Starbucks. Life's not so bad after all!

Lisa: Don't press your luck, son. That is, unless you prefer to *wear* that frappacino rather than drink it! (Lisa offers Ryan a big smile as she gives the drink order to the waiter.)

[Ryan and Lisa take their drinks and sit at table.]

Lisa: OK, I guess it's my turn to start this conversation. I was really wrong in how I overreacted to what you said about the whole terrorist thing.

Ryan: (interrupting) No, not really. I deserved it. Though you and I differ a lot about this whole God and faith thing, the comment about being a terrorist was way out of line. And you know Prof. Jacobsen's reputation—he tends to overemphasize in order to make a point. I should never have pinned his label on you.

Lisa: Fair enough. But I still shouldn't have overacted. Honestly, Ryan, when I left I felt as though I had totally blown it. Here I am talking about being a Christian and then, the next thing you know, I'm getting really angry at you.

Ryan: Yeah, you really were upset, weren't you?

Lisa: Yes.

Ryan: Well, you've been straight up with me, so I guess I should be the same with you. I felt badly that I had hurt your feelings.

Lisa: Really?

Ryan: Yes, really. I mean we've been friends since middle school. The last thing I wanted to do was to nail you like I did. In some ways, I wish we could put this whole "God thing" aside.

Lisa: I think you know I could never do that. At the same time, though, I think there is a way we could talk about it, like a discussion between really good friends.

Ryan: How's that?

Lisa: Well, someone recently suggested to me there were two key questions in life: Is there a God? And if so, can He be known? In other words, if there is a God, is it possible to have contact and communication with Him?

Ryan: That's interesting. I don't think I ever thought about it like that before.

Lisa: It makes sense, though, don't you think? Before one can think about knowing God, he must be sure there even is a God to know. And once someone concludes there is a God, he must think about the qualities of that God and whether or not God is impersonal or personal, the kind of God He is, and how He can be discovered and known.

Ryan: (laughing) So who's talking philosophy today?

Lisa: Well, maybe so, but I am not sure I'm content with just talking about God. I mean, if a God doesn't exist, or if He does exist but is so distant that He is virtually irrelevant, then why waste my time talking about it? I'm only willing to give so much time talking about matters that have little or no relevance to life! You know what I mean?

Ryan: You sound as though you can know whether or not God exists, like I can tell you for sure we are talking here today. Last I checked, science could not prove that which does not exist in the physical realm. And apart from tangible proof, Lisa, I could never believe in God. That's not to say that I think it is wrong to have faith; it is just that I always think facts and figures.

Lisa: So, am I correct in understanding you to say that apart from scientific inquiry, there is no way to know something for certain?

Ryan: Yes, I guess that would be a fair understanding of what I am saying.

Lisa: Ryan, how would you prove 10 minutes from now—*scientifically*—that we were having this conversation?

Ryan: Hmmm. That's a good question. I never thought about that. I guess I couldn't prove it. Perhaps it, too, will become simply a matter of faith.

Lisa: Ryan! Don't be silly! How could you *prove* we had this conversation?

Ryan: Now I see what you're driving at. I could have our waiter testify he took an order from us. I could also see if anyone else—like Tim and Amy over there—happened to see us talking. I could pull up your phone's log and find your message saved in my phone, and so on. Is that what you are getting at?

Lisa: Exactly! One of life's big questions, Ryan, is, "How do we know what we know?" All I'm attempting to suggest is that there are additional ways, beyond scientific inquiry, to know whether or not something accurately reflects the reality one perceives. For example, let's take your philosophy class.

Ryan: I think I see where you are headed with this one. In other words, how could I prove whether or not a philosophical statement is true or false, scientifically? Am I right?

Lisa: Yes.

Ryan: (smiling) You can't! It is just a matter of opinion, based on one's experience and conditioned by one's environment. It is just a matter of faith … just like religious belief!

Lisa: Now, my friend, Ryan, are you *really* willing to say there is no relationship between philosophical statements and real life observation?

Ryan: Now I'm lost.

Lisa: Let me think of an example. OK, It's like this. When a scientist writes an opinion based on an experiment, isn't she stating—in words—the results of the research? And aren't those words really combinations of abstract symbols? And because those abstract symbols represent far more than simply ink impressions on a paper, is not their meaning *beyond* scientific verification?

Ryan: I suppose. In other words, what you are saying is that even in the realm of scientific inquiry and study the deductions are communicated via a medium that transcends the ability of science to evaluate? In fact, I guess you could even back the process up one step and say that the opinion of the scientist—even before it is written—could almost enter the philosophical realm because the data is evaluated in the mind of the scientist, influenced by that particular scientist's background, compared with other information outside the realm of that particular experiment and a judgment made about the implications of the results that may even go beyond the limits of the experiment. Am I tracking with you? (Ryan displays his satisfaction with a wide grin).

Lisa: Impressive! Someone has said that reality is that which is, and truth consists of statements that mirror the same. When I asked you to meet me at Starbucks in Steinberg Hall, you read my message, understood the contents, and acted accordingly. Both of us are now sitting here at Starbucks in Steinberg Hall, talking. The statement I made you evaluated, responded to it by coming to an actual location, at an actual time, and the accuracy of my statement is reflected in the fact that you and I are both experiencing the same reality and can talk about that reality.

Ryan: Good point. Essentially you're saying that, in some way, we possess the ability to make real-life connections between the statements we make and the reality we experience.

Lisa: I couldn't have said it better, my friend! And even though those statements, as the events they describe, lie outside the realm of scientific inquiry, the resulting time/space realities they represent are able to be evaluated historically, philosophically and linguistically so that that which you and I communicate has meaningful correspondence and confirmation in our mutual experiences.

Ryan: So, maybe my philosophy class is not so much up in the clouds as I may have thought.

Lisa: No, and neither is the possibility of knowing the existence of God for certain.

Ryan: How's that? Now you've jumped from philosophical statements dealing with time/space realities to that which, by its very definition, is not a part of time/space reality; namely, God's existence. That is, if He *does* exist!

Lisa: Only one problem.

Ryan: What's that?

Lisa: That's if God chose to reveal Himself through various means *within* the realm of time/space existence. And that is exactly what I would like to talk about during our next meeting at Starbucks!

Ryan: You just love to leave me hanging, don't you, Lis? OK, I'll agree to it. You've got my curiosity up. Besides, you're a lot better looking than my philosophy prof! Next time, my treat.

Lisa: Well, at least my image has improved somewhat! So, how about next Thursday at 3: 00?

# CHAPTER 14

# Rational Reasons
# Suggesting God's Existence

*[Ryan is already seated at table when Lisa enters]*

LISA: (obviously very much in a hurry, almost dropping her book bag as she enters) Oh, Ryan, I'm so sorry! My test in Algebra went—

Ryan: (interrupting) Calm down; calm down, Lisa. I've just been catching up on some reading. Oh, and by the way, your mocha chip cappuccino should be just about ready. My treat this time. I have a feeling you are going to need it!

[Lisa picks up her drink from the counter and sits at the table across from Ryan. She takes a sip of her cappuccino.]

Lisa: Ahh! This tastes so good. Thanks so much, Ryan. But what did you mean by your having a feeling I'm going to need this?

Ryan: Well, I've been doing some thinking about our last conversation, and I've got some questions.

Lisa: OK. Sounds good, but don't expect me to have all the answers.

Ryan: To begin with, you are coming to this discussion with a lot of presuppositions.

Lisa: Such as?

Ryan: Well, first off, you have the concept in your head that God is a personal being; that is, that He somewhat resembles us—

Lisa: (interrupting) No, I don't believe God has a body with hands and feet and—

Ryan: (interrupting) Hold on; let me finish. No, I know you don't think of God as possessing a body, but you think of Him as definitely possessing personality. In that way, you consider Him to be a rational being who is able to think and communicate and so on.

Lisa: So, doesn't that make sense?

Ryan: To you, yes. But don't forget there are religions, such as Buddhism, where it is believed that ultimate reality is unity with the unquantifiable Void—though I confess I find that difficult to comprehend. And then there are other religions that are pantheistic, where God is more the Force behind all or the universal Mind—not really a personal being like in Christianity. So, my question is simply this: why do you think your picture of God is the correct one?

Lisa: Well, that's what the Bible communicates.

Ryan: I am trying to look at this whole thing objectively, and now you bring in the Bible. Who's to say the Bible has anything more to say on the matter than the Quran or the Hindu Scriptures or the writings of the Buddha or even, for that matter, Dan Brown or Sam Harris?

Lisa: OK, OK. I admit I moved way ahead with that one. Do you mind if I take it a couple of steps back?

Ryan: Be my guest!

Lisa: I would suggest that the design of the universe suggests personality.

Ryan: Now if you are going to start talking the whole Intelligent Design debate, you might as well point me to the Bible!

Lisa: And what, pray tell, do you mean by that?

Ryan: Intelligent Design is basically creationism with a new twist, right? It's Genesis with 21st century marketing.

Lisa: No way!

Ryan: Way!

Lisa: Let me ask a question, because I think we are saying one thing while both of us mean another. How would *you* define Intelligent Design?

Ryan: That's simple. Intelligent design is the belief that God created the universe in seven days.

Lisa: Well, I concur that some may think of it that way. But here's what *I* am talking about. Intelligent Design is the conclusion drawn from scientific observation that suggests, from the complexity of the systems observed that intelligence, rather that mere chance, is the best explanation of cause.

Ryan: Pretty fancy definition. But I still don't think that's what most people mean by Intelligent Design.

Lisa: OK. I'll admit there is a lot of debate on the whole I.D. question.

So, let me suggest an alternative. How about we stop talking about Intelligent Design, and let's start talking about *purposeful causation*. How's that?

Ryan: As I said, you're one bright kid!

Lisa: Well, there are several areas of scientific inquiry, all of which seem to exhibit a great deal of intricacy and complexity. I would suggest that when complexity and intricacy are apparent, one should consider intelligence as a factor in the equation.

Ryan: But given a sufficient amount of time virtually *anything* is possible, even order from disorder, wouldn't you agree?

Lisa: Well, that's actually an interesting question with a number of different angles. But at the outset, we've got to ask the basic question.

Ryan: And what is the basic question?

Lisa: One has to deal with the matter of first cause or causes. In other words, where did that which has been ordered come from in the first place? We could sit here all day and talk about the ability of time and chance to provide order and still miss the larger issue—where did it all come from to begin with? And that leads right to the first area of scientific inquiry, which provides some indication of intelligence in the equation.

Ryan: And what area is that?

Lisa: Cosmology. You know, the origin of the universe.

Ryan: But how does the Big Bang suggest intelligence?

Lisa: Great question! I was hoping you would ask that! Others suggest alternative models to the Big Bang, but I assume that you and I can agree that it is, at the present, the most popular model as to the origin of the universe. Right?

Ryan: I'll buy that one.

Lisa: And what was one of the most significant conclusions coming from the Big Bang theory?

Ryan: Well, if you mean that, previously, it was held that the universe was eternal, the Big Bang theorized that the universe had a beginning; that it was finite. Correct?

Lisa: Correct. Furthermore, the Big Bang—or maybe we should call it the Great Expansion or something—was the beginning of everything we know: time, space, matter and energy. Before the Big Bang, nothing existed—at least, nothing as we know it.

Ryan: So where or from what did that infinitesimally and infinitely small singularity of matter, energy and space first come? Is that where you are headed?

Lisa: Exactly!

Ryan: Well, I assume you will say God. But I may choose to say it was born out of another, mother universe or something.

Lisa: Well, you may do that, but just pushing its origin back one step doesn't really solve the problem. You can logically have an infinite regression of causes, but you can't have that in the real world. Somewhere, you *have* to have a beginning.

Ryan: So, then, where did God begin?

Lisa: The same place that your eternal reality—whatever that may be—began. I would say God is the uncaused first cause. If there is a God, He has always existed. And that really isn't a statement one has to get all hung up on. Everyone posits an uncaused first cause. Whether it be the concept of an eternal universe held by the Greek philosophers, Eastern pantheists or Steady State scientists or those who choose to somewhat ignore the issue by simply pushing back the process one step by suggesting a "multiverse" origin of our universe. My point is that something has to begin somewhere with something that is eternal and uncaused.

Ryan: I have a feeling this discussion could go on for a while, but I have a class coming up.

Lisa: OK. Let me put a wrap on this. I've been doing some reading recently on what has been called the fine tuning of the universe. Ryan, it is so totally awesome how all this has come together, even down to the mass and charge of the subatomic particles, to the level of gravitational force, as well as the level of the strong nuclear force that holds the protons and electrons together. If these were calibrated even the slightest bit differently, life would not or could not exist. For example, without the strong nuclear force, there would be no atoms. Without electromagnetic force, you would have no bonding between chemicals. If the force of gravity was changed slightly, complex life forms could not exist beyond the size of a pea without being crushed. These are constants our very existence depends on.

Ryan: Where have you been reading this stuff?

Lisa: Something else I've read has really struck me, and that's the discoverability of the universe. It is almost as though we have this connection with the universe, a connection that goes far beyond anything that we should have if our intelligence developed simply to make it easier for the human species to hunt and mate and migrate. It is as though we have an intelligence that has been designed to both discover and understand aspects of our existence that have nothing to do with survival alone. I have to ask why and from where? Ryan, it doesn't seem unreasonable to wonder if there might be a *Someone* who designed the universe and designed us.

Ryan: You are actually making quite a bit of sense. I've never thought much about what came before all that we know. The concept of a first cause has always seemed a bit theoretical to me. Maybe until today. Maybe I'm not totally committed to the position that God doesn't exist. But even if He does, I'm still not sure that He has much relevance for today.

Lisa: But do you understand, Ryan, that if there is a God and if He is knowable, that we can have contact and communication with Him? This adds a dimension to life, a sense of purpose, that doesn't otherwise exist. In my thinking, it is this sense of purpose—which all of us strive to know and experience—that also provides another area for consideration in our discussion. But I guess that's for another day.

Ryan: Yeah, definitely. I'm late for class. See you next week?

Lisa: Absolutely!

# CHAPTER 15

# Is Science the Only Way to Know Truth?

*[Lisa is sitting outside, reading at a picnic table, as Ryan approaches unexpectedly.]*

RYAN: Que pasa, Lisa?

Lisa: Oh, Ryan, you startled me!

Ryan: Sorry about that! When did you stop studying inside the library?

Lisa: Ever since the weather invited me back outside. Isn't this a great day?

Ryan: It is definitely a great day. Do you have time for one of our conversations, or do you need to finish your reading?

Lisa: Actually, just as you walked up, I was thinking, "What a great day for a conversation with Ryan!"

Ryan: (smiling) So, the other day I just happened to pick up an article that referenced Richard Dawkins.

Lisa: Dawkins? Do you mean the British ethologist?

Ryan: Yes, I have the article right here in my notebook ... Dawkins writes, "Scientific beliefs are supported by evidence, and they get results. Myths and faiths are not and do not."[1] I am still not sure that science, even if it's not the only way to know something, still isn't the best way. How do you respond to someone like a Dawkins?

Lisa: Just as I would respond to someone who says, "It is impossible to construct a sentence in the English language."

Ryan: (looking confused) I don't see where you are headed on this one.

Lisa: First of all, I don't know as much about science as Richard Dawkins, but I can still make rational observations about something, just like you and I commented earlier on what a beautiful day it is without either of us knowing much about meteorology.

Ryan: You mean the difference between first-order questions and second-order questions?

Lisa: Yes, that's right. Dawkins holds to the belief that I would call scientism.

Ryan: Scientism? What's the term mean?

Lisa: Scientism is the philosophical position that asserts that science is the only way, or at least the best way, to know something to be real or true.[2] The only problem with that position is that its very premise is self-refuting—like the statement I made about it being impossible to construct a sentence in the English language. Obviously, through that sentence I did exactly what the sentence says cannot be done. Thus, to use a sentence in the English language to express the idea that one could never construct a sentence in the English language is a self-referentially incoherent proposition. In other words, the statement is logically flawed. Science, by its very nature, proves the existence of things in the physical world—things that we can touch, taste, smell, hear, or see. Conversely, science is *not* able to validate things that lie outside that realm.

Ryan: You mean like philosophical statements?

Lisa: Exactly; just like the statement "Science is the surest way to know something to be true." Thus, it can't be proven—not by scientific means, at least—to be either true or false. The statement invalidates or refutes itself.

Ryan: I see what you are saying. I just can't believe it is just that simple. Guys like Dawkins are brilliant.

Lisa: I won't argue Dawkins's brilliance; I am just arguing that the premise of his philosophical position is wrong. Remember, he is a scientist and not a philosopher. And I think he has made a logical error that has nothing to do with real science. But I've got another problem with what he said.

Ryan: What's that?

Lisa: How would you feel if someone told your mom, "Ryan's three best friends are murderers and thieves"?

Ryan: Obviously, the statement wouldn't be true, and I would be ticked off.

Lisa: And might I suggest that you would be upset for at least two reasons? First, you would question which friends this person was talking about; no names have been attached to the person's assertion. Second, you would be right to question the person's motive. It would be guilt by association and would lead your mom to wonder if her son, too, was a murderer and a thief.

Ryan: OK. I would assume you are referring to that part of Dawkin's quote, where he aligns faith and myths, and are questioning his motive as a result. Right?

Lisa: Sure, absolutely. Wouldn't you? As you noted, this guy isn't stupid. But let's just give him the benefit of the doubt and assume that he is so into his position that he doesn't even realize what he did. It's just an honest mistake. Do you remember our earlier conversation about how there are ways to know something to be true other than science?

Ryan: Yeah, I almost forgot. You asked me whether or not I could prove, scientifically, that we had met and talked. And then you suggested there are other kinds of evidence, like historical evidence or the evidence of eyewitnesses.

Lisa: That's right. And Dawkins's statement is a perfect illustration of one who has limited the ability to know reality to scientific inquiry alone. If you want to limit understanding of reality to scientific inquiry alone, then there would be no way to validate events in history. We couldn't prove that you and I were friends, or that our moms loved us. Discussions about philosophy would be meaningless and unverifiable, and if you were to ask me to meet you at Starbucks, I just wouldn't show up—there would be no way for me to verify, scientifically, that you had actually invited me.

Ryan: Your point is well taken. But what does tangible evidence have to do with faith? Doesn't the term "faith" simply mean "believing in something you really can't prove"? I'm not knocking it. I'm just trying to understand where you are coming from in this.

Lisa: Frankly, if I really believed that faith was as you said—believing in something you really can't prove—I wouldn't have time for it. In fact, I would say it was a waste of time.

Ryan: That's an intriguing statement.

Lisa: Maybe, but it is an accurate statement, because the definition of faith you gave is nowhere near the Christian view of faith. The Christian view of faith is confidence or trust one places in a person or object that has been proven reliable. When it comes to a person, I can't put a person in a test tube, test his reliability under controlled circumstances, and then conclude this person is reliable. But you can consider relational and historical evidence in the time/ space dimension. In other words, I am talking about the kind of evidence that allows us to trust each other as friends. So, let me ask you, why do you think I'm your friend?

Ryan: I would have to say … you are my friend because you have always been there for me, like the time when my mom was diagnosed with cancer. You went with me to visit her in the hospital.

Lisa: Yes, I remember that well. I never thought that was a big deal; it just seemed like the *right* thing to do.

Ryan: But I had many other friends who could have done the same and didn't. And in thinking about what you did, I realize that there are so many times I have known the right thing to do and have chosen not to do it. Do you know what I mean?

Lisa: Yes, Ryan, I do. Could I tell you why I consider *you* a friend?

Ryan: Sure.

Lisa: I consider you a friend because I have come to trust you. You have always been straightforward with me, you have always shown up when you said you would, and you've always given me help when I've asked. That allows me to have faith that when you say you are going to meet me at Starbucks, I know that you will. That is really what the Bible is talking about when it speaks of having faith in God; it *trust* based on God's revelation of Himself in time/ space history. In the Old Testament, God revealed Himself to the Jewish people through various means, while in the New Testament He has done so primarily through the words and works of Jesus. People believed in God because of things they saw with their own eyes and heard with their ears. Does that make sense?

Ryan: Yes. But let's go back to that whole idea of self-refuting statements for a minute. So often I hear Christians say something like, "Your position is wrong because the Bible teaches this or that." Like you did just now—you appealed to the Bible to prove your point. Isn't that almost like a self-refuting statement?

Lisa: I don't think that would necessarily be self-refuting; after all, the Bible *is* a historical collection of writings that presents certain stories and ideas focused on God and His relationship to humanity. But to simply use the Bible's statements about itself to prove the validity of the Bible does border on circular reasoning, I'll agree. It would be much more helpful to demonstrate the Bible's reliability as a historical text before appealing to its authority. You know what I mean?

Ryan: But that, in part, is my point. The proof of the Bible's reliability— like the stories it has of Jesus, its being written by God, whatever—is taken from the Bible. How can you validate or invalidate something if you rely *solely* on the information source attempting to be validated?

Lisa: Let me suggest a couple of thoughts on the whole idea of the reliability of the Bible. If the Bible is *not* a reliable historical document, then we've got a major problem. If it is simply a collection of culturally-influenced stories then there would be little basis to suggest it contains transcendent truth regarding God. In fact, as I think about it, we really could say nothing more about Jesus than that He was simply a very good person whose message was misunderstood and, as a result, He died an unfortunate death. So, would you happen to have an extra five minutes?

Ryan: You're on.

Lisa: Evidence for the Bible's reliability is usually examined from three perspectives. First is the bibliographical test, which involves looking at manuscript evidence, such as numbers of manuscripts, condition of manuscripts, age of manuscripts, and so on. The second line of consideration deals with internal evidence; that is, claims the Bible makes for itself and consistency in what it teaches. Third is the area of external evidence, which examines the accuracy of the document and how it lines up with what we know about history, geography, and other things. So, when the Bible mentions a particular political ruler, for example, the external evidence would examine the record of history to verify accuracy.[3]

Ryan: So, Christians do allow for outside evidence in validating the Bible?

Lisa: Absolutely. Actually, there is an entire science devoted to the study of ancient writings, called textual criticism, which is applied to all ancient manuscripts—including the Bible—in determining their reliability. Recently, I did some reading on this and was really amazed at how the Bible stands unique among the books of the ancient world.

Ryan: How so?

Lisa: Well, first of all, remember that the Bible was not written by a few people in a short period of time. The Bible, both Old and New Testaments, was written over a period of 1500 years by over 40 different authors, who lived on three different continents—Asia, Africa, and Europe—and who wrote from various cultural backgrounds. The fact that they speak in continuity with each other on the variety of topics discussed is amazing in and of itself.

Ryan: Keep going; you're on a roll!

Lisa: Besides that, the manuscript evidence is just awesome. Remember, of course, that the first books of the Hebrew Scriptures—the Jewish Law or Torah—were written about 1400 BC. I say "first books" because the writings of the Old Testament alone encompass a period of almost a thousand years! Though it was always assumed that the Hebrew Scriptures, as a whole, had been transmitted with accuracy, we really didn't know how accurate until an *amazing* discovery was made. That discovery was the Dead Sea Scrolls.

Ryan: That's funny that you mention the Dead Sea Scrolls. I noticed that our museum is going to be hosting an exhibit with the scrolls later this year, but I wasn't sure of their significance.

Lisa: Here's the significance: when a Bedouin shepherd boy in 1947 discovered the first few scrolls, the earliest Old Testament manuscripts any museum had were dated from around AD 900.

Ryan: Why so late?

Lisa: As I understand it, Jews considered the Scriptures as holy so they would not allow a scroll to deteriorate. They feared that a deteriorating scroll would become illegible and would lose some of the words or phrases and that the message they considered as divine could be could be easily compromised. So, they often destroyed old manuscripts after carefully copying them onto new scrolls. The pains they went through to ensure the accuracy of that is a story in itself. With the discovery of the Dead Sea Scrolls, the result of the meticulous work of the copyists became evident.

Ryan: In what way?

Lisa: Of the hundreds of manuscripts found, one of the most incredible finds was a scroll of the prophet Isaiah. It was at least 1000 years older than any previously known copy of Isaiah that scholars had at the time. And you know what happened when they compared the later manuscripts with the Isaiah scroll discovered near the Dead Sea?

Ryan: Let me guess—they were almost identical?

Lisa: Exactly! About 95 percent! In fact, the five percent variation had to do primarily with some changes in spelling that had occurred in the natural development of the language and some obvious copyist errors.[4] No new teachings had been introduced, no portions added or whatever. In other words, Isaiah could pick up a copy of our Bible today and would accept the book named after him as a viable translation of what he had written 2600 years ago! Now, *that* is awesome!

I've got to go to class, but I should mention a couple of things about the

New Testament. Basically, there is more manuscript evidence for the New Testament than any other ancient document. Though the first complete copy of the New Testament is dated around the early part of the fourth century, there are older papyrus copies that are dated to the early AD 200s and from which almost the entire New Testament can be constructed. Of course, when you find copies that early, they obviously point to a much earlier original. For example, many scholars today will date the Gospel of Mark, one of the biographical books written by a follower of Jesus, within 20 to 30 years of Jesus's death. That means, of course, it would have to have been written at a time when eyewitnesses would still have been alive—those who could have verified or falsified what was written. The extensive numbers of manuscripts, as well as their distribution throughout the Mediterranean world, also suggests something else many people overlook.

Ryan: What's that?

Lisa: It means that these books weren't hidden away in some closet. They were written to be read and circulated broadly. That means—

Ryan: (excitedly) It means that the details of times, places, specific events—I suppose even like the miracles Jesus purportedly performed—were recorded so that people who had lived while Jesus lived could confirm the accuracy of the details. Am I right?

Lisa: Absolutely. And all I've really talked about is the bibliographical evidences for the Bible's accuracy and uniqueness. I haven't even mentioned anything about the Bible's consistency in the topics it discusses, or how archaeological discoveries over the past 150 years have only verified the specific civilizations and/or leaders it references, even those whose existence was questioned for years by historians. The really big question is, "Can a book reveal truth about God?" As I consider the uniqueness of both the Old and New Testaments, the manner in which they have been preserved so remarkably through time, regardless of the persecution of both the Jews and Christians, the consistency of the themes they address, the way in which those themes seem to mirror reality—is it possible that even language itself could be a link to discovering truth about God?

Ryan: Perhaps that's a question we can discuss next time.

Lisa: (hurrying off to class) Right. Text me when you want to get together again.

# Notes

[1] Richard Dawkins, *River Out of Eden: A Darwinian View of Life* (New York: Basic Books, 1995), 33.

[2] John C. Lennox, *God's Undertaker: Has Science Buried God?* (Oxford: Lion Hudson plc, 2007), 38–43. Lennox notes: "Scientism does not need to be refuted by external argument: it self-destructs…For, the statement that only science can lead to truth is not itself deduced from science. It is not a scientific statement but rather a statement about science, that is, it is a metascientific statement. Therefore, if scientism's basic principle is true, the statement expressing scientism must be false. Scientism refutes itself. Hence it is incoherent." (42)

[3] Jimmy Williams, "Are the Biblical Documents Reliable?," Probe Ministries, http: // www.probe.org/site/apps/nlnet/content2.aspx?c=fdKEIMNsEoG&b=4244795&ct=5 516753 (accessed April 26, 2007).

[4] Brantley, Garry K, "The Dead Sea Scrolls and Biblical Integrity," ApologeticsPress. org,http: //www.apologeticspress.org/articles/266 (accessed April 27, 2007).

CHAPTER 16

# Thinking About Self and Evil: One for God, One Against?

*[Lisa and Ryan sit down at a table in Starbucks, drinks in hand.]*

LISA: So what's the topic of conversation today?

Ryan: Well, I've got an admission to make—I have begun re-thinking my position on this whole "God thing." You have actually challenged me to give this a lot more thought than I ever have before.

Lisa: Oh, Ryan, I am so happy!

Ryan: Well, don't go overboard yet. I'm still trying to figure out exactly *who* this God may be. Going from not giving the existence of God much thought to thinking He *may* exist is a big step.

Lisa: Yes, it is.

Ryan: But my change in thinking, ironically, had more to do with some of those areas that you really can't prove scientifically; things like how one feels about others, relationships, even the thoughts I have about myself. It is interesting to me that I actually think about myself and will do certain things to improve that perception or even correct it, like when I offended you the other day by insinuating you were a terrorist.

Lisa: I do vaguely remember that!

Ryan: Lisa, only humans have those kinds of thoughts that cause us to do more than respond to stimuli, like eating when we are hungry or mating only with the desire to further our species. We actually think about those things and often evaluate our thoughts in the process. We talk about things like love and goodness and right and wrong.

Lisa: Yes, we do talk about a lot of seemingly abstract things, but those things seem to add a depth of meaning to the lives we live.

Ryan: Yeah…and why search for meaning to begin with? Beyond that, I have also come to realize that humans are distinct in the choices they make in regard to others. Sometimes we will even choose to do something that helps another more than it helps us, just like the time you gave up the starting position in your first high-school soccer game, just so you could go with me to the hospital.

Lisa: I didn't know you knew about that. That was *five* years ago. How did you find out?

Ryan: Lindsay told me. I knew you didn't want me to know, so I just didn't say anything. It is just that all of this is beginning to piece together. It is almost as though I am starting to see some things for the first time. But there is still an area that really bothers me.

Lisa: What is it?

Ryan: You remember Hillary?

Lisa: Sure, Ryan, Hillary was a good friend.

Ryan: She always seemed to struggle—her dad abusing her, then her parents' divorce, and all the rest.

Lisa: Yeah, it's easy to see sometimes why people go the whole drug route.

Ryan: But I guess I never thought her problems were so bad that she would OD. You know what I mean?

Lisa: I remember the last time I talked with Hillary. It was clear she was coming off a high; we could only get so far in our conversation. I told her to call me so we could get together. I so wanted to share with her how she could truly have hope—how God wanted to walk with her in the really tough times. And, then … well, then, I got the call from Jenny.

Ryan: So that's my question, Lisa.

Lisa: Question?

Ryan: Where was God?

Lisa: Oh, I see.

Ryan: Where was God for Hillary? I suppose what I am really asking is how there can be a good God who allows such pain and hurt. If God is all powerful, why doesn't He just put an end to all this? And if He is really good, how can He just sit there and do *nothing?* Honestly, it causes me to wonder if God is neither. Maybe He is not really God as we have traditionally thought—you know—in control over everything. Or maybe He can only see so far into the future. I don't know, Lisa. What do you think?

Lisa: I don't think any answer I could give would make us feel better about what happened to Hillary. I don't think I have ever met someone who was as kind and thoughtful as she was.

Ryan: I know what you mean. It is almost as though because of the pain she experienced, she was super-intuitive to the needs of others.

Lisa: Do you mind if I at least attempt to put some perspective on the pain and suffering we observe in the world?

Ryan: I really would like that.

Lisa: Let me ask you a question, Ryan. Is physical pain good or bad?

Ryan: That's an interesting question. I suppose I could say it is neither. Pain is simply an indicator of a problem. So maybe I could say, though unpleasant, it has benefit.

Lisa: Yes. And that benefit is to make us aware that something is wrong. My dad, for example, knew a guy who was injured in a shop accident. One of the vertebrae in his back was compressed which, in turn, put pressure on the spinal column. As a result, he lost feeling in his right arm. Ironically, though he could feel no pain, the doctors warned him that because of the work he performed in the machine shop, he had to be very aware of the potential for injury. I remember one time going to the shop with my dad; this guy would occasionally look over at his arm—like he was checking it out. That's when my dad explained to me that even a simple injury, left undetected, could lead to a much more serious problem.

Ryan: I assume you are suggesting that the same goes for emotional pain and the pain Hillary experienced?

Lisa: I am only suggesting that as a possibility. If God is truly good, and if humans are truly separated from God because of our rebellion and indifference to God, then would it be merciful of God to remove pain from our experience, only to have us discover, one day, that we had missed an eternal relationship with the God of the universe? Wouldn't it be better to have experienced pain so that we would seek solution?

Ryan: But surely God could have figured out another way.

Lisa: If God is God, then He is infinite in knowledge and wisdom and in every other way. Could He have? Sure. But is it also possible that, somehow, the current way is the best way?

Ryan: How could that be?

Lisa: Let me suggest there is something deeper going on in our discussion than simply the positive and negative results of pain and suffering. Ryan, why did Hillary's death bother us so? If all we are is here by chance, and if we are only a more advanced species of the animal kingdom, then why are we wasting our time talking about this? Aren't suffering and death just part of the territory of life?

Ryan: I can't believe you are saying this, Lisa. Hillary was a friend.

Lisa: Yes, Hillary was someone whose friendship and life you and I valued. It will never seem the same without Hillary. And that's my point. Hillary, among all the people you and I know, was unique. And, Ryan, you are a unique person to me, and I to you.

[Ryan sits back to think about Lisa's words.]

Lisa: Ryan, I don't always know the "why" for the pain and suffering, especially when it comes to friends like Hillary. All I know is that we are living in a world gone wrong; something is wrong. And the death of friends, like Hillary, causes all of us to take notice and to think much more deeply about life than we typically do. And what is so special about the death of one person is that there is something uniquely different about people, as opposed to all other members of the animal species.

Ryan: If there is a God, then perhaps the fact I react to the pain and suffering of a friend is an indicator that God has created humans as unique.

Lisa: And valuable. Personally, I think the relationship we share in friendship may be reflective of the high value God places on those He created. Ryan, the Bible declares that God loves the world and that He has chosen to build a bridge of relationship through His Son, Jesus. In fact, that raises another question for consideration: if there had been a better way or an easier way, then why wouldn't have God have chosen it? Was there a way where the sacrifice of His Son would not have been necessary? Then again, would we have missed the point?

Ryan: What point?

Lisa: The point that God had created us for a relationship, and He was willing to pay dearly for it because He valued us so highly. And that is what I really wanted to tell Hillary. But I never had the chance. I will always regret that.

Ryan: Well, at least you've told me. Right?
Lisa: Thanks, Ryan. You know I value your friendship.
Ryan: And I yours.

# CHAPTER 17

# Why Jesus?

*[Ryan and Lisa are seated at their usual table in Starbucks, both enjoying their favorite beverage.]*

RYAN: Hey, Lisa, would you still consider me a good friend, even if I *never* believed in Jesus?

Lisa: Wow, that question came from nowhere. What have you been thinking about?

Ryan: Well, would you?

Lisa: Of course I would consider you a friend, for all the same reasons I gave you during our talk the last time we met here.

Ryan: So it really wouldn't make that much difference then?

Lisa: Of course it would, but … Ryan, you know that I am a Christian. Right?

Ryan: I do think I've got that one down.

Lisa: But I am not sure you know exactly what that really means.

Ryan: Well, obviously, you believe in God. And you believe that Jesus lived a life that is worth following. So I guess that is why you do the good things you do, like helping me and going to church.

Lisa: So you think that by my being your friend that I'm somehow gaining points on my heavenly credit card?

Ryan: No, no. I think I know you better than that. I just think that you know you are supposed to do good to others.

Lisa: You mean sort of like the "What would Jesus do" idea?

Ryan: Yeah, that's right. And that's no criticism, Lisa. In fact, I think that is really cool! I wish I had more friends like you. You amaze me with your consistency. I am just not sure if I can live like that.

Lisa: Well, I can answer that: you can't! As the proverbial expression goes, "If you can't stand the heat, get out of the kitchen!" [Lisa smiles, obviously kidding with Ryan.] But let me get to the point. It is for the very reason that I can't live a life that is consistent that I believe in Jesus. If what the Bible says is true, then everyone has a basic problem, and that problem is sin. People are separated from God, and the evidence of that is seen all around us. Remember our discussion last time about pain indicators?

Ryan: You think that Hillary's death was caused because she was so sinful?

Lisa: All of us—including Hillary—live in a world that is deeply affected by rebellion and indifference to God. All of us—including Hillary—have done things that we don't even like to admit to others, much less worrying about what God thinks. And, yes, some of those things have more severe consequences than others. The point is we all need restoration in our relationship with the God who created us to know Him.

Ryan: But Lisa, what makes Jesus so special, as opposed to the other religious leaders of the world? Why is Christianity to be preferred over Judaism, Hinduism, Islam, or any other variety?

Lisa: Because of who Jesus was and what He did.

Ryan: What do you mean?

Lisa: I mean that Christianity, of all the world religions, is based on a *person*.

Ryan: Well, O.K. So what's so special about that? Islam is based on Mohammed's teachings, Judaism on Moses', and so on. Right?

Lisa: No, that's not what I mean. Harmony with God in most religions is based on the efforts of the individual. Christianity, on the other hand, is based on God's effort in reaching down with His solution for humanity. Most other religions assume man can merit God's favor or, at least, can attain that which he should be but now is not. On the other hand, Christianity teaches that nobody can earn God's favor. Indeed, no one can attain the goal of being all he should be; he will always fall short. And that is why Jesus came—to purchase God's favor for you and me, to make us right in God's eyes, so that we can have contact and communication with Him. As a result, we become who we were truly meant to be—beings in connection with the God who created us to know Him.

Ryan: But as much as I may want to believe that, Lisa, how can one really be sure that Christianity's way is better than any other way?

Lisa: You could not have asked a better question. Remember our talk a few weeks ago—the one where I suggested that the Christian definition of faith is very different from our culture's definition?

Ryan: Yes.

Lisa: Well, if you are to have faith in Jesus—at least in the way the Bible speaks of faith—you must be able to have confidence that Jesus really said and did the things He purportedly said and did. I mean, if Christianity is based on the person of Jesus and is not simply a system of works and merit, then you have to have a real Jesus. And He should have somehow demonstrated the truthfulness of His claims. Right?

Ryan: Makes sense.

Lisa: That's why I am going to suggest that you have to understand why Jesus's life is so totally unique; that He, above all of the world's religious leaders, lived a life that put Him ahead of the others. Jesus's life was unique for several reasons. It was unique because of the way He lived, the words He spoke and the way He influenced others. Think about it, Ryan. Here you have a Jewish carpenter—that is, someone not from the aristocracy or religious class—who was responsible for spawning a world movement. Remember that the Romans didn't really like the Jews. And the Romans also had one basic value: peace. So it didn't really matter what you believed, as long as you didn't rock the proverbial boat.

Ryan: Yes, the Pax Romana, which was initiated with the changes put into effect by Octavian, or Caesar Augustus, around 30 BC and continued for about 200 years.[1] Am I right?

Lisa: Very good, Ryan! So now enters Jesus, about 30 years into the rule of Augustus. Augustus' sweeping changes and the length of his reign caused many to consider him a god. Against this backdrop of strength and solidarity arose this Jewish carpenter, who did and said things that caused people to follow Him and the religious leaders to react against Him. Within 20 years of his death, against all kinds of odds—persecution from both the Roman government as well as the Jewish leaders—there are those calling themselves Christians throughout the empire and even in the Imperial City itself. Why would that be?

Ryan: Some have suggested that Jesus's followers developed folklore-type stories to increase His significance. Israel was looking for their religious deliverer, you know.

Lisa: Yes, the Jewish people *were* looking for a Messiah. No question. But there are a few problems with the legend scenario that some have suggested.

Ryan: For example?

Lisa: The Jewish people were anticipating a political deliverer. Jesus's crucifixion under the Romans pretty much ended that hope. So to suggest that Jesus's followers could have, or even *would* have, reconstructed Jesus to become some sort of miracle-working Messiah who temporarily left seems incredible. And don't forget that the rapid spread of Christianity to the Imperial City itself—within 20 years of Jesus's death—does not allow sufficient time for the development of a mythological figure.

Ryan: How's that?

Lisa: Because Rome is a long way from Palestine. For some sort of fairy-tale Jesus to have made it all the way to the city of Rome within 20 years of the crucifixion would have required those stories to have been fabricated and accepted by large numbers in Palestine before it ever would have been carried across the Mediterranean. And that just doesn't make sense, first, because the Jewish people wanted a political Messiah and not a dead fairy-tale one, and, second, because there were too many people living who would have remembered quite clearly the things Jesus said and did and would have had no motivation whatsoever to endure social ostracism for a legend.

Ryan: But, Lisa, many ancient cultures were given to mythology.

Lisa: True. But myths generally consist of fanciful beings and events that have little connection with time/space reality. Jesus lived among the very people who purportedly propagated the myth. And given the fact Jesus had fallen into disrepute with the Jewish religious leaders and subsequently was crucified, what motivation would the average Jewish person have to announce he was a follower of Jesus, especially knowing He wasn't really all everyone said He was? Would you risk social ostracism and potential persecution for something you knew was a legend?

Ryan: I get your point.

Lisa: Furthermore—and here's something I just learned the other day—the Jewish culture of the day was an oral culture. That means that information was primarily transferred by word of mouth which, of course, required the development of significant memorization skills.

Ryan: Are you saying that because the Jews had the ability to somewhat accurately pass on information, it would have been difficult to change the story about Jesus?

Lisa: That's right. Yet, oral cultures didn't transmit information about events, traditions, and sayings *somewhat* accurately; they did so *very* accurately.[2] And think about this—there is absolutely no historical evidence that the non-Jewish populace living in Rome had interest in Jewish folklore. You see, Ryan, the church in Rome was not primarily Jewish, as it was in Jerusalem, but it was comprised of *non*-Jewish people. So, one has to ask how this tiny religious splinter group survived to become the dominant religion of the Roman world.[3] I think something really happened in the land of Palestine that started a grassroots movement that led to Christianity's incredible expansion—despite persecution—up and until the time Constantine politicized it early in the fourth century.

Ryan: So what do you suggest happened?

Lisa: I think there is sufficient historical evidence to indicate that Jesus Christ came back to life after He was crucified!

Ryan: So you believe the whole "Jesus came back to life" idea?

Lisa: Yes. I can believe that could happen because I see God as part of the equation. If God is truly God, and if Jesus is really His Son, then why couldn't the resurrection have happened? Second, suggesting the viability of Jesus's resurrection as foundational to the Christian message is not just *my* idea. One of the early Christian apologists—that's someone who defends a particular position—was the Apostle Paul. This Jewish-skeptic-turned-apologist places the resurrection of Christ as the foundational event validating Christianity. From his perspective, if the resurrection never occurred, Christianity is pointless. Remember that we discussed that Christianity is all about the *person* of Jesus?

Ryan: Yes, but Jesus could have been just a good, moral teacher. What's wrong with that?

Lisa: Given the fact that Jesus taught that it was only through a relationship with Him that one could have a relationship with God, how could He have been a good moral teacher if, in fact, He was no different than you or me?

Ryan: So Jesus *did* say He was the only way to God?

Lisa: Yes. In fact, Jesus said "I am the way, the truth and the life. No man comes to the Father but through me." When he said "Father," he was referring to God.

Ryan: Where did you get this information?

Lisa: Well, besides the Bible, it is the book *Mere Christianity* that I found pretty insightful. It was written by a professor from Oxford professor, C.S. Lewis—you know, the same guy who wrote *Chronicles of Narnia*. He addressed the question of why Jesus couldn't be considered a good, moral teacher. I'll loan you my copy of the book. Lewis does a much better job than I do of explaining why that option just doesn't play out.

Ryan: I wish I could have the kind of faith you have—you seem so convinced of all of this.

Lisa: Ryan, have I ever told you *why* I became a Christian?

Ryan: No, I guess I thought you had always been a Christian.

Lisa: No, I've only been a Christian since my sophomore year in high school.

Ryan: Really?

Lisa: Yes. It was a pretty tough year. I worked hard to keep a smile on my face during that time, though inside I was … well … it was like I was dying. My dad had been laid off from his job, and it caused a lot of conflict at home. And I loved my home, Ryan. Then, all of a sudden, it was just gone. The fun times, the positive relationship between my mom and dad—it even changed the relationship with my brother, and that has never been the same since. And I contributed to the conflict as well. It was horrible. The only person who really knew what I was going through was Hillary.

Ryan: Hillary?

Lisa: Yes. Because she was going through tough times as well, it was like we had this bond. We would talk with each other and just vent our anger. Well, one of Hillary's friends came over one evening and brought some pot.

Ryan: You, Lisa?

Lisa: Yes, me, Ryan. We both began using pretty regularly. It was our only escape—or so it seemed. One night, however, I had a very bad reaction to the pot—I literally thought I was going to die. It scared me sufficiently that I was determined never to smoke again.

Ryan: I assume Hillary didn't have a reaction.

Lisa: No, she didn't. I only wish she had.

Ryan: Yeah. [Ryan pauses and looks off into the distance.]

Lisa: Do you remember Leslie Sardenaro?

Ryan: I haven't thought of her in a long time. Where is she?

Lisa: Leslie and her parents moved to Chicago a couple of years ago. We talk to each other through Facebook quite a bit. She's really doing great. But when we were sophomores, we were quite different—different interests, different friends, doing different things. But she cared.

Ryan: How so?

Lisa: One day I was sitting alone in the cafeteria and Leslie just came up, sat across from me, and started talking. Looking back on it, she really took a risk. I am sure I didn't appear all that interested in talking with anyone. But I played along, trying to keep up the "friendly Lisa" image.

Ryan: So what happened?

Lisa: I really can't remember how it all happened, but we began sitting together at lunch a couple of times a week. I just remember feeling so much better—like calm—after we would talk. Then one day, right in the middle of one of our conversations, she turned to me and said, "Lisa, I think there are two questions in life everyone has to answer. Is there a God? And if so, can you know Him? What do you think?" I didn't know what to say.

Ryan: No way!

Lisa: Ryan, believe it or not, I haven't always known, much less believed, the things we've been talking about the past several weeks. In fact, my life was really messed up. I was hurting inside. Though I had always thought there was some kind of "god" out there, I was no longer sure. Well, Leslie just let me talk for 15 or 20 minutes before it was time to go to class. Later, I told Leslie how much that time had meant. It was like a huge burden had been lifted; just having someone who was willing to listen. The next day at lunch, Leslie asked me if I had ever explored Jesus Christ's claims about the role He played in knowing God. Of course, I never had. Sure, I had occasionally been to church and heard a few Christmas and Easter sermons. But none of it made much sense. And that's when it happened.

Ryan: What happened?

Lisa: Leslie shared with me—right then and there—the words of Jesus from the Bible. She explained why Jesus had come and what He had done for me so that I might be able to know God personally. I admit, I never thought God really wanted a relationship with me. That seemed so ethereal. But Jesus's words seemed so compelling; it was as though I were hearing them super clearly. And what Leslie said seemed to make so much sense. God was making His truth clear to me. So much so that the choice to accept God's gift of life through His Son seemed hardly like a decision; it was like the obvious thing to do.

Ryan: I wish I could be sure that my experience would be like your experience.

Lisa: Ryan, though I want you to establish a relationship with Christ, I would never want you to do so based on my experience. But if there is something to be said about the reality of a relationship with God, then it must ultimately make a difference in our lives, somewhere and somehow. So many religions gain a following because of the experiences they claim, but I would suggest to you that only Christianity calls us based on the evidence, and the reality of its claims are proven true in the realm of experience. Ryan, I've faced tough times since my sophomore year in high school, and God has continued to validate my trust in Him in both good and difficult times. [Lisa pauses.] Ryan … why don't you just ask God?

Ryan: Ask God?

Lisa: Yes. If you are sincere in wanting to know if God exists and if His Son, Jesus, is who He claimed to be, why not simply ask God to make it clear to you as He did for me? If the God of the Bible is all the Bible says, then He desires for you to know Him and is fully capable of helping you clearly see the evidence He has left for discovery.

Ryan: I think I will, Lisa. You've given me a lot to think about today.

Lisa: I've been praying you would get to this point, Ryan.

Ryan: Yeah, I sort of figured that.

# *Notes*

[1] Steven Kreis, "Lectures on Ancient and Medieval European History / Lecture 12: Augustus Caesar and the Pax Romana," The History Guide, http: //www.historyguide.org/ancient/lecture12b.html, (accessed April 30, 2007).

[2] J.P. Moreland, "Searching for the Historical Jesus," in the compact disc series *The Case for Christianity* (available through the Department of Christian Apologetics, Biola University, 13800 Biola Avenue, La Mirada, CA 90639).

[3] Gillian Clark, *Christianity and Roman Society* (United Kingdom: Cambridge University Press, 2004), 13.

# Just Believe? Why the Christian Faith Is Not Without Substance

*"On the other hand, what concerns me most as I survey the scientific and social landscape…is the increasing assertiveness of elements within American society who wish to blur the distinction between science and religion. The two offer fundamentally different means of understanding the universe and must be clearly differentiated if they are to fulfill their respective and, I believe, fully compatible roles in our society. Scientists…pose questions and test hypotheses…until the evidence is overwhelmingly in favor of one solution over others. Believers, in contrast, are asked to trust without the proof, which is what makes faith at once so daunting and inspiring."*

(Shirley M. Tilghman, president, Princeton University, in a speech at the Memorial Sloan-Kettering Cancer Center Academic Convocation, May 2005)

CHAPTER 18

# How God Engaged Humanity Through Jesus (Or, Evidences Which Suggest the Deity of Christ)

YESTERDAY I was engaged in a conversation with Eric, a young man who disdains "organized religion." He *does* believe there is a God, even though he is not sure that God is knowable. It is just that he grew up in a church that—at least to him—had emphasized form over function; his faith consisted simply of performing particular rituals. He had grown up observing an empty, organizational structure.

Given the fact I had engaged Eric in talking about spiritual matters, he could guess my take on the matter. He pointed out the injustices. throughout history, perpetrated by organized religion. And, of course, not just any religion, the Christian religion in particular.

One cannot disagree with the assessment that the Church has overextended its reach at various times in history, or even that many horrendous things have been done in the name of Christ. So what does one say?

I simply pointed Eric to the life of Jesus. You see, every religion has the potential for being misjudged on the basis of how it has been abused, and Christianity is no different in this regard. Yet, if one truly desires to see an unobstructed view of Christianity, one must evaluate both the message Jesus conveyed as well as the manner in which He lived.

When talking to people about the Christian faith, it often is quite apparent that few have little idea as to the significance of Jesus's claims or the life He lived. Most may think of Christ as a good person, but there are not many who have made the connection between His exemplary life and the many very bold claims He made. Fewer there are still who have investigated the evidence that lends such great support to the unusual nature of Christ's life.

Indeed, Christ's life serves as one of the most compelling evidences of the Christian faith. As with any philosophy or religion, one must consider the life of its founder when evaluating the validity of the principles set forth. Given the extraordinary nature of Jesus's claim to be God's Son—the revelation of the one and only God—one should expect equally extraordinary evidence.

So, what are some of the compelling traits of Christ's life, those qualities and characteristics that help set His life apart from the other "greats" of history? And what evidence does exist that may help our friends establish confidence in Jesus and the claims He made?

Three particular areas of consideration pertaining to Jesus's life often prove helpful in building the case for Christianity with those willing to listen:

- the unusual nature of His words and works

- the uniqueness of His resurrection

- the incredible influence He had on His followers

## The Unusual Nature of Jesus's Words and Works

If you were to ask most students who they considered one of the most just men of history—that is, who they think treated people more fairly and mercifully than any other—you would discover that a majority would answer "Jesus Christ." Now, they might not be able to quote for you even one phrase of Jesus's many teachings, but the consensus is that Jesus was a man who was both fair and kind to others.

The reason for this is that the things Jesus said, attested by the life He lived, sets Him apart from the other great leaders of history. Moreover, the connection between His words and His works is indisputable—what He "preached" is what He practiced. And that connection is what has left an indelible impression on the history of the world.

Let's take, for example, Jesus's teaching in the Beatitudes (Matthew 5). In describing to His Jewish audience the characteristics of the citizens of the much-anticipated Kingdom of God, Jesus proclaimed:

> Blessed are the poor in spirit, for theirs is the kingdom of heaven.
> Blessed are those who mourn, for they shall be comforted.
> Blessed are the meek, for they shall inherit the earth.
> Blessed are those who hunger and thirst for righteousness, for they shall be satisfied.
> Blessed are the merciful, for they shall receive mercy.
> Blessed are the pure in heart, for they shall see God.
> Blessed are the peacemakers, for they shall be called sons of God.
> Blessed are those who are persecuted for righteousness' sake, for theirs is the kingdom of heaven. (Matthew 5:3–10)

Do you know of any other kingdom, throughout history, whose leader would choose to bless the down-and-out, the merciful, the kind, and the righteous? No. And neither had Jesus's Jewish audience. As a nation, they were under the firm hand of Roman rule. As a people, they were under the very rigid control of the religious elite.

Perhaps Jesus's fellow Jews had come to question the reality of God in their experience. Or maybe they just felt disenfranchised, as though God gave little, if any, notice of them at all.

Jesus's message was a radical one, both then and now. It was a departure from the norm. It was a message of hope and freedom in a world where dread and oppression ruled. And it is a message for today as much as it was a message for then. And it is the kind of message that compels people to follow.

Yet many leaders have spoken kind words, only to be later discovered as brutal tyrants. How did Jesus fare in the ultimate test of the life He lived? How did He treat those closest to Him, as well as the masses that looked on from afar?

It was Jesus who said "Love your neighbor as yourself" (Mark 12: 31 NLT). Likewise, it was He who instructed His followers that "if someone slaps you on the right cheek, offer the other cheek also" (Matthew 5: 39 NLT) and "Do to others as you would like them to do to you" (Luke 6: 31 NLT). And it was He who pleaded, "Come to me, all of you who are weary and carry heavy burdens, and I will give you rest" (Matthew 11: 28 NLT).

In my many interactions with people from a variety of cultural and religious backgrounds, there has never been anyone who suggested that Jesus's character was not as history has recorded—few will question the incredibly positive virtue of Christ's life.

Indeed, it is the amazing quality of Christ's life that has fanned the flame of those ascribing to His divine nature. If one could destroy the foundation of the incredibly virtuous life Christ lived, then belief in His divinity would surely falter.

Yet it is certainly because of the uniqueness of the life Jesus lived that one is compelled to consider the words Jesus spoke. Indeed, both Christ's life *and* words must be considered in tandem; otherwise, one will end up with a very sweet Jesus whose life may motivate someone to be nice but which would hardly explain the tenacity of the early Christians, who were willing to enter the Coliseum rather than defect from their faith.

**Jesus's kindness and love can only be completely understood when one considers the purpose He ascribed to it. If one fails to deal with Christ's mission, one fails to comprehend the significance of His words and, ultimately, His life**.

Jesus stated His mission clearly: "For the Son of Man came to seek and save those who are lost" (Luke 19: 10 NLT). When one understands the compelling nature of this mission, one can come to grips with the radical side of Jesus. On the one hand, His love invited people into relationship; on the other, His zeal actively opposed anyone who would attempt to deter that mission and, thereby, prevent others from experiencing the grace He offered.

It is the redemptive purpose that He claimed as His mission that forms the context of His most radical claim of all—that He was the Son of God. And it is the compelling witness of Jesus's life (including the miracles He performed) that provided the context for one to seriously consider any claim of deity. Conversely so, it is this claim that enables us to understand *why* He, at times, acted so vehemently against those who opposed Him and His mission. He was acting at God's bequest, and anyone opposing Him was, in fact, opposing God.

The exclusivity that Jesus claimed when He declared "I am *the* way, *the* truth, and *the* life. No one can come to the Father *except through me*" [emphasis mine] (John 14: 6 NLT) now makes perfect sense. He had both the authority and ability (see Mark 2: 1–12) to address the universal problem of humanity's separation from God. It is from this perspective, then, that we see that Jesus's exclusive message is one of open-handedness (offering restored relationship with God) rather than close-mindedness and intolerance.

But the one facet of Christ's life that may most impress those with whom you interact is that *He gave His life for the claims and teachings He presented.*

I challenged Eric to consider the merits of Christianity because of the claims and life of Christ, and it was at this very point that Eric conceded. "You've got to respect a guy who was willing to die for His beliefs," he commented.

Indeed, even on the cross Jesus was willing to forgive. And it was by the cross He purchased the right to do so. I went on to explain to Eric that Jesus's death had particular significance: it was God paying *my* sin debt at His expense. Because of Jesus's death, the path is open for relationship with God. No other leader of the world's major religions has ever claimed the ability to forgive sins.

It is the fundamental longing of the human soul—the desire for unconditional love and acceptance—that is addressed, with finality, in Christianity alone, in Christ alone.

Though Christ's death was far more than simply a model of ultimate commitment, it was surely that. And it has provided a model for Christians throughout the centuries. Though abuses can be attributed to the followers of every religion, it was Augustine who rightly cautioned that one must never judge a philosophy by its abuse. The life of the leader always serves as a point of reference for the follower. And when it comes to the leaders of history, there is not one whose life has been more carefully scrutinized, nor more carefully modeled, than the one who claimed divine authority, even demonstrating divine ability: Jesus of Nazareth.

## The Uniqueness of Jesus's Resurrection

It is a recognized fact of history that Jesus lived and died. Yes, you can always find the scholar or two who will deny Jesus ever lived. And yes, you will find those who suggest that the "Jesus of history" is much different from the Jesus of the Gospels, although the basis for which they make such assertions often has more to do with their presuppositions than the objective evaluation of historical evidence.

Given the extraordinary evidence of the biblical record, however, and the extra-biblical references to His life and death (including the writings of the Church

Fathers as well as Roman historians), the facts of Jesus's life and death by Roman crucifixion can be substantiated historically. Few people will question either.[1]

So why is it that some have a more difficult time accepting Christ's resurrection as historical fact? Why is it that our friends who do not know Jesus question this particular facet of the Christian narrative?

Because in affirming the resurrection of Christ, we have moved from the natural to the supernatural. And in the Western world, anything of supernatural content is immediately suspect.

Some suggest it is one thing to historically attest the life and words of an individual but quite another to historically substantiate a supernatural occurrence. Today, there are those who posit that historical evidence is limited to describing and affirming probable natural events and that, given the fact that the resurrection is a supernatural event, it is therefore deemed improbable and cannot be historically verified.[2]

But why is that so? Why can't the same evidence that gives credence to Jesus's life and death also support the possibility of His resurrection? In other words, if the natural evidence suggests the least probable (i.e., supernatural) cause of a particular effect, why can't history at least allow the evidence to lead where it may?

I would suggest that throughout the course of history, there have been innumerable "improbable" causes of certain effects and yet history has validated those with impunity. (The Industrial Revolution of the 1800s and the Technological Revolution of the 1900s would be good examples; causes of particular effects considered improbable just a few years earlier became quite probable because of the advancements made. As new causes arose, so did the potentiality of those causes influencing particular effects.)

Moreover, it is one thing to say that a supernatural cause is least probable (granted, we do live in a world dominated by natural causes and their effects); it is quite another to assign "zero" probability (or impossible "knowability") even before collecting the data. That approach is prejudiced from the start. If there is a God, then it may be assumed that, at some point, He may desire to make Himself known in the natural realm. Thus an anti-supernatural bias may be considered more a commentary on the historian than on the merits of the argument which dismisses the potential of assigning a supernatural cause to a particular effect in the natural world.

Most people will not have a problem with allowing the evidence to lead them where it may. And there are many today who do not rule out the supernatural. Yet it remains that most of those with whom you discuss the relevance of a relationship with Jesus have never been presented the idea that there is credible, *historical evidence* underlying the belief in Christ's resurrection. And some may question why it is so important to make that case.

It is our role to break the typical perception of Christianity as an "experience-based-only" belief system. I want the person with whom I am conversing to understand, clearly, that there is a direct connection between the *credibility* of the evidence and the *validity* of the message.

The New Testament authors appealed to concrete evidence in validating the words and works of Jesus. They were *not* satisfied to leave Christianity in the "just believe" realm of experiential faith. In fact, they entered the world of time-space reality and appealed to particular events and occasions, wherein Jesus acted and spoke, so that what He said and did could either be validated or falsified by those who were present or knew those who had been. Therefore, it is quite typical for the writers to describe particular events in Jesus's life by including where He was, who He was with, what He said and even, on occasion, the time of day it all took place.

For example, take the story of Jesus's healing of the Roman centurion's servant, found in Luke 7. Luke records the place (Capernaum), the person who was the recipient of the miracle (a centurion's servant), the people who were part of the process (the centurion making the request; Jewish elders sent to Jesus with the request from the centurion; other friends also sent by the centurion), the exact words of the centurion's request, Jesus's response and, finally, the result (the servant was healed). Furthermore, Luke notes "When those who had been sent returned to the house, they found the slave in good health."

Did you ever stop to think how the New Testament writers would have set themselves up for failure if what they recorded was not accurate? Let's consider the above example.

First of all, though the city of Capernaum was strategically located (situated on one of the major trade routes of the ancient world, the Via Maris), it was a city of perhaps only 1000 to 1500 inhabitants.[3] That means the news of such an event would have traveled quickly, both within the city itself and beyond. Furthermore, if the event was simply a fabrication, it would have been incredibly difficult to suggest that an event of such an extraordinary nature had escaped notice.

Second, though the name of the centurion is not mentioned it is reasonable to assume that the city would have had only one centurion at the time. So as to avoid any confusion as to the centurion's identification (e.g., perhaps Capernaum had, over time, several centurions overseeing the Roman garrison stationed near there), Luke records the testimony of the Jewish elders (i.e., city fathers) that it was *this particular centurion* who had even built the local synagogue for them. The absence of his name, combined with this description, suggests he was likely well known.

Third, the number of people involved (including the leaders of the city) makes this event all the more open to verification or refutation. There is good evidence to suggest that at least the three Synoptic Gospels (Matthew, Mark and Luke) were written by AD 70 and Mark, quite likely, much earlier. This means, of course, people who had been alive at the time of the event's occurrence would still have been available for cross-verification and would have had children and friends privy to a firsthand account of the remarkable events surrounding the miracle.

Fourth, Luke records that the servant was found to be "in *good* health" [emphasis mine]. No, Luke did not say "improved" or "in good spirits" but "in *good* health." Thus, a servant who was dying did not simply improve; he became healthy and had likely returned to serving in the home.

It is this same clarity that surrounds the resurrection accounts of Christ. Though the New Testament authors could have spoken of a *spiritual* resurrection (thus avoiding testability of the fact), they proclaimed a *physical* resurrection of Jesus from the grave.

In fact, the Apostle Paul makes it clear in I Corinthians 15 that if Christ was not resurrected, the Christian faith is "in vain" (15: 14), "futile" (15: 17), and believers are to be "pitied" (15: 19). In other words, the reliability of the Gospel message is directly proportional to the *reality* of the resurrection.

It is for this reason that I want to anchor the Christian message historically in my interactions with people. I will often offer the following suggestion for the individual's consideration: "There is one particular belief that serves as the pivotal point in Christianity. That belief is in the bodily resurrection of Christ. If it is true, then Christianity is true; if it is false, then Christianity is false, because Christianity is all about a relationship with the person of Jesus. I believe there is credible historical evidence that suggests a supernatural resurrection is the best explanation as to what happened to the body of Jesus following His death."

Since the time of Christ's resurrection, various natural explanations—call them "counter-theories"—have been offered to explain the supernatural event of

Jesus's resurrection. Those explanations can be combined into three broad categories as follows:

- **Jesus did not die on the cross.** Either it was someone else (the Quran, for example, says that Judas was placed on the cross in Jesus's stead) or Jesus *was* crucified only to be resuscitated by the cool, damp tomb.

- **Jesus's followers, beginning with the women, went to the wrong tomb, thus allowing the idea of a resurrection to be propagated.** A sub-set of this theory is the suggestion by some that Jesus was never buried *in a tomb* but was cast into a common grave reserved for crucified criminals.

- **The disciples stole Jesus's body.**

Realize that it is important that you do understand why the account of Christ's resurrection is a defensible fact of history; *it is the foundation of the Christian's faith.* I would highly encourage you to check out the resources given in the notes at the end of this chapter for that reason.

In my experience of interacting with students, they have rarely questioned me concerning the specific details of Christ's resurrection or proposed one of the three alternative theories listed above. Many are intrigued by my proposal that the resurrection of Christ is a fact of history, subject to verifiable evidence. And that is how I would begin to position my response.

As I reach the point of explaining the Gospel in my conversation, I will oftentimes begin by making the following summary statement: "It is a fact of history that Jesus Christ lived in Palestine in the first century. It is also a fact of history that He was put to death by Roman crucifixion—that was part of His mission, of the why He came to this earth in the first place. And the evidence also seems to support that He lived again.[5] It is the resurrection of Jesus that separates Christianity from every other religion."

Historians cannot ignore that the Gospel of Mark (considered the earliest Gospel by the majority of scholars and a reflection of Peter's teaching) and Luke's Gospel (the author is considered by most scholars to be an exceptional historian) record the life and death and resurrection of Jesus. If you accept their testimony of Jesus's life, then it seems inconsistent not to accept their testimony concerning the events surrounding His death and resurrection as well.

The same Luke who wrote the Gospel also penned the book of Acts, which picks up the story with a resurrected Christ who interacted with at least 120 of His closest followers. It was that group which, very shortly following Christ's departure, would lead a vibrant and growing Christian community, energized by the belief in Jesus's resurrection (see Peter's sermon in Acts 2).

So what *does* one make of the alternative theories which have been offered to explain away the resurrection of Jesus? What evidence should one point to in order to bolster the account of Jesus's resurrection, as well as refute the counter arguments?

My recommendation is that you respond with broad arguments, rather than a detail-by-detail assessment. For example, I have often said something like this: "If someone ever wanted to prove Christianity was false, all he would have to do is discredit the central teaching that Jesus was resurrected from the dead after His crucifixion. In fact, one of the early defenders of the Christian faith declared that if the resurrection of Christ was not true, then the Christian faith was pointless and Christians were to be pitied in their belief.

"You see, Jesus said that He would return to life after being dead for three days. And it is this statement, combined with the fact that the followers of Jesus were ignited because they believed He had resurrected, which compels me to believe the resurrection is a fact of history. All that the Jewish religious leaders or Roman government officials had to do in order to quell the spread of Christianity was to prove that Jesus's body was still in the tomb. All they had to do was to display the body of Christ publicly. And they never did this.

"That is one of the most interesting questions of history—assuming, of course, if Jesus remained dead and buried. The religious leaders of Palestine, as well as arguably the world's most powerful government, could never produce the body of Jesus thus effectively ending the spread of Christianity."

In a very real sense, this *one* point controverts all the counter theories.

However, for the sake of discussion, let's examine the first theory: Jesus did not really die. If, in fact, Jesus simply "recovered" from His crucifixion and was only a man, He eventually would have had to die *at some point,* thus still having the effect of discrediting the prophecy concerning His resurrection, as well as His claim of being the Jewish Messiah.

Furthermore, what exactly would a "recovery" from crucifixion look like? And could a severely wounded and weakened Jesus have returned to declare victory in such a manner that His followers would spawn the kind of movement they did, as well as risking their own lives in the process? The very thought seems incredulous and lacks historical verifiability.

Quite simply, *if Jesus had not perished and had continued to live in Palestine (or elsewhere, for that matter), how does the bulk of historical record lack documentation pertaining to the remainder of the life of one of the world's most influential individuals?*

I have alluded above to the fact that Islam teaches that Jesus did not die on the cross, that someone—either Judas Iscariot or Simon—took His place. Though the response to this position is beyond the scope of this book—the difficulty is enhanced by the Muslim belief that the Quran is beyond human scrutiny and evaluation as to its historicity—it is imperative you are aware of the Muslim position, due to its growing, worldwide significance.[6]

Concerning the second theory, what should one make of the suggestion that Mary Magdalene, Mary the mother of James, and Salome (Mark 16: 1)—apparently the first to arrive at the tomb early on that Sunday morning—went to the wrong tomb? Even those who discount Christ's resurrection accept the historicity of this account (it is consistently included in virtually every account of the resurrection narrative); they simply assert that the women ended up at the wrong tomb. Even the comment, "See the place where they laid him" (Mark 16: 6), made by the young man the women came upon in the open tomb, is taken as meaning, "You are in the wrong place; over there is where they have laid him."[7]

If the women went to the wrong tomb then, given the rapid spread of the Christian message as well as the fact that the body of Jesus was never found, we must assume that *everyone else* also went to the wrong tomb! And that would include the Jewish leaders and Roman government officials who surely could have dispelled the belief in the resurrection, if based on such a silly error.

The same would hold true if the Romans had *not* allowed Jesus to be buried in the tomb of Joseph of Arimathea but had chosen to throw his body in the pit or gravesite set aside for common criminals. Given Pilate's propensity to maintain peace among the Jewish populace, a Christian sect—now energized by a belief in Jesus's resurrection—would have been the least of his desires. Once again, *if anyone* would have known the whereabouts of Jesus's body, surely Pilate would have.

Moreover, it seems quite unlikely that the Jewish religious leaders, knowing the prediction Jesus made concerning His return to life after three days, would not have ensured that they knew the place of burial and would do everything in their power to prevent Jesus's followers from producing a resurrection scenario.

This leads to the final argument for consideration: the disciples stole Jesus's body. Though it was the earliest argument put forth by the religious leaders of Jesus's day (see Matthew 28: 11–14), few scholars today give this theory serious consideration.

All accounts of Christ's followers after His crucifixion show them to be both confused and afraid. To suggest that Jesus's disciples overcame their fear and devised a plan to overpower the guards and rob the tomb, and that they then hid Jesus's body and swore secrecy (even preventing leaks to and/or from members of their own families) is hardly within the realm plausibility. It borders more on purely fanciful thinking for this simple reason: those same followers, once successfully accomplishing all the above, would have then had to formulate the fabric necessary to create a movement that would transform history and one for which they would give their lives.

Does one really need to say any more?

The resurrection of Jesus Christ is the cornerstone of the Christian faith. It stands as a testimony to the uniqueness of the person of Jesus Christ. As you explore the evidence imbedded in the biblical narrative, your confidence in the Gospel message will be all the surer.

Dr. William Lane Craig is a Christian historian and philosopher who has extensively examined the evidences for the resurrection. A summary of his key points are as follows: [8]

- **Jesus was buried by Joseph of Arimathea in a tomb**. This is affirmed by multiple authors using early and independent sources. These sources include the four Gospels and the writings of the Apostle Paul. These writings can be demonstrated to be credible historical sources. It is likely, as well, that some of this source material (Paul's creedal statement in I Corinthians 15: 3–7, for example) goes back to within two to eight years of the resurrection.[9] Furthermore, it is unlikely that the early Christians would have invented the story of Joseph of Arimathea in that he was a member of the same religious group—the Sanhedrin—who arranged the trial that resulted in Christ's being crucified.

- **On the Sunday after the crucifixion, Jesus's tomb was found empty by a group of His women followers.** Once again, multiple and independent early sources affirm this. Though some of the secondary details (number of women, exactly which women, etc.) differ among the accounts, the core affirmation is the same: Jesus's tomb was empty and discovered by some of His women followers.[10]

  In view of this particular detail, it is of interest to note that, in first-century Jewish society, the testimony of a woman was not highly regarded nor viewed as credible (i.e.—it was inadmissible as evidence in a court of law). Therefore, had the resurrection account been *fabricated* by the Christian community, it seems unlikely that such a construct would have included *women* as the first witnesses of the empty tomb. (It is also extraordinary that the visit by the women even "trumps" the visit by the apostles John and Peter! Surely a fabricated account would have highlighted the dual testimonies of these two key apostles over that of the women's!)

- **On different occasions and under various circumstances, different individuals and groups of people experienced appearances of Jesus as alive from the dead.** One of the characteristics that sets the story of Christ's life apart from legendary literature is the appeal that is made to specific places, times, people, and events. No less an emphasis is placed on such specificity in Christ's post-resurrection appearances; those appearances being documented in the Gospels and the writings of the Apostle Paul (I Corinthians 15).

  In regard to this particular point, William Craig points out that the early date of the Apostle Paul's information, combined with the fact that he had personal acquaintanceship and even friendship with the key individuals involved, makes it virtually impossible to dismiss the post-resurrection appearances of Jesus as merely legend. And, when one considers Paul's account along with the accounts offered by the Gospel writers, "The appearance narratives span such a breadth of independent sources that it cannot be reasonably denied that the earliest disciples did have such experiences."[11]

| Resurrection Appearances[13] | | | | |
|---|---|---|---|---|
| # | Appeared to | Location | Time | Scriptures |
| 1 | Mary Magdalene | Jerusalem (tomb) | Sunday | Mark 16: 9-11; John 20: 11-18 |
| 2 | Some other women | Jerusalem (tomb) | Sunday | Matthew 28: 9-10 |
| 3 | Peter | Jerusalem | Sunday | Luke 24: 34; I Corinthians 15: 5 |
| 4 | Emmaus disciples | Emmaus | Sunday | Luke 24: 13-35 |
| 5 | 10 disciples (and unnamed others) | Jerusalem | Sunday | Mark 16: 14; Luke 24: 33-43; John 20: 19-25 |
| 6 | 11 disciples | Jerusalem | A week later | John 20: 26-31; I Corinthians 15: 5 |
| 7 | 7 disciples | Galilee | ? | John 21: 1-25 |
| 8 | 500 at one time | ? | ? | I Corinthians 15: 6 |
| 9 | James (brother of Jesus) | ? | ? | I Corinthians 15: 7 |
| 10 | 11 disciples | Galilee | ? | Matthew 28: 16-20; Mark 16: 15-18 |
| 11 | 11 disciples | Jerusalem (Mount of Olives) | 40 days later | Luke 24: 44-53; Acts 1: 3-12 |

The fact of the matter is that had the details corroborating the resurrection account been false, there would have been people alive who would have known they were false (see I Corinthians 15: 6). Furthermore, those same inconsistencies and/or fabrications would have been known by the Jewish leaders as well, and they would have publicly decimated them.

It is also telling that the earliest Jewish refutation of the resurrection (see Matthew 28: 11–15) presupposed an empty tomb.[12] Had Jesus's body remained in the tomb (the location of which would surely have been known by the Jewish religious leaders as well as the Romans), rather than fabricate a story as to its disappearance (i.e., that the disciples stole the body), all they would have had to do would have been to publicize its whereabouts.

Finally, Christ's resurrection appearances involved multiple participants, at various times, in a variety of circumstances. He appeared to Mary Magdalene, Peter, and James (individually); two men walking on the road to Emmaus; the women at the tomb; the disciples [on five different occasions]; and 500 followers at one time. The identification of actual places, events, and named individuals adds strength to the validity of Christ's resurrection as an historical event.

- **The original disciples suddenly and sincerely came to believe that Jesus had risen from the dead, despite their having every predisposition to the contrary.** The Jews had always anticipated their Messiah to be a victorious, political deliverer. The concept of a Messiah who would suffer and die, though suggested in the prophets (e.g., Isaiah 53), was not clearly understood until the prophetic passages were viewed through the lens of Christ's teachings following His resurrection.

If the resurrection were not true, however, it is inexplicable why a Messianic movement would even begin at all; the Jewish people had always anticipated a Messiah who would deliver them from political oppression. Something of great significance needed to occur for the Jewish men and women who followed Jesus to adjust their traditional understanding and be willing to put their lives on the line to teach a new understanding concerning Messiah. The British scholar N.T. Wright concludes: "That is why, as a historian, I cannot explain the rise of early Christianity unless Jesus rose again, leaving an empty tomb behind him."[14]

Finally, one must not forget the context in which these early followers of Jesus proclaimed this new teaching of a resurrected Messiah (Christ): *Jerusalem.* Yes, you got that right—the religious capital of the nation! Is it really plausible to think that if this group of early Christians had *not* been completely convinced of the reality of Christ's resurrection they would have so boldly risked confronting the same religious leadership who crucified their Leader?

Frank Morison (a pseudonym for Albert Henry Ross, 1881-1950) was a British skeptic who set out to disprove the resurrection of Christ. He knew that it served as the cornerstone of the Christian faith—disprove it and you would undermine the entire structure of the faith. As a result of his research, however, he became convinced of the historicity of Jesus's resurrection and became His avid follower instead. He went on to detail his search in a book titled, *Who Moved the Stone?*

Morison points to the amazing boldness of these early Christians—a boldness that was unquestionably, in his estimation, rooted in nothing less than the conviction that what they believed to be true was true indeed. That conviction resulted in the significant expansion of a movement that, from a purely human standpoint, should have been destined for failure rather than success. He writes:

> The terrors and the persecutions these men ultimately had to face and did face unflinchingly, do not admit of a halfhearted adhesion secretly honeycombed with doubt. The belief has to be unconditional and of adamantine strength to satisfy the conditions. Sooner or later, too, if the belief was to spread it had to bite its way into the corporate consciousness by convincing argument and attempted proof.

> Now the peculiar thing about this phenomenon is that, not only did it spread to every single member of the party of Jesus of whom we have any trace, but they brought it to Jerusalem and carried it with inconceivable audacity into the most keenly intellectual center of Judea ... *And they won.* Within twenty years the claim of these Galilean peasants had disrupted the Jewish church [religious system] and impressed itself upon every town on the Eastern littoral of the Mediterranean from Caesarea to Troas. In less than fifty years it had begun to threaten the peace of the Roman Empire.

> When we have said everything that can be said about the willingness of certain types of people to believe what they want to believe, to be carried away by their emotions, and to assert as fact what has originally reached them as hearsay, we stand confronted with the greatest mystery of all. *Why did it win?*[15]

# The Incredible Influence Jesus
# had on His Followers

*How did a tiny, politically suspect, religious group become the dominant religion of the Roman world?*[16] Given the worldwide influence of Christianity, that is perhaps one of history's more significant questions.

When one simply looks at the makeup of Jesus's rather ordinary group of some 120 followers (Acts 1: 15), the odds against their having success in creating a movement opposed by the Jewish leaders—and eventually by Rome itself—as well as a movement that would change the landscape of history, seems insurmountable. Morison makes a good point when he notes:

> I do not want to minimize the character of the historic nucleus from which Christianity sprang, but, seriously, does this rather heterogeneous body of simple folk, reeling under the shock of the Crucifixion, the utter degradation and death of their Leader, look like the driving force we require? Frankly, it does not, and the more we think of it disintegrating under the crisis, the less we can imagine it rewelding into that molten focus that achieved those results. *Yet the clear evidence of history is that it did.*[17]

Moreover, had it simply been a religio-political movement spawned among members of a disenfranchised class, the question would have far less significance. History records many such movements. But it is the sheer difficulty, potentially inflicted on the life of the convert, that causes one to pause and grant consideration to this question.

> Jesus died on a cross: a public, agonizing death, legally inflicted by a Roman provincial governor as the standard punishment for rebels. For almost three hundred years, His followers were also at risk of legally inflicted death, sometimes as a public spectacle. Roman law allowed Christians to be burned alive or thrown to wild animals or inventively tortured.[18]

People do not enjoy being tortured and put to death. And when the potential of such is backed by the political and religious elite of the world, the threat is *very* real. What, therefore, would motivate one—even a member of some disenfranchised class—to give up poverty and hardship to follow the crucified Jesus, only to face the potential of torture and death?

And yet Christianity thrived and spread throughout the Roman Empire.

Seutonius, the Roman historian who served the Emperor Hadrian in the early second century AD and author of the *Lives of the Caesars*, records for us the expulsion of Jews from Rome under Claudius (10 BC–AD 54): "Since the Jews constantly made disturbances at the instigation of Chrestus [scholars suggest a garbled version of the Latin *Christus*[19]], he [Emperor Claudius] expelled them from Rome."[20] This would have been around AD 49.[21]

Whether or not these were Jews who were reacting against Christian teaching, Jewish believers who were teaching the reality of Christ, or a combination of both, we do not know. What *is* clear, however, is that the news of Jesus had made it all the way to Rome and had made such impact that it came to the attention of the emperor—and this was *within less than 20 years of Jesus's crucifixion.*

The significance of Christianity's impact on the Imperial City can also be inferred from the mention of Christians in relationship to another, well-known historical event. It was in AD 64 that fire ravaged the interior of Rome, only to have Nero (AD 54–68) subsequently begin building his palace on top of the ruins. The citizenry of Rome began to suspect Nero's complicity in the matter, thus motivating him to ascribe blame elsewhere—and he chose *Christians!* The Roman historian Tacitus documents this scenario when he writes (ca. AD 110):

> But all human efforts, all the lavish gifts of the emperor, and the propitia- tions of the gods, did not banish the sinister belief that the conflagration was the result of an order. Consequently, to get rid of the report, Nero fastened the guilt and inflicted the most exquisite tortures on a class hated for their abominations, called Christians by the populace. Christus, from whom the name had its origin, suffered the extreme penalty during the reign of Tiberius at the hands of one of our procurators, Pontius Pilatus, and a most mischievous superstition, thus checked for the moment, again broke out not only in Judaea, the first source of the evil, but even in Rome, where all things hideous and shameful from every part of the world find their centre and become popular. Accordingly, an arrest was first made of all who pleaded guilty [i.e., of following Christ]; then, upon their information, an immense multitude was convicted, not so much of the crime of firing the city, as of hatred against mankind. Mockery of every sort was added to their deaths. Covered with the skins of beasts,

they were torn by dogs and perished, or were nailed to crosses, or were doomed to the flames and burnt, to serve as a nightly illumination, when daylight had expired.[22]

Thus, within a little over 30 years of Christ's death, followers of Jesus Christ had grown to such numbers in the capital city that Nero could use them as a scapegoat for his burning of Rome.

What was it about this Jewish carpenter that resulted in so many following His teachings, even potentially at the expense of one's life? What other reasons, apart from the miraculous event of His resurrection, might one suggest?

- Could it be because He was viewed as a martyr for the Jewish people? Unlikely, because Jesus was only one of 30,000 Jewish males crucified in Palestine by the Romans![23] That He was vilified by the religious elite *and* the masses would more normally have led, or so it seems, to the belief that Jesus deserved what he got and was the perpetrator of a sham.

- Could it be because His followers fabricated the supernatural aspects of His life, creating a more or less legendary Jesus? One must ask, "And for *whose* benefit?" If His followers knew that Jesus were merely a man (even if He did have all the right intentions), why should they put their lives on the line to make Him something different? Do not countless people today hold Jesus in high esteem, simply because of the life He lived and the words He spoke, apart from ascribing to His deity or supernatural works?

    Furthermore, Christian apologist J.P. Moreland notes that from the time Jesus was crucified (AD 33) until the time that we can date the New Testament materials, there is an insufficient amount of time "for a simple carpenter from Nazareth to become deified and blown up into a legendary figure." He continues by pointing out that the presence of both friendly and hostile eyewitnesses would have made the creation of a legendary Jesus a formidable task. Moreland cites the work of A.N. Sherwin-White who, in his classic work, *Roman Society and Roman Law in the New Testament* (1963), asserts that "even two generations are too short a span to allow the mythical tendency to prevail over the hard historic core." [24/25]

The bottom line is this: given the very early dates we are able to affix the writings of Jesus's followers (several within 25 years of Jesus's crucifixion), there is an insufficient amount of time for the creation of a legendary Jesus. *The Jesus of history is the Jesus of faith.*

- Could it be that the teachings of Jesus (e.g., to love one's neighbor, to care for the needy, etc.) and the Christian community that was spawned by those teachings attracted the Roman multitudes because Christianity provided a better option than the other religions of the day? Indeed, even as today, one could have easily followed Jesus's teachings without worshipping Him as God's Son—*if* Christianity were simply a different brand of religious system.

The Roman world was replete with numerous other deities and religions. With the blessing of the Roman government, it was a multicultural, tolerance-oriented empire. So what was it that caused problems for Christianity? I would like to suggest that it was the *exclusivity* of the message—that Jesus *alone* was the way to have a relationship with God and that He *alone* should be worshipped.

It is in view of this that I find the comments of Dr. Sophie Lunn-Rockliffe (Lecturer in Roman History at King's College, London) insightful as she has explored the history of the growth and development of Christianity within the Roman Empire:

> Pagans were probably most suspicious of the Christian refusal to sacrifice to the Roman gods. This was an insult to the gods and potentially endangered the empire which they deigned to protect. Furthermore, the Christian refusal to offer sacrifices to the emperor, a semi-divine monarch, had the whiff of both sacrilege and treason about it.[26]

Pliny the Younger, the governor of Bithynia-Pontus (two provinces located in modern-day northern Turkey and bordering the Black Sea) served under the rule of Emperor Trajan. In one of his letters to Trajan, Pliny wrote:

I have never been present at an examination of Christians. So, I do not know the nature or the extent of the punishments usually dealt out to them…For the moment this is the line I have taken with all persons brought before me on the charge of being Christians. I have asked them in person if they are Christians; if they admit it, I repeat the question a second and third time, with a warning of the punishment awaiting them … I considered that I should dismiss any who denied that they were or ever have been Christians, once they had repeated after me a formula of invocation to the gods and had made offerings of wine and incense to your statue (which I had ordered to be brought into court for this purpose along with images of the gods), and furthermore had cursed the name of Christ. Real Christians (I understand) can never be induced to do these things …[27]

I often summarize some of the information above after I have challenged someone to examine the claims of Jesus Christ. My desire is to provide that individual with the impetus to look at Jesus's claims differently from the way they might contemplate the words of the friend at school, the neighbor next door, or their favorite Bantam Books philosopher.

Jesus Christ stands alone among all the religious leaders of history.

The *positive* influence He has had through His words and works, the mystery of the resurrection that defies explanation apart from supernatural means, and the willingness to give one's life as demonstrated by His first-century followers, is sufficiently compelling to cause one to ask the question, "Could it be that God has walked among us?"

# Notes

[1] Grant Jeffrey notes: "The remarkable truth is that the life of Jesus of Nazareth occurred in historical time as opposed to some mythological period in the distant past. There is no other period in the ancient past that is so well documented as the first century of the Christian era during the rule of the Roman emperors. Some of the greatest historians of the ancient world were contemporaries of Jesus and His disciples, including the Roman writers Livy and Seneca, as well as the Jewish historian Flavius Josephus, whose works have survived through the centuries." (Jesus: The Great Debate, [Toronto: Frontier Research Publications, 1999], 42)

[2] *Is There Historical Evidence for the Resurrection of Jesus?* Transcript of a debate between William Lane Craig and Bart D. Ehrman, College of the Holy Cross, http://www.holycross.edu/departments/crec/website/resurrection-debate-transcript.pdf (Accessed January 10, 2008).

[3] BIBARCH. "Capernaum," http://www.bibarch.com/ArchaeologicalSites/Capernaum.htm (accessed January 15, 2008).

[4] See *The New Evidence that Demands a Verdict* (chapter 9) by Josh McDowell (Nashville, TN: Thomas Nelson Publishers, 1999), *Who Moved the Stone?* by Frank Morison (Grand Rapids, MI: Zondervan, 2002) and "Contemporary Scholarship and the Historical Evidences for the Resurrection of Jesus Christ," an on-line article by William Lane Craig (www.reasonablefaith.org/site/News2?page=NewsArticle&id=52 14).

[5] I am indebted to Dr. Craig Hazen (Director, Graduate Program in Christian Apologetics, Biola University) for this cogent summary of the historical record. One is often apt to miss the obvious when delving into the details of the historical record!

[6] Norman L. Geisler and Abdul Saleeb, *Answering Islam: The Crescent in Light of the Cross* (Grand Rapids, MI: Baker Books, 1993), 271–286.

[7] Frank Morison, *Who Moved the Stone?* (Grand Rapids, MI: Zondervan, 2002), 96–103.

[8] Ibid., 4–6.

[9] Lee Strobel, The *Case for Christ* (Grand Rapids, MI: Zondervan, 1998), 230.

[10] Critics have used these secondary details (which can be reconciled) to suggest that the Gospel accounts are not reliable. The slight variations in the accounts actually add credibility to the source material and demonstrate that independent and different sources were used; otherwise, every account would be exactly the same. If the resurrection narrative had been invented by the Christian community, it would seem more likely that the variations would have been reconciled before being recorded and distributed in order to artificially enhance the credibility of the various accounts. (See Strobel, 213–217).

[11] *Is There Historical Evidence for the Resurrection of Jesus?* Transcript of debate between Bart D. Ehrman and William Lane Craig, College of Holy Cross (Accessed January 10, 2008).

[12] Strobel, 221.

[13] Charles C. Ryrie, ed., *The Ryrie Study Bible* (Chicago: Moody Press, 1995), 1672.

[14] N.T. Wright, "The New Unimproved Jesus," Christianity *Today* (September 13, 1993): 26.

[15] Morison, 115.

[16] Gillian Clark, *Christianity and Roman Society* (Cambridge: Cambridge University Press, 2006), 1.

[17] Morison, 105.

[18] Clark, 38.

[19] See "Non-Biblical Sources for the Historical Jesus" in *The Archaeological Study Bible*, ed. Walter C. Kaiser, Jr and Duane Garrett (Grand Rapids, MI: Zondervan, 2005), 1751, where the following scenario is suggested:

"The Roman authorities in 49 could easily have misunderstood the cause of Jewish upheavals in their city. If Jews had rioted because of the presence of Christians [presumably Jews who were followers of Jesus] among them, Romans seeking to make sense of the troubles could have jumped to the conclusion that someone named "Chrestus" was at the center of it. Local authorities in Rome at this very early stage of Christian history would have possessed little knowledge of this new religion or the degree of discord it had already created among the Jews. It is worth noting that this expulsion of Jews from Rome is also mentioned in Acts 18: 2."

[20] J.C. Rolfe, ed, "Suetonias: De Vita Caesarum—Divus Claudius, c. 110 CE" in *Suetonias,* The Loeb Classical Library (New York: The MacMillan Co, 1914) II, 3-83, Internet Ancient History Sourcebook, http: //www.fordham.edu/halsall/ancient/suet-claudius-rolfe.html (accessed May 30, 2007).

[21] Clark, 18.

[22] Tacitus, *The Annals*: Book XV, trans. Alfred John Church and William Jackson Brodribb, The Internet Classics Archive, http: //classics.mit.edu/Tacitus/annals.11.xv.html (accessed May 30, 2007).

[23] J.P. Moreland, "Searching for the Historical Jesus," in the compact disc series *The Case for Christianity* (available through the Department of Christian Apologetics, Biola University, 13800 Biola Avenue, La Mirada, CA 90639).

[24] Ibid.

[25] Adrian N. Sherwin-White, *Roman Society and Roman Law in the New Testament* (Oxford: Clarendon Press, 1963), 189-190.

[26] Sophie Lunn-Rockliffe, "Christianity and the Roman Empire," British Broadcasting Company, http: //www.bbc.co.uk/history/ancient/romans/christianityromanempire_article_02.shtml (accessed March 28, 2007).

[27] Chris Heaton, "Christian Persecution," United Nations of Roma Victrix, www.unrv.com. http: //www.unrv.com/culture/christian-persecution.php (accessed March 28, 2007).

# CHAPTER 19

# How God Engaged the World Through the Bible (Or, The Bible as a Reliable Record of God's Truth)

EVENTUALLY, you will get to the Bible as you engage your friends in conversations about God. And you will discover that people have a variety of ideas about who or what God is and how to get to know Him—and if that is even possible. So how does one really know? Apart from a source of revelation, one cannot know, absolutely, who God is. There must be a divinely revealed source of information. Otherwise, everyone's opinion stands on equal footing.

Even as Jesus was God's living Word (see John 1: 1), so the Bible claims to be God's written Word—His communication to us in written form. To posit the Bible as God's revelation to humanity, one must accept the premise that there is a God who desires to be known. Yet, once this premise has been stated, some likely will ask, "But why the Bible?" What about Islam's Quran, the Buddhist's Tripitaka, or the Vedic texts of Hinduism? What sets the Bible apart from the holy books of other world religions?

And how can one be sure that what was written in biblical times has been transmitted accurately through the ages? What about all those variants, versions, and various interpretations? And wasn't its transmission influenced by groups of individuals who had political and/or religious agendas to support?

Let's consider some of the questions you will undoubtedly be asked and consider answers that will help others understand more clearly why you believe the Bible to be unique and the only reliable source of divine communication.

**Q—Men wrote the Bible, so why do you think it is so special?**

**A—The Bible claims to be divinely authorized.**

The Apostle Paul asserts, "All Scripture is inspired by God" (2 Timothy 3: 16). Though the term Scriptures was used to refer specifically to the Old Testament documents (see Matthew 21: 42), the concept of inspiration can be understood to apply to the New Testament documents as well. In 2 Timothy 3, the case may be made that Paul considered his own teachings (see verses 10 and 14, in particular), along with the Scriptures (Old Testament) as being inspired of God. It for this reason he includes the modifier "all" immediately before the word Scripture (suggesting that other writings, in addition to the Hebrew Scriptures, had God as their divine Author).

Jesus Himself affirmed the divine authorship and authority of the Old Testament and indirectly affirmed the same of the New Testament, as He promised His disciples that the Holy Spirit would "guide you into all the truth" (John 16: 13). This guidance of the Spirit would surely extend to the expression of truth in written form and would serve to complement the responsibility Jesus gave His disciples immediately before His ascension, when He commanded them: "Therefore, go and make disciples of all the nations, baptizing them in the name of the Father and the Son and the Holy Spirit. Teach these new disciples to obey all the commands I have given you. And be sure of this: I am with you always, even to the end of the age" (Matthew 28: 19–20 NLT).

Throughout the New Testament, the writers clearly convey their confidence that the words they wrote were of God and, as such, their writings came with divine authority. For example, the Apostle Paul, near the conclusion of his second letter to the church at Corinth (in which he had been tough in dealing with the sins of that church), explains: "I am writing this to you before I come, hoping that I won't need to deal severely with you when I do come. For I want to use *the authority the Lord has given me* to strengthen you, not to tear you down" (2 Corinthians 13: 10, NLT). Emphasis mine.

Yet this belief the individual writers held is not something they alone affirmed; it is a shared belief by the other New Testament authors. Consider that Peter includes Paul's writings along with "other Scriptures" (2 Peter 3: 15–16) and in 1 Timothy 5: 18, Paul quotes from Luke 10: 7 and Deuteronomy 25: 4, placing both on equal par by referring to them as Scripture.

Furthermore, the Apostles' confidence in the authoritative nature of their writings is also indicative of the fact that they had both Gospels and epistles circulated so that they could be read among the churches throughout the Mediterranean world. Even shortly after Christ's resurrection, the believing Jews of the Jerusalem church were said to have "devoted themselves to the apostles' teaching" (Acts 2: 42).

Thus, even the Christian community can be seen as giving affirmation to the very tenet of divine inspiration and authority claimed by the apostles, initially, and by all the New Testament authors, ultimately. It is the testimony of the Christian community to particular writings that is crucial in our understanding of why certain books were included, and others excluded, from the New Testament we have today.

Finally, the Old Testament prophets and New Testament apostles confirmed their authority through miracles. The Old Testament Law was quite clear as to its penalty for one who might assert himself to be God's prophet if he was not: the penalty was death (Deuteronomy 18: 20–22). Furthermore, the test for being God's prophet was quite simple: 100 percent accuracy! Thus, a false prophet would never have been able to write and circulate a book in the nation of Israel. A prophet was only considered a prophet of God if he spoke with complete accuracy.

In the New Testament, the authority of the apostles was also verified through miraculous works (see in particular the book of Acts). The Church of the first century consisted of many individuals who possessed firsthand knowledge of the apostles' character and purported miraculous works. Jewish individuals who ascribed to the apostolic message that Jesus was God's Messiah faced family and social ostracism and even persecution. Therefore, it seems highly improbable they would have taken such a step without a significant degree of proof as to the integrity of Jesus or to His apostles, including evidence supporting the miracles they purportedly performed.[1]

**Q—"But isn't this claim by the biblical authors simply a self-claim? Is there any evidence to back it up?"**

**A—If the Bible is from God, then it should demonstrate unique qualities that would serve to substantiate its claim. For example, it should be accurate, both historically and in its transmission. Also,**

it should include some kind of evidence—direct and indirect—
that would point to a divine origin. Consider the following:

# #1—MANUSCRIPT EVIDENCE

**The New Testament** has extensively more manuscript evidence than any
other book of antiquity. More than 5000 Greek manuscripts of portions of
the New Testament have been catalogued.[2] It is important for you to be aware
of several key facts concerning New Testament manuscripts so you won't be
caught off guard in a discussion:

- **First**, there are no existing original manuscripts (or autographs) of
  the New Testament, but that is the same for every other book of
  antiquity. Therefore, we must rely on copies, just like we rely on
  copies of all other books of antiquity. So, the key question is, "Can
  we rely on the copies as reliable?"

- **Second**, the copies we have can be divided into four primary categories (according to the material on which they were written, the type
  of script used, and/or the purpose of their use).[3] The four groupings
  are:

  » *papyri* (the earliest manuscripts written on paper made from
     the papyrus reed)

  » *uncials* (manuscripts written in all-capital Greek letters)

  » *minuscules* (manuscripts written in a cursive-like script
     consisting of primarily lower-case lettering that developed
     around AD 800)

  » *lectionaries* (books containing Scripture readings for partic-
     ular days of the civil and church calendar, written in both
     uncial and miniscule script)[4]

  As of January 2006, the grand total of all manuscripts from these
  four sources was numbered at 5,745.[5]

- **Third**, many of these manuscripts (especially the papyri, written
  on perishable material that disintegrated with the passage of time)
  are often fragmentary and may contain only a few lines of text.

However, scholars trained in the study of textual criticism[6] (the study of ancient manuscripts, their authenticity, and transmission) can learn a great deal from even fragmentary evidence.

For example, the type of writing, the composition of the manuscript (whether it was written on papyrus, parchment, or vellum) and how it was compiled (whether it was bound as a book or was part of a scroll), and the location of the manuscript helps the trained textual critic to determine the most plausible time frame for its writing, as well as the most likely place for its origin. Even when the manuscript represents only a fragment from a much longer manuscript, its words and lines may be compared to later and more complete copies for accuracy of transmission.

Let's look at a historical example that demonstrates how the application of the discipline of textual criticism helped in the dating of John's Gospel.

It had been traditionally taught that the Gospel of John was not written until the mid-second century (around AD 160). Of course, this would exclude the Apostle John from having written the book and would serve to confirm the assessment of German theologians of the nineteenth century that the miraculous nature of Jesus's life was simply a fabrication created by the Christian community.

In 1934, however, one discovery changed all. C.H. Roberts of St. John's College, Oxford, was studying pieces of papyri at the John Rylands Library in Manchester, England, when he came across a fragment with writing on both sides. He realized it contained several verses from John's Gospel (John 18: 31–34 and 18: 37–38). Based on the style of script used, he determined it was penned between AD 100 and 150. But here's the important point—the papyrus came from a community along the Nile River, a significant distance from Ephesus (located in modern-day Turkey), where the Gospel was believed to have been written. In order for a copy of John's Gospel to end up that far away from its point of origin suggests a much earlier date for its composition.[7]

As a result of this discovery, it was now not only possible to assert that the Apostle John may have written the Gospel named for him, but it would have been penned during a period when first-century believers, who had either been eyewitnesses of Christ or knew first-hand accounts of the events recorded, were still alive and could affirm or deny that which was written (including the miraculous nature of Jesus's life).

Textual criticism, however, does not deal only with a manuscript's *external* evidences (e.g., dating, style of script, type of manuscript, etc.); it also evaluates *internal* evidences as well. When it comes to the Gospels, for example, the authors' accuracy in pinpointing particular locations, as well as the descriptions they provide of the political climate and social characteristics of the time, suggests those having had a firsthand knowledge of the culture as well as the geography of the region. Indeed, only those having lived at the time when the events occurred would have been able to record the details with such great accuracy and familiarity with the cultural milieu. These evidences, of course, help provide the basis for a strong appeal to a first-century dating of the Gospels.

It is also significant to note that not one of the Gospel authors mentions the Roman/Jewish war (AD 66–70), which culminated in the Roman army under Titus destroying the city of Jerusalem, including the Temple, in AD 70. Jesus had clearly prophesied the coming destruction of Jerusalem, as well as the Temple (Matthew 23: 37; 24: 2; see also Mark 13 and Luke 21). Thus, given the religious significance of both, the authors would have surely recorded these events, had such already occurred.

**The absence of any mention of Rome's siege, and its destruction of Jerusalem and the temple, is a compelling reason to consider ascribing a date of no later than AD 70 to each of the three Synoptic Gospels, even including the Gospel of John.**[8]

- **Fourth,** the New Testament manuscripts we possess can be categorized according to three major groups, also known as manuscript traditions, families of manuscripts, or text-types. The three major text-types are the:

&raquo;   *Alexandrian* (produced primarily in Egypt around the ancient city of Alexandria). The dryness of the climate in this region has allowed manuscripts representative of this text-type to be some of our most ancient. Important witnesses to this textual family are $P^{66}$ and $P^{75}$ (two papyri from the Bodmer Papyrus collection / see chart later in this chapter), Codex Sinaiticus, and Codex Vaticanus.

&raquo;   *Western* (developed in or around Rome and circulated primarily in Italy, Gaul [France], and North Africa). Important witnesses to this textual family are $P^{48}$ (a papyrus containing portions of Acts 23) , $P^{38}$ (a papyrus containing portions of Acts 18 & 19), and Codex Bezae.

&raquo;   *Byzantine* (developed in Antioch of Syria and the area historically identified as the Byzantine Empire). Most of the Greek manuscripts of the New Testament are from the Byzantine text-type, which has led to its being referred to as the Majority Text. The King James version of the Bible has as its source manuscripts representing the Byzantine text-type.[9]

These text-types have their origin from the second century; with the Alexandrian and Western being earlier than the Byzantine.[10] The text-type (which is a hypothetical model of manuscript distribution) was developed by comparing the manuscripts of the New Testament and "grouping them into the largest possible groups of [manuscripts] which generally share the same readings."[11] Historically, the text-types suggest "the strong probability that three very early copies (or groups of copies) were carried to different geographical locations of the ancient world and they became the regional 'originals' of almost all the rest of the [New Testament manuscripts]."[12]

The existence of text-types, of course, does not preclude the existence of earlier manuscripts. Rather, their existence suggests quite the opposite: the three manuscript families began to form as the earlier manuscripts were copied for preservation and distribution. Thus, *the existence of the three text-types assumes, and provides evidence for, the existence of earlier manuscripts.*

For example, let's assume that over the course of the next 20 years, the manuscript of this book was published by three different publishers: one publisher is located in Britain, another in New York, and a third in South Africa. If we dismiss the world of the digital transfer of information, one can begin to understand how each of the text-types could develop its own identifiable "personality".

You can see, for example, how the British publishing house would likely adjust the spelling of certain words to the British norm. Perhaps the South African publishing house would desire to empha-size the deity of Jesus and, therefore, add the term *Lord* before Jesus in the dialogue I created between Lisa and Ryan. And perhaps in the transfer of data, the publishing firm in New York might inadver-tently leave out a sentence in one of my conversations. The changes made at each of the publishing houses would be reflected in the books that particular publisher produced.

Though the variants between the manuscripts would clearly demonstrate changes had occurred in the transmission process, the fact that the vast majority of material was the same would point to a common ancestor; a common source that would predate the publishers' copies and take us back to an earlier manuscript or even the original manuscript itself.

Here is something else to consider: The existence of text-types—especially as it is applied to the New Testament and its manuscripts—may even be construed as additional evidence for the reliability of the New Testament.

Given that it is generally agreed that the text-types had their develop-ment at the beginning of the second century and that each text-type was separated geographically, thus developing independently, does much to preclude the possibility of collusion by a regional church council in changing the text of the New Testament. Rather than causing confusion, the existence of the three manuscript traditions allows for broad comparative analysis between manuscripts. This only aids New Testament textual critics in their quest to determine the reading that most accurately resembles the original.

For example, in my illustration above, it would be easy to see how a studied textual critic would be able to able to discern the reason behind the variants, as well as any omissions. The factors of geographic distance and independent development would add to the confidence of the textual critic in his or her ability to develop a manuscript that would closely resemble the original.

- **Fifth**, the distance in time between the composition of the original manuscripts and the copies we possess is significantly less in comparison to other ancient works. Consider the following chart:

| Author | Book | Date Written | Earliest Copies | Time Gap | No. of Copies |
|--------|------|--------------|-----------------|----------|---------------|
| Homer | *Iliad* | 800 BC | c. 400 BC | c. 400 yrs. | 643 |
| Herodotus | *History* | 480–425 BC | c. AD 900 | c. 1350 yrs. | 8 |
| Thucydides | *History* | 460–400 BC | c. AD 900 | c. 1300 yrs. | 8 |
| Caesar | *Gallic Wars* | 100–44 BC | c. AD 900 | c. 1000 yrs. | 10 |
| Livy | *History of Rome* | 59 BC–AD 17 | 4th cent. (partial) Mostly 10th cent | c. 400 yrs. c. 1000 yrs. | 1 (partial) 19 |
| Tacitus | *Annals* | AD 100 | c. AD 1100 | c. 1000 yrs. | 20 |
| New Testament | *27 Books* | AD 50 – 100 | c. 125 (fragment) c. 200 – 250 (books) c. 250 (most of NT) c. 340 (complete NT) | 50-75 yrs. 150-200 yrs. 200 yrs. 250 yrs. | 5745 |

Chart adapted from *The New Evidence That Demands a Verdict* by Josh McDowell (Nashville: Thomas Nelson Publishers, 1999), 38. New Testament manuscript information updated with material from *Reinventing Jesus* by Komoszewski, Sawyer and Wallace (Grand Rapids, MI: Kregal, 2006), 75-82. See also *The New Testament Documents: Are They Reliable?* by F.F. Bruce (Downers Grove, IL: InterVarsity Press, 1964), 16-17.

The New Testament (AD 50–100), its books and portions of passages, have been attested to by over 5,700 manuscripts. As of January 2006, this number includes 118 papyri, 317 uncials, 2,877 minuscules, and 2,433 lectionaries.[13] A number of significant manuscripts have been dated to within the first three centuries of Christ's life, the papyri fragments and texts being the oldest. Consider the following examples:

» The earliest extant New Testament manuscript fragment (the story of its discovery which I detailed earlier in the chapter) is the **John Rylands papyrus** (designated p52 and named for the museum near Manchester, England, by which it is owned). It is dated around AD 125 – 150; within 50 to 75 years of when John originally penned his Gospel.

» **The Bodmer Papyri** collection (purchased by M. Martin Bodmer of Switzerland in 1955–1956 and currently residing at the Bibliotheca Bodmeriana in Cologny [near Geneva]), contains Greek and Coptic papyri and three parchment manuscripts from both codices and scrolls. The three most important papyri are **p**[66], **p**[72], and **p**[75] which, considered together, preserve for us a significant portion of the Gospel of John, the earliest known copies of Jude, 1 and 2 Peter and, as well, our earliest copy of the Gospel of Luke (dated between AD 175 and 225).14

| PAPYRUS | DATING | CONTENTS |
|---|---|---|
| **p**[66] | AD 200 | Portions of John's Gospel |
| **p**[72] | 3rd cent. | Jude, 1 & 2 Peter (and other non-canonical books) |
| **p**[75] | AD 175 – 225 | Most of Luke and John (earliest known copy of Luke) |

Material for chart adapted from *A General Introduction to the Bible,* Rev. ed. by Norman L. Geisler and William E. Nix (Chicago: Moody Press, 1986) 389–390.

» An almost complete copy of the New Testament has been

preserved in the **Chester Beatty Papyri** (dating from c. AD 250—Most of the collection of the 11 codices is housed in the Chester Beatty Library and Gallery of Oriental Art located near Dublin, Ireland. The library's Web site can be accessed at www.cbl.ie.). Perhaps the most important papyri found in this collection are three papyrus codices (or books) catalogued as $p^{45}$, $p^{46}$, and $p^{47}$. Considered together, these three papyri contain portions representing most of the New Testament.

| PAPYRUS | DATING | CONTENTS |
|---|---|---|
| $p^{45}$ | 3$^{rd}$ cent. | Portions of Matthew, John, Mark, Luke, and Acts. |
| $p^{46}$ | c. AD 200 - 250 | Portions of Romans, 1and 2 Corinthians, Ephesians, Galatians, Philippians, Colossians, 1 Thessalonians and Hebrews. Portions of Romans, 1 Thessalonians, and all of 2 Thessalonians are missing. The books were arranged in descending order according to size. |
| $p^{47}$ | 3$^{rd}$ cent. | A portion of the book of Revelation (9: 10–17: 2). |

Material for chart adapted from A General Introduction to the Bible, Rev. ed. by Norman L. Geisler and William E. Nix (Chicago: Moody Press, 1986) 389–390.Please note: The papyri listed above were collated at least 60 years prior to Constantine's commission to Eusebius (AD 332) to make 50 copies of the New Testament. It is instructive that though the Bodmer Papyri collection, for example, also contains apocryphal literature along with Scripture, it does not contain the "competing gospels" (e.g., Gospel of Thomas) that some suggest were intentionally eliminated by Eusebius under Constantine's command. In fact, the letters and Gospels included are those that strongly support the orthodox Christian picture of Jesus as the miracle-working Son of God: wholly human, yet wholly divine.15

» The Codex Sinaiticus (c. AD 340): This is an uncial manuscript (the script consisting of all capital letters—a format which began to develop in the fourth century) and abbreviated in manuscript shorthand by the first letter of the Hebrew alphabet aleph [א]. Codex Sinaiticus preserves half of the Old Testament and virtually all of the New (with a few missing verses from Mark and John).

» Given the fact that the New Testament books were independently written and circulated, the collation of all the books in א (as well as collections of papyri noted above) obviously attests to the earlier composition of the individual works.[16] Furthermore, one must remember that it was a luxury to possess books in the ancient world, as all required the painstaking effort of a scribe to produce. Thus, the existence of a codex, such as Sinaiticus, was a rare commodity.

It is the relatively early attestation to the New Testament books, combined with the extensive distribution of independent families of manuscripts throughout the Mediterranean world and the Middle East, which allows for the strong comparative analysis of the manuscripts. This comparative analysis—using manuscripts representing different regions, text-types, and time periods— helps affirm the consistency and accuracy of the Gospel message as well as the manuscripts themselves.[17]

• **Sixth**, the writings of the Church Fathers give early attestation to the books of the New Testament, as well as its content. The Church Fathers were the leaders of the Church who followed the apostles. Their role took on greater prominence by the first half of the second century, as Jesus's apostles, by this time, had either been martyred or died a natural death.

The writings of the Fathers were read in the churches; the instruction and exhortations they give clearly was based on the Apostles' teaching and writings (which are evidenced in how they quote the writings of the Apostles with Scriptural authority as they battled heretical groups and cultural vices).[18] As one moves into the second half of the second century, the Fathers begin to write commentaries on the Scriptures (e.g., Papias' *Exposition of the Lord's Oracles* and Heracleon's commentary on the Gospels), and Tatian (a follower of Justin Martyr) compiled his famous *Diatessaron* (AD 170), a harmonization of the four Gospels.[19]

Though the patristic writings do not serve as primary witnesses to the text of the New Testament (due to Fathers' tendency to quote from memory, make allusions to scriptural content, or even quote from other noncanonical written or oral sources similar in content[20]), they do give strong testimony to the essential content of the New Testament, as well as serve as witnesses to the authority and authenticity of the 27 books comprising our New Testament.

During the nineteenth century, Oxford scholar and Anglican vicar John William Burgon (1813–1888) embarked on a project to identify the New Testament quotations from many of the writings of the Greek and Latin Fathers. His assistants then compiled his research, extracted the passages (arranging them in order according to the New Testament books), and placed them in 16 large scrapbooks, which are now stored in the British Museum. The quotations catalogued numbered a staggering 86,439.[21]

In the twentieth century, the American Committee of the International Greek New Testament Project worked to assemble a full critical apparatus for the Gospel of Luke (Note: A New Testament *critical apparatus* lists all available manuscript evidence for the reading(s) of particular passages from Greek manuscripts and various versions and patristic writings, and is used to help determine the most accurate rendering of a passage.) During that process, scholars collected all the Gospel citations from the Greek Fathers through the fifth century. Nearly 8,500 verses or portions thereof were discovered to be from the Gospel of Luke alone! [22]

It is the notable New Testament textual critic Bruce Manning Metzger who comments:

Besides textual evidence derived from New Testament Greek manuscripts and from early versions, the textual critic has available the numerous scriptural quotations included in the commentaries, sermons, and other treatises written by early Church Fathers. Indeed, so extensive are these citations that if all other sources for our knowledge of the text of the New Testament were destroyed, they would be sufficient alone for the reconstruction of practically the entire New Testament.[23]

## Early Citations of the New Testament

| FATHER | GOSPELS | ACTS | PAUL'S EPISTLES | GENERAL EPISTLES | REVELATION | TOTAL |
|---|---|---|---|---|---|---|
| Justin Martyr (d. 192) | 268 | 10 | 43 | 6 | 3 | 330 |
| Irenaeus (d. 202) | 1038 | 194 | 499 | 23 | 65 | 1819 |
| Clement of Alexandria (d. 215) | 1017 | 44 | 1127 | 207 | 11 | 2406 |
| Origin (d. 254) | 9231 | 349 | 7778 | 399 | 165 | 17922 |
| Tertullian (d. 220) | 3822 | 502 | 2609 | 120 | 205 | 7258 |
| Hippolytus (d. 236) | 734 | 42 | 387 | 27 | 188 | 1378 |
| Eusebius (d. 340) | 3258 | 211 | 1592 | 88 | 27 | 5176 |
| TOTALS: | 19368 | 1352 | 14035 | 870 | 664 | 36289 |

Chart from *A General Introduction to the Bible,* Rev. ed. by Norman L. Geisler and William E. Nix (Chicago: Moody Press, 1986), 431 and based on information from Burgon's index.

**The Old Testament** does not have the extensive manuscript tradition of the New Testament. In fact, "There are no manuscripts in existence dating from before the Babylonian Captivity (586 BC)."[24] This is due, perhaps, to at least two factors:

1.  The destruction of Jerusalem and the Temple in 586 BC by King Nebuchadnezzar of Babylon likely resulted in a majority of manuscripts of the time being destroyed.

2.  Jewish scribal tradition required that severely worn manuscripts (i.e., scrolls) be removed from use and placed in a room attached to each synagogue called a geniza (or gheniza) until they could be disposed of properly (a practice still carried on to this day). Eventually, these worn manuscripts were often burned or buried or simply disintegrated from age.[25]

Since the Old Testament was written over a period of approximately 1000 years (ca. 1400 BC–400 BC), the primary question relates to the reliability of the text of the Old Testament today

As one considers the question as to the accuracy of the Old Testament, it is imperative to understand that the transmission of the Hebrew Scriptures was not done haphazardly. The Jewish people held their Scriptures to be divinely given. Later scribal tradition (beginning formally with Ezra around 400 BC[26]) demonstrates that greatest care was exercised in copying texts considered of God-given origin. Throughout the centuries, though different criteria were used—often depending on whether the scroll was to be used in the synagogue or privately—scribes took great care in preserving the accuracy of the text.[27]

Yet how reliable were these copyists? Given the hundreds of years and multiplied thousands of manuscripts copied and recopied, how accurately could they have preserved the text?

Until 1947, we really did not know the degree of accuracy.

It was in that year, through a chance discovery by a young shepherd boy, that the reliability of the Hebrew Scriptures was profoundly demonstrated. When looking for a lost goat near the canyon of the Wady Qumran, 13 miles east of Jerusalem and about a mile west of the Dead Sea, the boy wandered into a cave, where he discovered some large jars containing leather scrolls. A few highlights of this discovery are as follows:

- The few scrolls would only represent the initial find (explorations were initiated in 1949 and continued until 1956), which ultimately comprised 11 caves and thousands of fragments and manuscripts, representing every Old Testament book (except Esther) and 400 books from the Essene community. (The Essenes were a religious sect from about the time of Christ that had separated themselves from the Jewish community).[28]

- One of the most significant finds: two scrolls of the book of Isaiah. These were dated at about 100 BC, thus providing a manuscript sample of Isaiah having been copied over *1000 years earlier* than the earliest known copy at the time (a copy dated ca. AD 980).

  The text of these early manuscripts was compared to the later manuscripts and found to be "word for word identical with our standard Hebrew Bible in more than 95 percent of the text."[29]

- The discovery of what has become known as the Dead Sea Scrolls substantiated the accuracy of the scribes' transmission of the Hebrew text throughout the centuries.

I've attempted to acquaint you with arguably the most significant archaeological discovery of the past 100 years with regard to the textual accuracy of the Old Testament. I have always found a knowledge of the Dead Sea Scrolls an important element in discussions with my Jewish friends, in particular, as I am able to affirm the textual basis of their faith in evidence of the God who revealed Himself through His prophets then, and who has done so today through Jesus, as well as the authors (all of whom, except Luke, were of Jewish descent) of the New Testament.[30]

# #2—HISTORICAL ACCURACY

It is the sheer historical accuracy of the Bible that attests to its textual accuracy and, ultimately, does much to support the claim of its authors— that it records and reflects the very words of God. One of the classic texts which explores the Bible's inspiration, transmission and historicity is *A General Introduction of the Bible* by Norman Geisler and William Nix. In that volume, the authors make this important point:

> No historical discovery is a direct evidence of any spiritual claim in the Bible, such as the claim to be divinely inspired; nevertheless, the historicity of the Bible does provide indirect verification of the claim of inspiration. Confirmation of the Bible's accuracy in factual matters lends credibility to its claims when speaking on other subjects.[31]

Indeed, the historical accuracy of the Bible has been verified archaeologically through numerous discoveries. Geisler cites the assessment of Nelson Glueck (1900–1971), the American-born Jewish archaeologist who excavated over 1000 sites in the Middle East, who wrote:

> It may be stated categorically that no archaeological discovery has ever controverted a biblical reference. Scores of archaeological findings have been made which confirm in clear outline or exact detail historical statements in the Bible.[32]

**The Old Testament**

The degree of accuracy of the Old Testament record is startling. Robert Dick Wilson (1856–1930) was an American linguist and scholar—during his lifetime he purportedly learned 45 languages, including Hebrew, Aramaic, and Greek—who made it one of his life's pursuits to determine the accuracy of the biblical manuscripts.

Wilson once noted that the Hebrew Scriptures cite the names of 26 or more foreign kings. Even in his day, the names of these kings had been verified through archaeology, having been discovered in documents contemporaneous with the kings or on monuments dedicated to them. In a section of his classic work, *A Scientific Investigation of the Old Testament* (originally published in 1926), he details how accurately the spelling of these names had been transmitted in the biblical documents and summarized as follows:

> Thus we find that in 143 cases of transliteration from Egyptian, Assyrian, Babylonian and Moabite into Hebrew ... the evidence shows that for 2,300 to 3,900 years the text of the proper names in the Hebrew Bible has been transmitted with most minute accuracy. That the original scribes should have written them with such close conformity to correct philological principles is a wonderful proof of their thorough care and scholarship; further that the Hebrew text should have been transmitted by copyists through so many centuries is a phenomenon unequaled in the history of literature.[33]

Consider *three* additional examples where the Old Testament record has been affirmed through archaeological research:

### 1. The Hittites[34]

There are nearly 50 references to the Hittites in 15 books of the Old Testament. God promised Abraham (Genesis 15: 20) that part of the land his descendants would inherit would be that possessed in his day by the Hittites. Uriah, Bathsheba's husband, was a Hittite (2 Samuel 11: 3). And Solomon transacted business with the Hittites (I Kings 10: 29).

- Until the late nineteenth century, however, nothing was known of the Hittites, and many suggested their existence was a fabrication of the biblical authors.

- In 1876, however, British Assyriologist and linguist A.H. Sayce (1846–1933) discovered inscriptions carved on rocks in Turkey and suspected they might be an indication of the Hittite nation. Eventually, working with William Wright (1830–1889), a British Orientalist and professor of Arabic at the University of Cambridge, they determined that the ruins of *Boghaz-koy* (located approximately 93 miles east of Ankara, Turkey) were those of the Hittite capital, Hattusha. The capital city itself covered an area of 300 acres, and the empire even extended at one time from the Aegean Sea to the banks of the Euphrates River.[35]

## 2. Sodom and Gomorrah

Many scholars considered the story of Sodom and Gomorrah as simply a story fabricated by the biblical authors to communicate moral principles (and some even suggesting a condemnation of the sin of inhospitality).

- Once again, the Old Testament records the destruction of Sodom and Gomorrah as a factual event (Deuteronomy 29: 23, Isaiah 13: 19, Jeremiah 49: 18). The two cities' location is placed somewhere in the region of the Dead Sea (Genesis 14: 3) in the valley of Siddim.

- Sodom and Gomorrah were included as two of the five "cities of the plain" (Genesis 13: 10–13; 14: 18–19), traditionally considered to have been located at the south end of the Dead Sea.

- In 1924 the renowned archaeologist William Albright (1891–1971), director of the American School of Oriental Research at John Hopkins University, excavated the site of an Early Bronze Age (3500–2000 BC) settlement or town, Bab edh-Drha', located at the lower southeast end of the Dead Sea (present-day Jordan) and lying almost 800 feet below sea level. During the site's survey and excavation, a walled town area was discovered, along with several structures located outside the wall and an apparent graveyard away from the town area. Albright suggested that Bab edh-Drha' was a ceremonial site for these five ancient cities, the ruins of these cities likely lying beneath the shallow waters of the southern basin of the Dead Sea.[36]

- With renewed interest in the site, excavations continued in the 1960s, sponsored by the American Schools of Oriental Research and under the direction of Paul Lapp. In the fall of 1965 a major stone wall was discovered at Bab edh-Dhra', measuring 23 feet wide and made of stone and mud bricks. This wall enclosed a city area of nine to 10 acres and likely having a having a population of between 600 and 1200. Lapp concluded that Bab edh-Dhra' was not simply a site for religious or ceremonial center but was indeed a city.[37]

- A survey of the area in 1973, led by Walter Rast and Thomas Schaub, resulted in the discovery of four additional sites (Numeira, Safi, Feifeh, and Khanazirwith) with Early Bronze cultural materials. This led them to suggest a possible linkage to the biblical "cities of the plain." The discovery of these four additional sites led to the formation of a new expedition, the Expedition to the Dead Sea Plain (EDSP), which continued periodic expeditions to the area until 1989 (a project affiliated with the American Schools of Oriental Research and funded in part by the National Endowment for the Humanities as well as the National Geographic Society).[38]

- In 1984 Walter Rast suggested that the two Early Bronze towns of Bab edh-Dhra' and Numeria may have given rise to the biblical tradition of Sodom and Gomorrah. [39]

- Both cities give evidence of a violent end, with burnt debris discovered in virtually every area excavated.[40]

- Excavations of five charnel houses (buildings where corpses and bones are stored) of Bab edh-Dhra' revealed that the buildings had been burned. Though it was suggested that these were intentionally destroyed by enemy invaders, there is no historical parallel that would explain *why* an invading force would burn the charnel buildings, which were located several hundred meters away from the city and its walls.[41]

- In 1979, however, the largest charnel house was excavated. In studying the structure it became apparent that it, too, had been destroyed by fire. The archaeologists also discovered it had been burned *from the inside out*. Apparently, the roof had caught fire and subsequently collapsed, thus spreading the fire to the interior of the building. Archaeologists first thought the burning of the charnel houses had been due to some cult practice or possibly for hygienic purposes, but the excavation clearly evidenced *how* the building had burned, which dismissed such explanations. [Such destruction would parallel the biblical account of God's judgment as recorded in Genesis 19.][42]

- All five of the cities were abandoned about the same time, from 2450 BC to 2350 BC. According to the Old Testament, four of the five cities were destroyed by fire, leaving only the city of Zoar, to which Lot fled. Zoar, however, would also be abandoned later.[43]

## 3. King David

Though a prominent figure in the Hebrew Scriptures, King David's existence had not been affirmed by any extra-biblical evidence until near the end of the twentieth century. Some scholars had even called into question his existence and the historicity of events surrounding his purported fame. Yet, once again, because of archaeological discovery, the biblical record concerning King David was validated.

- Israeli archaeologist Dr. Avraham Biran had been directing excavations at the ancient city of Dan, located at the foot of Mount Hermon in the northern part of Israel, since 1966. During that time, little had been produced in the way of significant written materials or inscriptions.

- On July 21, 1993, however, a broken fragment of basalt stone was discovered to have been reused (in situ—in secondary use) in the construction of a wall. (In the ancient world it was not uncommon to reuse materials from previous structures in the construction of others.) Upon closer examination, it was evident the surveyors had found an inscribed stone, a fragment of an ancient stele (an upright stone pillar or slab which served as a monument or marker). Two additional fragments of the stele were discovered in June 1994.

- The stele was dated to the ninth century BC (based on pottery fragments unearthed beneath the flagstone pavement at the base of the wall). Its date could not have been later than 732 BC, in that the pavement was covered by debris from the Assyrian invasion of Palestine in that year.

- Though the 13 lines making up the inscription (which was written in ancient Aramaic) require significant reconstruction, the ninth line clearly contains the phrase "House of David," a formulation typically employed to identify one's dynastic heritage. This discovery, then, was the first extra-biblical evidence pointing to the existence of a king of the Jewish nation by the name of David.

- It is surmised that the stele, which commemorates the conquest of Dan by one of the Aramean kings of Damascus (possibly Hazael; who reigned from 844/42 – 798? / see 2 Kings 8: 7–15, 28; 2 Chronicles 22: 5), was possibly broken by either Jehoash (798 – 782) or his son, Jeroboam II (793, co-regent 782 – 753) in order to remove this memorial to Aram and its conquest of Dan.[44]

- In another archaeological dig (beginning in mid-February 2005), Jewish archaeologist Eilat Mazar initiated excavations immediately to the north of the City of David in search of King David's palace. (Note: The City of David is at the northern end of Jerusalem and is its most ancient area. Originally, the area consisted of a Jebusite—a Canaanite tribal group—fortress, which David conquered.)

- To date, a building referred to as the "Large-Stone Structure" (awaiting more specific identification) has been discovered immediately north of the northernmost wall of the ancient city. Mazar notes that this structure "was not just any public building but a structure that was clearly the product of inspiration, imagination, and considerable economic investment." Though the structure's construction involved, over time, three separate phases, the discovery of pottery shards were helpful in dating the initial phase of construction "close to the beginning of Iron Age IIa, probably around the middle of the tenth century BC, when the Bible says King David ruled the United Kingdom of Israel."[45]

- Interestingly, both the inspiration for and location that prompted Eliat's quest came from historical references to David's palace found in the Hebrew Scriptures:

  » Samuel 5: 11, which speaks of the construction of such a palace

  » Samuel 5: 17, "which describes David in the City of David going down, or descending (*yered*), from his residence to the citadel or fortress (*metzudah*) … It is clear from the topography of the City of David that David could have gone down to the citadel only from the north, as the city is surrounded by deep valleys on every other side."[46] One cannot help but appreciate the precise detail that has been accurately preserved in the text for the past 3000 years…so much so that it helped guide the efforts of a modern-day archaeologist in this potentially-significant discovery!

## The New Testament

If you had lived at the middle of the nineteenth century you would have had little of the historical or archaeological evidence we have today confirming the historicity of the New Testament authors. The Gospel of Luke (now considered authored by a historian of the first rank) was questioned because so many of the names, places, and other historical allusions he makes were unknown. For example, the name of Pilate had no extra-biblical reference; the city of Capernaum (where Jesus spent a great deal of time) had no known historical counterpart; and the evidence for Roman crucifixion, within first-century Jerusalem, had not been discovered. Some were even beginning to suggest the possibility that the person of Jesus was the figment of some misguided people's imagination. The list could go on.

But that was then, and now is now. And now is a different matter—a *much* different matter.

Despite numerous significant archaeological discoveries, not one has discredited a single New Testament citation of historical reference. It is for this reason that when scholars attempt to discredit the New Testament writers today, they do so from a literary or sociological perspective, not a historical one. The following *three* discoveries will help substantiate the historicity of the biblical accounts.

### 1. Pontius Pilate

For nearly 2000 years, the only extra-biblical references we had to Pilate were from Josephus, Philo of Alexandria, and Tacitus. Yet no epigraphical inscriptions had been discovered.

- Josephus affirms that Pilate was the fifth Roman governor of the province of Judaea, whose rule lasted from AD 26 to AD 37 (Antiquities 18.32f, 35, 89). In his works Antiquities and The Jewish War, Josephus describes four incidents involving Pilate—one of these even potentially referring to Jesus's execution or, at the very least, some kind of disturbance involving Jesus's followers following His death.

- Philo describes a fifth historical incident involving Pilate in his story Legatio and Gaium (Legatio, 299–305).[47]

- Tacitus confirms Pilate's role in Jesus's crucifixion in his Annals (15.44).[48]

In 1961, however, Italian archaeologist Antonio Frova and his team of researchers were excavating a site in the ancient town of Caesarea. (It is believed that during Jesus's time, Caesarea served as the headquarters for the Roman governor [or *prefect*] and his troops.) During the excavation, Frova discovered a slab of limestone rock measuring two feet by three feet and bearing the following Latin inscription:


. . . . . S TIBERIEVM
. . . . . NTIVS PILATVS
. . . . . ECTVS IVDA E
. . . . . . . . . . ' . . . . .


- Though the inscription is not able to be reconstructed in its entirety with absolute confidence, three things are clearly discernable:

    »    The second line refers to Pontius Pilate.

    »    His title praefectus Iudaeae, prefect of Judea, is cited in the third line.

    »    This inscription was evidently some kind of dedicatory marker placed on a building known as a Tiberiéum, having been dedicated to Tiberius (presumably by Pilate).[49]

•    This was the first time any inscription bearing Pilate's name had been discovered.[50] It is of particular interest to note that the inscription bears Pilate's more complete name, something that neither Josephus nor Philo used in their writings but is recorded in Luke's Gospel (3: 1).

## 2. Politarchs in Thessalonica

As the Apostle Paul and his associate Silas began making inroads throughout the Mediterranean world in proclaiming the good news of Jesus Christ, they met acceptance as well as rejection. Such was the case in the ancient city of Thessalonica, where the team spent perhaps several months. Initially it was Paul's custom to take the Gospel message to the Jews of the city and then to the Gentiles. As both Jews and Gentiles began to respond to Jesus as Messiah, the Jewish leaders incited a mob reaction with the intent of extricating Paul and Silas from Thessalonica.

As a result, Luke records that several Christians, as well as the owner of the home who had hosted Paul and Silas, were taken before the "rulers of the city" (Acts 17: 5–6). The phrase "rulers of the city" (NKJV, ASV; "city officials" NIV and "city authorities" ESV) is translated from the Greek word politarchas and occurs only in Acts 17: 6, 8 in all the New Testament.[51]

•    Critics believed that Luke had made an error in referring to the city leaders of Thessalonica as politarchas, given that it is a term used nowhere else in Greek literature. The more common terms, "magistrates" (Gk. strateegoi) or "authorities" (Gk. exousiais) should have been employed.[52]

- It is likely that the Apostle Paul traveled to Thessalonica on the famed Egnatian Way (Via Egnatia), the main thoroughfare that extended from the western shore of the Adriatic in Greece, all the way to what is known as Istanbul today. A Roman arch, known as the Vandar Gate, once stood over the Egnatian Way. In 1867, the arch was torn down and its stones used to repair the city walls. The inscription from that arch, now stored in the British Museum, begins with the phrase "In the time of the Politarchas ..."[53]

- In 1960, Carl Shuler published a list of 32 inscriptions bearing the title of "politarchas," 19 of the inscriptions having been discovered in Thessalonica, with three of the inscriptions dating to the first century. (Indeed, as noted with the previous example, the title began surfacing in archaeological excavations in the 1800s.)[54]

- It is in view of these discoveries that noted biblical archaeologist John McRay notes:

"It is interesting that scholarly discussion has now shifted from whether politarchs existed at all to the question of when the institution originated! It is now incontrovertible that politarchs existed in Macedonia both before and during the time of the Apostle Paul."[55]

## 3. Ossuaries

In years past, some scholars, such as Rudolph Bultmann, questioned the personal names recorded by the New Testament authors as not being characteristic of names found in the first century. Rather, the names had been chosen for their meaning rather than for the purpose of historical record.[56] For over 100 years now, however, the discovery of burial boxes, known as ossuaries, has laid that claim to rest!

An ossuary was a stone box designed for the purpose of storing the bones of a deceased person, which were cleaned and collected several years after death. Given the fact that such a practice is foreign to our experience, the following explanation will give you some perspective:

The family would return several years after a death, clean the bones of the skeleton, and then re-bury the bones in a stone ossuary, usually forty inches long, twenty inches wide, and twenty-five inches high. The lids of these ossuaries are triangular, semicircular, or rectangular with either plain sides or ornamentation consisting of a motif using a geometric rose pattern...Greek or Hebrew inscriptions containing the name and identification of the deceased were often painted or engraved with an iron pointer on the sides or on the lids of the ossuaries.[57]

The following will provide details of several significant discoveries involving these stone burial boxes as well as the insights gained from the inscriptions on them:

- In 1873, famed French Orientalist/archaeologist Charles Clermont-Ganneau (the one credited with saving the Mobite or Mesha stele) wrote a report to England's Palestine Exploration Fund (a group created in the 1860s to further archaeological exploration of the Middle East) concerning his discoveries.[58] That report was subsequently published under the title Archaeological Researches in Palestine during the years 1873–1874.[59]

  » He details therein an incident in which an Arab sheik, Effendi Abu Saud, unintentionally discovered the existence of a large cave beneath his house, located on the Eastern slopes of the Mount of Olives.

  » Clermont-Ganneau was called to investigate and determined that Abu Saud had unwittingly discovered an ancient storehouse for ossuaries, containing 30 limestone coffins as well as a number of terra-cotta vases.

  » Of significance was the fact that on several of the ossuaries the likeness of a cross had been engraved or the Hebrew name Jesus (ישוע), leading him to conclude that these were early Christians.[60]

  » Clermont-Ganneau had his assistant carefully copy the

inscriptions from the sides of the ossuaries. Those inscriptions, included in his 1874 report, detail many names that are found in the New Testament (e.g., Salome, Judah, Simeon, Martha, Eleazar).[61]

- In 1953 excavations on the Mount of Olives produced a large cemetery consisting of hundreds of burial sites, including over 120 ossuaries. More than 40 of the ossuaries contained inscriptions that bore such names as Joseph, Judas, Solome, Sapphira, Simeon, Yeshua (or, Jesus—That's right, the name Jesus was not uncommon in first-century Jewish society!), John, and others very typical of the names we find mentioned in the New Testament.[62]

- In 1990, several ossuaries were discovered accidentally as workers were building a water park in Jerusalem's Peace Forest (located on the southwest side of Old Jerusalem). It was this accidental discovery that has produced one of the most significant archaeological finds pertaining to ossuaries: the ossuary of Caiaphas the high priest, who played a key role in Jesus's trial before the Sanhedrin. This ossuary is currently housed, along with the Pontius Pilate inscription noted earlier, at the Israeli Museum in Jerusalem.[63] The Caiaphas Ossuary toured the United States in 2007, along with the Dead Sea Scrolls exhibit.[64]

I would encourage you to explore additional examples of how archaeology has affirmed the accuracy of both the Old and New Testaments. You will be challenged by the studies that have been conducted over the past 150 years, in particular, and conducted by those committed to Christ as well as those who are pursuing understanding of ancient history without any particular faith at all.

Given the precise historical detail employed by the biblical authors, it does not seem rational that these writings were designed to convey legendary stories, whether of a miracle-working God in the Hebrew Scriptures or a divine Son in the New Testament. The writers' attention to such detail suggests they believed that which they were writing accurately recorded historical fact.

# #3—FULFILLED PROPHECY

The Old Testament was written over a period of 1000 years and contains nearly 300 prophecies concerning the coming Messiah. These prophecies were offered by the authors of the New Testament as proof that Jesus was the Jewish Messiah.

- It is the *specificity* of biblical prophecy, however, that sets it apart from the "guesses" of fortune tellers throughout history.

- Specific prophecies were given relating to Jesus's birth, life, miracles, death, and future rule. When using prophecy as a means of verification of the uniqueness of Jesus's life, I focus attention on the prophecies and their fulfillment, as related to His first coming. The chart on page 186 could be of particular interest to your Jewish friends:

The Old and New Testaments both contain prophecies concerning the rise and fall of world nations, often as their histories relate to that of  Israel's—its exile and return to the land, and its being a focal point of world conflict. Note several specific examples cited in the chart on page 187.

- Especially today, with the worldwide attention placed on the Middle East, I enjoy pointing out that the Bible paints a picture of the final conflict of civilization being centered in *the Middle East!* That *is* significant. Here is a book containing prophecies pertaining to the end of time (the latest written approximately 1,900 years ago) that places the locus of world attention on a tiny piece of desert real estate—the nation of Israel.

- All these prophecies have been (and are currently being) fulfilled, exactly as foretold. It is the inclusion of fulfilled prophecy and seemingly uncanny insight into future events that sets the Bible apart from any other religious book. Fulfilled prophecy begs the question: "How could this simply be a book of human origin?"

| Specific prophecy | Old Testament Passage | New Testament Fulfillment |
|---|---|---|
| Born of a woman | Genesis 3: 15 | Galatians 4: 4 |
| Tribe (family) of Judah | Genesis 49: 10 | Matthew 1: 2; Luke 3: 33 |
| Born of a virgin | Isaiah 7: 14 | Matthew 1: 23 |
| Born in Bethlehem | Micah 5: 2 | Matthew 2: 6 |
| Coming to be announced | Isaiah 40: 3, 5; Malachi 3: 1 | John 1: 23; Luke 3: 3-6 |
| Fulfilled role of prophet | Deuteronomy 18: 15-18 | Matthew 21: 11; cmp. John 3: 2 |
| Would bring hope & freedom | Isaiah 61: 1-2a* | Luke 4: 18-19 |
| Would enter Jerusalem on a donkey | Zechariah 9: 9 | John 12: 13-14 |
| Would be mocked | Psalm 22: 7-8 | Matthew 27: 39,43 |
| Would be scourged | Isaiah 53: 5 | John 19: 1,18 |
| Hands and feet would be pierced | Zechariah 12: 10; Psalm 22: 16 | John 20: 25, 27 |
| Bones would not be broken | Psalm 22: 17 | John 19: 33-36 |
| Would be resurrected | Psalm 16: 10; 22: 22 | Matthew 28: 6; Acts 2: 27-28 |
| Would ascend | Psalm 68: 18 | Luke 24: 50-53; Acts 1: 9-11 |

Adapted from *Ryrie Study Bible*, Expanded Edition. Chicago: Moody Press, 1995, 1503.

* In some instances you will discover that in a singular prophetic passage both the first and second comings of the Messiah are discussed (as in Isaiah 61: 1-2). At His first coming the Messiah would come as Savior; at His second as King. At Christ's first coming He extended the grace of God; at His second He will administer God's judgment, yet restoration for Israel and the "remnant" of the Jewish people who will believe in Jesus as Messiah. It is for this reason that Jesus stops halfway through His reading of the Isaiah passage (recorded in Luke 4: 18-19) and proclaims, "Today this Scripture has been fulfilled in your hearing" (Luke 4: 21). The last part of the passage still awaits fulfillment.

| Prophecy | Scripture | Fulfillment |
|----------|-----------|-------------|
| Israel (Judah) would be taken captive by Babylon for a 70-year period. After that, Babylon would be destroyed. | Jeremiah 25: 11 (written ca. 627 – 585 BC) | In 586 BC Nebuchadnezzar destroyed Jerusalem and took the Jewish people into captivity. The Medes and Persians captured Babylon in 539 BC, thus allowing Cyrus to issue his decree. (see below) |
| King Cyrus would direct that Jerusalem be rebuilt and the Temple foundation laid. | Isaiah 44: 24-28; 54: 1 (written ca. 700 BC) At the time of writing both Jerusalem and the Temple were still standing! | King Nebuchadnezzar of Babylon conquered Israel in 605 BC and, in 586 BC, destroyed Jerusalem and the Temple. In October of 539 BC, Persia conquered Babylon. Shortly thereafter (538 BC), King Cyrus of Persia decreed that Jews could return to Israel to rebuild the Temple (Ezra 1: 1-4). Later (444 BC) King Artaxerxes of Persia would allow Nehemiah to return and complete the building of the city (Nehemiah 2: 1-8). |
| God would make of Abraham a great nation (the Jewish people) who would forever possess the land of Palestine. After dispersion, they would, one day, return to that land. | Genesis 12: 2-3; 13: 14-15 (written ca. 1400 BC); Ezekiel 37 (written ca. 592-570 BC) | Though the Jewish people were allowed to return to their land under the Medes and Persians, they were scat-tered again in AD 70, when the Roman general Titus destroyed Jerusalem. After nearly 1,900 years, however, the Jewish people were granted title to the land of Israel in 1948 and a historic return (an ancient people returning to their ancient homeland) was instituted as prophesied by Ezekiel in fulfillment of God's promise to Abraham. |
| At the end of time, Israel will come under attack by nations to its north and will be delivered supernaturally. | Ezekiel 38-39 (written ca. 592-570 BC) | This is yet to be fulfilled though the land of Magog was identified by the Roman historian Josephus as the land of the Scythians—now occupied by the nations of Russia, Ukraine, and Kazakhstan.[65] |

Material adapted from *The New Evidence that Demands a Verdict* by Josh McDowell, Nashville: Thomas Nelson, 1999 (see pp 164–192), and Global Media Research Web site: www.greatcom. org/resources/areadydefense (Accessed on June 18, 2007).

## #4—Central Role of Jesus Christ

It is intriguing that this unique book includes as its central character the world's most controversial person, Jesus Christ. Though there have been attempts to call into question the historicity of the Gospel accounts, it is clear that to deny their historicity often has more to do with particular presuppositions (e.g., Jesus could not have performed miracles because the miraculous doesn't occur; history cannot study that which lies outside the scope of what normally/naturally occurs, etc.) held by the scholar rather than any evidence that controverts that which has been recorded by the Gospel writers. Furthermore, the significance of Jesus's teachings and the influence they have had on Western culture is unparalleled.

Throughout His lifetime on earth, Jesus consistently appealed to the Scriptures and clearly attested to their divine origin. If Jesus lived the kind of life as recorded in the Bible, and if His life has had such marked influence on people and cultures worldwide and throughout the centuries, then His affirmation of the Old Testament Scriptures should be seriously considered.

Furthermore, given the strong manuscript evidence attesting the accuracy with which the claims of Christ have been recorded, and coupled with the dynamic influence and transformational nature of His teachings throughout the centuries, it would seem that the New Testament has accurately reflected the words that Jesus said.

**Q—I understand that the manuscripts of the New Testament are riddled with error. For example, isn't it true there are hundreds of textual variants (disagreements) in wording between the texts? Given such disagreement, who can really know what the authors said much less rely on the accuracy of the words of Jesus they record?**

**A—Actually, there are thousands of variants between the manuscripts! Yet there is a field of study known as textual criticism that evaluates the manuscripts of ancient works, and which enables scholars to determine the reading which is closest to what was originally written, including the words of Jesus recorded by the New Testament authors.**

Of the approximately 138,000 words in the Greek New Testament (the language in which the New Testament was written), there are between 300,000 and 400,000 variants.[66]

But what does this staggering number of variants imply? Does it suggest that we cannot have confidence in the New Testament? Do the many variants mean that the words of Jesus and the apostles are up for grabs? Consider the following important points:

- **First**, we must define a textual variant, which is "any place among the manuscripts of the New Testament where there is not uniformity of wording."[67] *Any* variation between manuscripts—whether a simple spelling error, addition or deletion of a word or phrase, or a change in sentence structure without impacting its meaning—will be noted as a variant.

   It is also important to remember that Greek is an *inflected* language. Particular suffixes are used with nouns, indicating, for example, the subject and direct object of a sentence, as well as using prefixes, suffixes, and infixes on the verbs that modify. Therefore, in Greek, the order of a particular sentence is *not* as important as it is, for example, in the English language. Regardless, any change in manuscripts involving even word *order* is considered a variant.[68]

- **Second**, it is important to understand how variants are counted. Anyone hearing that there are 300,000 to 400,000 variants among the manuscripts of the New Testament is liable to immediately toss it out the window! Each and every variant is multiplied by the number of manuscripts in which it appears.

   For example, let's assume that in one of the printings of this book, a member of the editorial team inadvertently misspelled the word *manuscript* as "manusscript" in just one place. Let's also say that this particular printing consisted of 5000 additional copies of the book to be published, all with the word "manusscript" in that one location. This *variant* (a spelling error) would be counted as a variant as many times as the word was misspelled. In other words, this *one spelling error* would be tallied as *5000 variants*!

- **Third**, when most people hear of variants, they immediately assume that one is speaking of matters of major disagreement. In fact, according to Dr. Bruce M. Metzger (perhaps the foremost expert on New Testament textual criticism), there is not a single foundational doctrine of Christianity that is brought into jeopardy by any variant.[69]

That is not to say that no variant concerns a major doctrine. For example, the Jehovah's Witnesses, in attempting to undermine the deity of Christ, will point out that the following, *italicized* portion of I John 5: 7–8, reflected in the King James Version of the Bible, does not appear in the earliest of manuscripts:

> For there are three that bear witness *in heaven, the Father, the Word, and the Holy Ghost: and these three are one. And there are three that bear witness in earth*, the Spirit, and the water, and the blood; and these three agree in one.

Though it may be true that the italicized portion of the passage above does not appear in the earliest of manuscripts, it is wholly inaccurate to conclude that because of the absence of these two verses the doctrine of the trinity and Christ's deity is not attested elsewhere.[70] John 1, Ephesians 1, Colossians 1, and Hebrews 1 contain key passages clearly demonstrating that the New Testament authors viewed Jesus as divine. Also consider the manner in which the Apostle Paul interchangeably uses the terms *God* and *Savior* for God the Father <u>and</u> Jesus; also, in your reading of John's letters in particular, the manner in which that apostle consistently connects relationship with the Son as the foundation of relationship with the Father, his theology assuming that both shared in the divine nature.

- **Fourth**, the multiple hundreds and thousands of manuscripts we have from various time periods and locations throughout the Mediterranean world, as well as the Middle East, provide textual critics with the resources they need to reconstruct the text of the New Testament as closely to the original as possible (and, it might be added, more closely than is possible *with any other ancient text*).

**Indeed, it is the pervasive distribution of the New Testament manuscripts that helps ensure that the text has not been**

**significantly altered or its message changed by a single individual or group of individuals.**

Using these manuscripts, textual critics investigate two lines of evidence in determining the most likely original reading of a particular text.[71]

» **External Evidence** involves examination of the various "readings" of a particular passage, whether the variations of the passage consist of a single letter, word, or phrase. External evidence will examine all pertinent manuscripts (papyri, uncials, minuscules, lectionaries), versions (Syriac, Coptic, etc.) as well as quotations of the same found in the writings of the Church Fathers.

In his examination, the textual critic will consider the following:

1. *Date and character* (Character has to do with a manuscript's compliance with the text-type from which it comes; the more faithfully it models the text-type, the more accurate the transmission process has been for that manuscript.)

2. *Genealogical solidarity* within the text-type. Does the particular reading agree with the readings of other manuscripts within the same text-type?

3. *Geographical distribution.* Is this reading more localized, or does it seem to have broad consensus thus being found in other manuscripts of independent origin?

Generally speaking, the reading or variant of the earliest manuscript(s) is *usually* to be preferred, simply because logic would tell us that with less time between the original manuscripts (which we do not have) and the ones we possess, there are fewer intermediary manuscripts, thus potentially fewer errors, and a text that more closely resembles the original.[72]

» **Internal Evidence** involves examination of **two** kinds of probabilities.[73]

*Transcriptional probabilities,* which evaluate the characteristics of the scribes and the errors they committed, whether those errors are intentional or unintentional.

- *Intentional errors* can result from a scribe's attempt to correct an apparent theological discrepancy in a difficult-to-understand passage, the desire to keep particular details the same between parallel passages, or a tendency to smooth out the grammatical construction of a passage.

- *Unintentional errors* can occur due to something as simple as failing eyesight or difficulty in discerning between particular letters of the Greek alphabet, some of which appear very similar. (i.e.—"One of the most common variants involves the use of the first person plural pronoun and the second person plural pronoun. There is only one letter difference between the two in Greek."[74]). Other errors can be attributed to memory (i.e.—inadvertently switching the order of words in the transcription process), adding words from another perhaps more familiar and similar passage, or difficulty of reading a faded original.[75]

*Intrinsic probabilities* consider what the author would most likely have written. Two key factors are *context* and *style.* Pertinent to context, the textual critic is concerned with the flow of the passage and if one variant reading fits the passage better than another.

For example, if one manuscript tradition features the present tense of a verb, and another features the future tense, the focus of the passage (and even perhaps the broader context of the book as a whole) may well help determine the correct variant. A good example of this is found in John 14: 16, where some manuscripts have Jesus telling His disciples the Spirit *"is* in you," while other manuscripts have Jesus instructing His disciples that the Spirit *"will be* in you." The immediate context of John 14—the chapter as a whole looking to the future—as well as the anticipation of the Spirit's coming—anticipated elsewhere in John—argue for the future tense.[76]

As to evaluating an author's style, "here the question concerns what an author normally does, how he normally expresses himself, what his motifs and language usually involve."[77] Stylistic similarity helps textual critics determine the most viable reading, whether it be concerning the use of a single word or an extended passage (i.e.—as the debated, extended conclusion of Mark's Gospel / Mark 16: 9-20).[78]

Consider the following three parameters used by textual critics as they evaluate the internal evidence of a manuscript. Given the many factors involved in assessing a particular manuscript's authenticity and reliability, these should be considered as general guidelines.[79]

1. **The shorter reading is preferred**. (Scribes had a tendency to *add* words or phrases rather than omit them.[80] Often, this was done in order to clarify a passage that, at least to the scribe, seemed a bit ambiguous grammatically or theologically.)

2. **The more difficult reading is preferred** (unless too difficult or nonsensical). (Scribes tended to smooth out perceived difficulties in the text.)

3. Finally, and perhaps the most important guideline of the three, **the reading that best gives rise to the others is preferred**. Thus, given the known scribal tendencies, the characteristics of the text-type, and other considerations, which reading is most likely original?

The discipline of textual criticism helps scholars determine the reading that is closest to the original. With the vast numbers of New Testament manuscripts available—traversing both the geographical spectrum of the Mediterranean world and the Middle East, as well as the centuries—we can be assured that the words recorded, as having been spoken and written by Jesus and His apostles, have been meticulously transmitted and preserved for us. Even today, the study of the New Testament manuscripts continues (with over 90 percent of all known

Greek manuscripts being preserved on microfilm at the Institute for New Testament Textual Research in Munster, Germany[81]), so that the testimony to the uniqueness of the New Testament as a reliable source of information concerning the person and work of Jesus Christ will not be lost to future generations.

**Q—"OK, but I've heard it said that the faith of Christ's disciples overpowered their memories. How do you know that what has been recorded about Jesus's miraculous works, as well the things He said indicating He was more than a man, weren't simply made up?"**

**A—The idea that the Jesus's disciples came to believe and teach a divine Jesus who was not the Jesus of history is a viewpoint that fails to account for the following:**

**#1—The role of oral tradition in the Jewish culture of the day**

- Though the first Gospel written is thought to be Mark (written in the mid-to-late 50s or early 60s[82]), there still would have been many people living who would have heard Jesus's teaching, seen His miraculous works, or heard firsthand accounts of the same.

- The Jewish, first-century culture was an oral culture. Given the fact there were relatively few scrolls (books or codices were not developed till later), and no newspapers or other forms of transmitting written information, it was an essential requirement of life to remember what one had heard. Thus, people in Christ's day developed a high degree of memorization skill.[83]

- It was typical of followers of rabbis in Jesus's day to memorize a significant amount of their teacher's sayings. Jesus's disciples may well have thought of themselves in this way and, therefore, would have memorized much of what He taught.[84] (Surely, much of that which the Gospel writers recorded was repeated and restated by Jesus on many different occasions.) Furthermore, as one evaluates the manner in which Jesus taught, He often used stories and other literary forms which would have accommodated memorization as well as the need of the majority of those listening to transmit His teaching orally.

- The memory of Jesus's disciples was a collective memory, a "memory in community," and as such, incorrect recollections would have been easily filtered and corrected by members of the group.[85]

## #2—The rapid spread of the Gospel message

- After Christ's death, resurrection, and ascension, the disciples were actively involved in speaking of His miraculous life and works.[86]

- Fabrications and/or inaccuracies of any sort could have easily been corrected by the community. The disciples did not make their proclamations in a vacuum. They proclaimed the words and works of Jesus publicly, thus exposing the Gospel message to public scrutiny, including scrutiny by those who were hostile to the Gospel message, including the Romans and Jewish religious leaders.

- The first public proclamation of the Gospel was by Peter at Pentecost (50 days after Christ's crucifixion) to Jews who had traveled to Jerusalem from around the Mediterranean world for this annual feast. Once the message about Jesus left Jerusalem, the apostles and other disciples would have lost the ability to monitor and control its content. For those who suggest that the disciples' faith overpowered their memories, it seems unlikely that such could have happened so quickly, especially given the fact that Jesus had lived His life in such public domain.

## #3—The view of Christ as expressed by the Apostle Paul

- The Apostle Paul wrote most of his letters to the churches before the Gospels were written. (The New Testament books are not in chronological order.) Paul was martyred in AD 66 or 67 under Emperor Nero; he began writing no later than the early 50s (with most of his major letters appearing during that decade), and he continued writing until shortly before his death (2 Timothy is generally believed to be his last letter). The dating of Paul's writings is affirmed by both liberal and conservative scholars.

- Paul made three significant trips (often referred to as his "missionary journeys") throughout the Mediterranean world in order to proclaim the Gospel to the Gentile world. These journeys began in the mid-40s and continued until the mid 50s. He wrote most of his major epistles while traveling; they served as follow-up and instructional letters to the churches that had been established, reaffirming that which he had taught and addressing matters of concern. (Paul's remaining letters were written after his arrest in approximately AD 56, which subsequently led to his trip to Rome and house arrest in that city—which is the point at which the record of Acts concludes. It appears from history he was apparently released, may have traveled some more and was, once again, imprisoned a second time leading to his eventual martyrdom in AD 66 or 67.)

- In his first letter to the church of Corinth (I Corinthians, written around AD 52), there is a strong statement asserting the importance of Christ's resurrection. In I Corinthians 15, the Apostle Paul affirms not only his belief in the bodily resurrection of Christ but also posits the resurrection of Christ as the basis of the Christian's faith and hope.

- Within the context of this same chapter, Paul succinctly expresses the core beliefs he had passed on to the believers in Corinth when he writes the following:

  v. 3) "I passed on to you what was most important and what had also been passed on to me. Christ died for our sins, just as the Scriptures had said.

  v. 4) He was buried, and he was raised from the dead on the third day, just as the Scriptures said.

  v. 5) He was seen by Peter and then by the Twelve.

  v. 6) After that, he was seen by more than five hundred of his followers at one time, most of whom are still alive, though some have died.

  v. 7) Then he was seen by James and later by all the apostles."

  (I Corinthians 15: 3–7, NLT)

  » The manner in which this is stated in the original language suggests that it was likely a rather fixed statement and reflects an oral tradition passed on to him by either the Christians, with whom he met immediately following his conversion, or by the apostles. Quite likely, too, given its formulation, it was a creedal statement known by the Christian community as well.[87]

» This creedal statement contains what Paul (and, presumably, the Christian community from which it undoubtedly originated) considered the essentials of the Gospel message to be. It is imperative to note that the statement affirms the bodily resurrection of Christ. Given that history records that Paul's conversion happened within a couple of years following Christ's crucifixion, one can argue persuasively that this creedal statement finds its origin within two to five years of that time.[88]

### #4—The attestation of early manuscripts that affirm a divine Jesus[89]

• The suggestion of some that it was Constantine who invented the doctrine of Christ's deity ignores the early manuscript evidence.

• Explicit reference to the divinity of Jesus is found in pre-fourth-century papyri (p) codex (book) manuscripts. For example, three of the papyri manuscripts including direct reference to Christ's divinity are among our most important. They are:

  » $p^{46}$ - includes eight of Paul's letters (Romans, I and II Corinthians, Ephesians, Galatians, Philippians, Colossians, I Thessalonians) and the letter to the Hebrews.

  » $p^{66}$ includes most of John's Gospel.

  » $p^{75}$ includes most of Luke and part of John

• The following chart identifies some of the specific passages included in the manuscripts described above, which explicitly affirm Jesus as being divine. Other passages in the papyri give ample evidence implicitly as to the same.

| Manuscript | John 1: 1 | John 20: 28 | Romans 9: 5 | Hebrews 1: 8 |
|---|---|---|---|---|
| **p⁴⁶** (AD 200) | | | X | X |
| **p⁶⁶** (AD 175 – 225) | X | X | | |
| **p⁷⁵** (Early 3ʳᵈ century AD) | X | | | |

Chart taken from *Reinventing Jesus* by J. Ed Komoszewski, M. James Sawyer and Daniel B. Wallace (Grand Rapids: Kregal Publications, 2006), 116.

**Q—"What about all the other Gospels, like the Gospel of Thomas, which the Church chose not to recognize? Isn't that evidence that church leaders picked the books that painted a picture of Jesus that they liked?**

**A—The four Gospels predate the Gospel of Thomas by at least 75 years and were accepted as canonical (the word canon is a transliteration of the Greek word kan n meaning "rule" or "standard") because they had long been considered authoritative. The church councils met to affirm which books were authoritative; the content of these meetings is a matter of historical record.**

This question has two parts:

1. The questioner wants to know why the Gospel of Thomas or others like it is not part of our New Testament today. Some have suggested that church leaders under Constantine's influence chose writings that only reflected the divine Jesus that they wanted.

2. The questioner assumes that the process of collecting and affirming the authoritative books of the New Testament (a process referred to as *canonization*) was accomplished by a few church leaders apart from any input from the Christian community.

   Let's review the history. The Gospel of Thomas was part of the Nag Hammadi Library discovered in December 1945 near the town of Nag Hammadi (located in Upper Egypt). The 13 codices (books) discovered contained over 50 texts (including the Gospel of Thomas, the Gospel of Philip, and the Gospel of Truth).[90] The Gospel of Thomas contains 113 or 114 sayings attributed to Jesus (one can read it in its entirety at the Gnostic Library Society Web site, www.gnosis.org) and was written in Greek, in Syria, about AD 140.[91]

The Gospel of Thomas reflects the philosophy of Gnosticism. Gnosticism was "a second-century phenomenon that had to do with salvation through enlightenment for an elite few. It emphasized the goodness of the spirit and the badness of the material or physical."[92] Therefore, in view of Gnosticism's dichotomy between body and spirit (physical and spiritual) this gospel rejected the deity of Christ (because the divine can in no way be intermingled with flesh) as well as His *bodily* resurrection. These two divergent teachings, alone, were cause sufficient to have the Gospel of Thomas excluded from the canon. Several other reasons also help explain its exclusion:

- Though one-third to one-half of the 113 or 114 (if you include the final saying: *"Simon Peter said to them, 'Make Mary leave us, for females don't deserve life.'"* --some think this was added later) of the sayings listed do have parallels in the Gospels, the others reflect Gnostic philosophy and have absolutely no parallel in the other Gospels.

- If it had been written in the first century (as some have suggested), and if it had been considered as authoritative, it seems logical to assume that it would have been distributed as pervasively as were the other Gospels. History indicates otherwise.

- Again, if Thomas were a first-century document, and if at least the roots of Gnosticism found their ground in the teachings of Jesus, it would seem logical to assume that at least some of these sayings (e.g., reflecting incipient Gnosticism) would have been picked up by the other writers. Interestingly, Thomas quotes from the other Gospel writers, whereas none of the other Gospel writers quote from him.

- To suggest that the Church decided to squelch the teachings of the Gospel of Thomas (choosing to picture Christ as Redeemer, which the Gospel of Thomas does not) would have required a massive effort of removing and destroying vast numbers of manuscripts from around the Mediterranean world. Furthermore, this effort would have had to somehow escape the notice of history.[93] There is absolutely *no* evidence for such a conspiracy.

- Just encourage someone to read the Gospel of Thomas, along with one of the other Gospels, and ask for his or her evaluation.

Let's now address the second question pertaining to the collection and collating of the books of the Bible. Conspiracy theories abound in our day! The process of canonization is one of the latest victims of attempts by the conspiracy theorists (*Da Vinci Code,* et. al.). However, to consider the attempts to undermine the reliability of the Bible as simply a "fad" would be imprudent. Quite likely this discussion will be around for a while, in that its attack is aimed at the very foundation of the Christian faith. It is in view of this that an overview of this process is in order.[94]

- Jesus told His disciples that the Holy Spirit "will teach you all things and bring to your remembrance all that I have said to you" and "he will guide you into all the truth" (John 14: 26; 16: 13). The idea that there are certain authoritative Christian writings (as well as those that are not), finds its basis in the belief that the apostles could be trusted because of their connection with Christ and the promises He made to them, to speak on behalf of God.

- From the very beginning, the apostles anticipated that their writings would be considered authoritative and even read by others than the recipients (see I Corinthians 14: 37; I Thessalonians 2: 13 and 5: 27; Revelation 1: 3). The idea that particular books were arbitrarily chosen by church leaders, apart from the purview of the Christian community, and deemed authoritative in some secretive manner, flatly ignores the historical record.

- Books written by those who were not apostles (i.e., Mark, Luke, Acts, James and Jude), yet which became part of the New Testament, were considered as having apostolic authority or having been granted apostolic approval.[95] This authority or approval may have been granted explicitly because of the author's position in the church (i.e.—James being a leader in the Jerusalem church and Jude his brother) or implicitly because of the author's association with the apostles (i.e.—Mark being one of Peter's assistants; Luke one of Paul's). The substance of the book or letter—and how it aligned itself with accepted apostolic preaching—was considered in all cases.

- One further crucial point must be made: the fact that the Christian community had a role in this affirmation cannot be minimized. The books that were eventually included in the canon were those that were affirmed as being authoritative by the Christian community. At first, such affirmation would have been granted at the local or regional level. Quite simply, this was because the books were either written or given to a particular community of believers in a particular geographical location by the author or his emissary.

  **It was a book's acceptance—at first, locally and/or regionally—that ultimately led to its being considered as authoritative for the entire Church. The case for the canonicity of a particular book or letter did not develop in a vacuum.**

- Evidence suggests that, within the first half of the second century AD, the Gospels and Paul's letters were accepted and read by the Church. Furthermore, the early Church Fathers (i.e.—Clement, Polycarp [a disciple of the apostles] and Ignatius) give credence to the New Testament books in that they quote freely from all except Mark (which closely parallels Matthew), 2 and 3 John, Jude, and 2 Peter. Before them, Clement of Rome wrote to the Christians in Corinth (AD 95), using material from Matthew and Luke and demonstrating familiarity with Romans and I Corinthians.[96]

- The reasons for canonization were never shrouded in mystery; they were practical in nature. Due to the growth of the Church, the increasing persecution of believers, the destruction of biblical manuscripts[97] by decree of Rome, the introduction of heretical teachings and writings and, finally, the desire of the Christian community to know exactly which writings were to be read with authority in the services, provided the ground swell for the canonization process.[98]

- Even the fact that several of the books were contested only serves to highlight the careful, evaluative process invoked. Again, it is clear that the canonization process did not simply involve a few church leaders but the Christian community at large, both East and West.

- Within 25 years of Diocletian's edict to destroy all biblical manuscripts (AD 302), Constantine commissioned the historian Eusebius to prepare 50 copies of the Scriptures, largely in response to the need resulting from the effectiveness of that edict. In his letter to Eusebius, Constantine states: "I have thought it expedient to instruct your Prudence to order fifty copies of the sacred Scriptures, the provision and use of which you know to be most needful for the instruction of the Church ..."[99] These copies contained the same 27 books of the New Testament we have today. Surely Eusebius was "fully aware of which were the sacred books for which many believers had been willing to lay down their very lives ..."[100]

- In AD 367, in his Festal Letter for Easter, Bishop Athanasius of Alexandria affirmed the 27 New Testament books we have today as being canonical. At the councils of Hippo (AD 393) and Carthage (AD 397), both under Augustine's influence, the New Testament canon of 27 books was ratified, thus uniting both East and West in this crucial matter.[101]

- The books ultimately included in the canon passed *three* tests:

1.  **Authority**

    »   Was the book authored by an apostle or one closely associated with him?

    »   Did its content conform to the teachings of other books knowingly written by the apostles?

2.  **Antiquity**

>   » Was the book written before or after the apostolic era (when the apostles were still alive)?

>   » If it was written *after* the death of the apostles, it was rejected without question.[102]

3.  **Acceptance**

>   » Was it widely circulated and read by the Early Church?

>   » Was it often quoted in the writings of the Early Church Fathers (thus demonstrating its acceptance by those who would have known it to be credible or not)?

The fact that there never was an official pronouncement concerning the canon is telling. In their excellent book, *Reinventing Jesus*, Ed Komoszewski, James Sawyer, and Daniel Wallace suggest that the lack of such a pronouncement,

> tells us implicitly that *the canon was a list of authoritative books rather than an authoritative list of books* [emphasis mine]. Those books that belong in the canon belong there because of their intrinsic worth and authenticity as witnesses to Jesus Christ, not because some church council declared them to be authoritative.[103]

The table on the following page will serve to compare and contrast the development of the canon over an approximately 150-year period, representing the consensus of the Christian community in diverse parts of the Roman Empire. In that so much attention is given today on the "disputed books," it is important to note the Church's agreement on a *majority* of the books of the New Testament. In fact, by "as early as the second century AD, there were 20 or so books that were never questioned—and these are the writings that reflect the most essential truths about Jesus."[104]

| The Fragment of Muratori Mid-second century AD / Rome | Codex Claromontanus Late third century AD / Egypt or North Africa | Eusebius of Caesarea's Church History Early fourth century AD / Palestine and Asia Minor |
|---|---|---|
| *Accepted Books:* Matthew Mark Luke John Acts Romans 1 and 2 Corinthians Galatians Ephesians Colossians 1 and 2 Thessalonians 1 and 2 Timothy Titus Philemon 1 John 2-3 John (counted as one) Jude Revelation <br><br> Disputed: Apocalypse of Peter <br><br> Rejected: | *Accepted Books:* Matthew Mark Luke John Acts Romans 1 and 2 Corinthians Galatians Ephesians Philippians Colossians 1 and 2 Thessalonians 1 and 2 Timothy Titus Philemon Hebrews (possibly disputed) James 1 and 2 Peter 1, 2 and 3 John Jude Revelation <br><br> Disputed: Apocalypse of Peter Epistle of Barnabas | *Accepted Books:* Matthew Mark Luke John Acts Romans 1 and 2 Corinthians Galatians Ephesians Philippians Colossians 1 and 2 Thessalonians 1 and 2 Timothy Titus Philemon Hebrews 1 Peter 1 John Revelation (possibly disputed) <br><br> Disputed: James Jude 2 Peter 2 and 3 John |
| Laodiceans Alexandrians The Shepherd of Hermas | The Shepherd of Hermas Acts of Paul | Rejected: <br><br> Apocalypse of Peter Acts of Paul The Shepherd of Hermas Epistle of Barnabas Teaching of the Twelve Apostles Gospel of Peter Gospel of Thomas Gospel of Matthias Gospel of the Hebrews Acts of Andrew Acts of John |

Chart taken from *Misquoting Truth* by Timothy Paul Jones (Downers Grove: InterVarsity Press, 2007), 135.

**Q—One of my professors made the comment that we really don't even know who wrote the Gospels. If that is so, then how can we be sure we have the true story of Jesus's life?**

**A—It is true that not one of the four Gospels included in the New Testament directly claims to be written by the author associated with it. However, there is strong and early tradition affirming the canonical Gospels as authoritative as well as the authorship of each as traditionally ascribed.**

- **First** of all, when you approach the field of New Testament studies you will discover that since the mid-1800s, in particular, many attempts have been made to explain away the supernatural aspects of the New Testament, with a primary focus being on the Gospels. That is not to say that *every* aspect of these efforts has been negative (e.g., German "form criticism" which examines the literary form(s) or *genre*(s) of a book and the influence of such pertaining to the interpretation of the same). In fact, as a result of some of the research, New Testament scholars who *affirm* the supernatural aspect of the Gospels, have gained new insights on the one hand (e.g., as to, perhaps, the extent to which God chose to communicate His truth *within* the cultural framework) and, on the other, have become even more firmly committed to the Gospels' reliability as they have risen to the challenge of their defense.

  The fact that the authors' may have used other sources of information (see Luke 1: 1-4) and may have chosen particular literary devices to communicate their message in *no* way detracts from the divine origin of the Bible. In fact, it serves to highlight the fact that God chose to work *through* His people—using their particular gifts and abilities. Yet, they wrote *under the direction of the Holy Spirit* so that they were able to record God's message without error (see 2 Peter 1: 21).

- **Second**, you will discover that just about every conceivable idea has been put forth by scholars who do *not* affirm the divine origin of the Bible, in general, and who do not believe in a supernatural Jesus, in particular, to explain the origin(s) of the teaching of a divine Jesus as presented in the Gospels. Remember, however, one important axiom: Not everything that is *possible* is *plausible*. And not every idea deserves equal attention.

Perhaps a good evaluative question is this: Has the suggested test or process applied to evaluate the authenticity/accuracy of the Gospels been applied, in concept as well as extent, to other ancient documents as well? If the answer is "no" then the test or process has quite possibly been motivated by presuppositions designed to undermine the message of the Gospels, rather than simply ascertain the historicity of the transmission process.[105]

- **Third**, though there are many who attempt to explain away the divine origin of the New Testament Gospels, there remains the incredibly significant impact left in the lives of individuals and the cultures exposed to their message. It would seem that one's explanation of the origin of the books standing behind such a movement must at least equal the impact of the same.

- **Fourth**, remember that the message conveyed in the Gospels was not a popular one. Both the Orthodox Jewish community and the multicultural and religiously inclusive mindset of the Roman world were opposed to the core message of Christianity: that Jesus was the divine Son of God and that one could receive eternal salvation through Him alone.

Let's consider some of the reasons why there is a high degree of probability that the Gospels that have been passed on to us are the "right" ones. Much of the following has been summarized from information contained in *The Origin of the Bible*, edited by Philip Wesley Comfort,[106] with complementary facts footnoted:

1. The Church Fathers' use of the books of the Bible (as well as the Gospels) suggests their authenticity. Of all people, they would have known whether or not the four Gospels were genuine. One of the earliest Church Fathers was Polycarp (AD 69–155). Tradition says he was mentored by the Apostle John. In AD 95, he wrote a letter to the Corinthian church using material from Matthew and Luke (as well as Hebrews, Romans, and Paul's letters to the Corinthians; also, possibly 1 Timothy, Titus and Ephesians).

2. Polycarp is joined by Clement (d. AD 99), perhaps the Clement mentioned by Paul in Philippians, and Ignatius (d. AD 110), a disciple of the Apostle John. Comfort notes: "In the writings

of these men only Mark (which closely parallels the material of Matthew), 2 and 3 John, Jude, and 2 Peter are not clearly attested."[107]

3.    Irenaeus (d. ca. AD 200), the Church Father and apologist, quotes in his *Against Heresies* from Matthew, Mark, and Luke (as well as a number of Paul's writings, James, and 1 Peter).[108]

4.    Papias (ca. AD 130–140) mentions by name the Gospels of Matthew and Mark.

5.    Even the heretic Marcion (d. 160) in his canon—which excluded the entire Old Testament and many of the New Testament books—accepted the Gospel of Luke (except for the first two chapters) as authentic. Even Marcion did not mention or include any other "competing" gospels.

6.    Toward the end of his life, Tatian (d. AD 180) wrote his famed *Diatessaron* (meaning "through the four"), which was a harmony of the four Gospels. Of interest is the fact that Tatian was a pupil of Justin Martyr, the second-century Christian apologist who defended Christianity before the Roman Senate as well as before the Emperor Antoninus Pius. (In his writings, it is clear that Justin considered the writings of the apostles on par with the Old Testament Scriptures by his use of the phrase "it is written" preceding quotations from the New Testament.) Again, notice that Tatian, as well, did not include any other "competing" gospel in his arrangement.[109]

7.    The Muritorian Fragment is a seventh-century Latin manuscript discovered by Italian historian Father Ludovico A. Muratori as he was doing research in the Ambrosian Library in Milan. This manuscript fragment (hence the name) was subsequently published by him in 1740; it contains a copy of what is arguably the earliest known listing of New Testament books considered as canonical by the author (who is unknown).

    The list is considered to have been originally compiled around AD 170, due to the fact that it refers to Pius I as having recently been the Bishop of Rome (Pius I served as bishop, AD 142–157). Though the document is mutilated at both ends and only mentions the Gospels of Luke and John by name, there is strong indication it originally included a reference to Matthew and Mark having been listed in their traditional order. (You can view a digital image of the Muritorian Canon on the Web by conducting a search via Google™ images. See previous table for listing of books included.)

Now, a few additional remarks specifically related to the authorship ascribed to each of the Gospels:

» **Matthew**: Strong tradition supports Matthew's association with the Gospel named for him. Indeed, "it may reasonably be claimed that the title was affixed at least as early as AD 125."[110] In Papias' writings (*Interpretations of the Lord's Logia*), he accepts Matthew's authorship of the *Logia*, most reasonably understood as a reference to the Gospel he wrote. Furthermore, Irenaeus, Pantaenus, and Origen all referred to the Gospel Matthew wrote.[111] Finally, there is no significant competing tradition to the contrary.

» **Mark**: The authorship of this Gospel is attested by Papias, Irenaeus, Clement of Alexandria, Origen, and Jerome. It is also likely attested by the Muratorian Canon (as noted above, though the first part of the manuscript is mutilated, most scholars agree that Matthew and Mark [names absent] should be included along with Luke and John [names present] in their traditional arrangement). Furthermore, the majority of scholars connect Mark with Peter and, it is assumed, the author is one and the same with the John Mark (Barnabas' nephew), who traveled with the Apostle Paul (as recorded in Acts).[112]

» **Luke**: The earliest known witness to the authorship of this Gospel is the Muratorian Canon (ca. AD 170). However, Luke's authorship for this Gospel, as well as the book of Acts, is also affirmed by Irenaeus, Clement of Alexandria, Origen, and Tertullian. Furthermore, there is strong internal evidence to suggest (in line with the fact that both Luke and Acts are dedicated to the same person, Theophilus) that they share the same author. Both books have strong similarity linguistically and stylistically and Acts does seem to follow the Gospel account naturally (as though it is the second part of a two-part work).

- Some have suggested that the late witness to Luke's authorship could suggest that the Muratorian Canon simply inferred Luke's authorship from the "we passages" of Acts (wherein the author refers to himself in the first person indicating he was an eyewitness of the events he was documenting / see 16: 10-17; 20: 5-21: 18; 27: 1-28: 16) and that the error was simply accepted and advanced by those who followed.

- Though by no means a conclusive proof of Lucan authorship, the "we" passages do suggest the strong possibility that the author of Acts (and, likewise, of the Gospel traditionally ascribed to Luke) *was* a traveling companion of the Apostle Paul's. Furthermore, since Luke is mentioned by name in three of Paul's "prison epistles" (Colossians, 2 Timothy and Philemon), yet he is *not* mentioned in any of the letters Paul wrote during his second and third missionary journeys (1 & 2 Thessalonians, 1 & 2 Corinthians, Romans and, some would suggest, Galatians), representing travels which *preceded* those that would have included the author (assuming the "we" passage scenario), this assumption finds additional corroboration. Finally, additional internal evidence (e.g., the author's precise detail which would fit his profession as a medical doctor), along with the process of elimination (e.g., the author would obviously *not* be one of Paul's companions mentioned by name during the "we" passages), yet was undoubtedly one of the companions the Apostle mentions by name in his prison epistles (Mark, Jesus, Justis, Epaphras, Demas, Luke and Epaphroditus), Luke becomes a strong candidate for both the authorship of Acts and of the Gospel.

- Yet if Luke was not the author, then *three* important questions must be answered:

  1. Why are there not competing traditions that suggest another individual as author?

  2. Why would the Church choose, from all the available options, to advance the non-apostolic Luke, rather than a more prominent figure if, in fact, he was not the author?

  3. Why did such a suggestion gain such a footing in the opinion of the Church Fathers if there was no firm basis for such an opinion?[113]

» **John**: Irenaeus (second half of second century) is the first writer who names John, Jesus's disciple, as the author of this Gospel. According to Eusebius, Irenaeus' source of information was Polycarp, who was to have gained his information from the apostles. Some have suggested that Irenaeus' recollection of Polycarp's reference to John was a case of mistaken identity; in fact, he was thought to be the apostle when it was really another John. It seems unlikely, however, that Irenaeus (having lived in the East as well as having close connections to Rome) would have so forthrightly affirmed the Apostle John's authorship without additional support.[114] Though this final point is really a matter pertaining to internal evidence (coming from within the Gospel itself), it is interesting to note that not once is Jesus's disciple, John, mentioned in this Gospel. This seems extraordinary given his apparent status as one of the three closest to Jesus—a status clearly indicated in the other Gospels where his name is mentioned 20 times (including parallel passages). The absence of his mention would certainly seem quite strange unless, of course, the Gospel was written by him and/or under his direction.[115]

Let's assume for the sake of argument that we really do not have a clue as to who wrote the four Gospels. Consider, then, the following scenario: Let's say that someone showed me an old newspaper article detailing the events of November 22, 1963, and the assassination of John F. Kennedy. In order to ascertain the validity of the article, should my primary question be "Who wrote this article?" or would the truly significant question be "Does the document accurately describe the events of that day, according to the testimony of others and the record of history?" Though it would perhaps be of interest if the author was identified as one of the Secret Service men who guarded the president on that day, it would not invalidate the article in the least if the author were simply a bystander. In fact, some might argue that a member of the Secret Service might even be a less objective witness (i.e., be inclined to play down the significance of his role in the protection of the president or lack thereof), as opposed to a bystander, who would likely record the events of that day exactly as he observed them.

In like manner, if we do not truly know who authored the Gospels, then I would suggest that we have additional and independent sources verifying the life of Christ as reflected throughout the New Testament. Thus, if you remove the apostolic authors of the Gospels (Matthew and John), as well as their close associates (Mark and Luke), you have effectively removed those most likely to have had the agenda of making Jesus something He was not (a miracle-worker and Son of God). So, to those skeptical, I would suggest that to do so would arguably even *raise* the level of objectivity of the Gospel writers and their message. In other words, such a result does little to undermine the record of the authors as to Jesus's teachings and their attribution to Him of a divine nature. The material included in the Gospels would have been subject to the scrutiny of the Christian community at large and the evaluation of those who could have affirmed or denied the teachings therein based on first-hand testimony of the events themselves as well as the words of Jesus that had been heard in person or had been passed on through oral tradition.

The Bible stands unique among all other books of ancient history. The fact of the Bible's uniqueness is attested by:

- its pervasive influence throughout the centuries

- its endurance despite persecution, resulting from those who affirm its message

- the significant inclusion of verifiable fulfilled prophecy

- manuscript evidence that attests to the accuracy of transmission

- the inclusion of the teachings of Jesus Christ, resulting in life transformation of people in every century and culture since His time on earth

Though uniqueness does not prove divine authorship, the Bible's compelling uniqueness suggests a book of extraordinary origin. Given these ingredients, however, and given that not another book like the Bible exists, it is reasonable to suggest *the potential* of divine authorship for its origin.

# *Notes*

[1] For comprehensive treatment of this subject see *A General Introduction to the Bible* by Norman L. Geisler and William E. Nix (Chicago: Moody Press, 1986) and *The Origin of the Bible*, Philip Wesley Comfort, ed. (Wheaton: Tyndale House Publishers, 1992).

[2] Lee Strobel, *The Case for Christ* (Grand Rapids, MI: Zondervan, 1998), 60.

[3] Bruce M. Metzger, *The Text of the New Testament: Its Transmission, Corruption and Restoration* (Oxford: Oxford University Press, 1968), 31.

[4] Ibid., 32–33.

[5] J. Ed Komoszewski, James Sawyer and Daniel B. Wallace, *Reinventing Jesus* (Grand Rapids, MI: Kregal Publications, 2006), 77.

The authors cite the number of manuscripts per category as follows: papyri/118, uncials/317, minuscules/2,877, and lectionaries/2,433, thus making the total 5,745.

[6] Metzger comments on the origin of the discipline of textual criticism as follows: "The classical method of textual criticism arose during and after the Renaissance when attention was drawn to spurious papal decretals and when questions were raised regarding falsifications in Church history and in the credentials of certain religious orders." (156.)

[7] Strobel, 62.

[8] Grant R. Jeffrey, *Jesus: The Great Debate* (Toronto: Frontier Research Publications, 1999).

See discussion in chapter two, "The Fundamental Issue of When the Gospels were Written," 49–56. Pertaining to an early dating of John's Gospel see article by Daniel B. Wallace, "The Gospel of John: Introduction, Argument, Outline," Bible.org, http://www.bible.org/page.php?page_id=1328.

Komoszewski, Sawyer, and Wallace point out that many scholars who date the Synoptic Gospels after AD 70 do so because they do not believe Christ could have prophesied the impending conquering and destruction of Jerusalem and the Temple. They assume, "Since predictive prophecy does not occur, and since Jesus's words reflect an event that has yet to occur, these Gospels necessarily were written after the fact of Jerusalem's fall." However, they go on to point out that J.A.T. Robinson (*Redating the New Testament* [Eugene: Wipf and Stock Publishers, 2000]) notes the details contained in Christ's Olivet Discourse do not exactly parallel the events surrounding the fall of Jerusalem and destruction of the Temple in AD 70. Thus, for the Gospel writers to preserve, much less invent, a partially unfulfilled prophecy would only detract from, surely in no way enhance, their presentation of a divine Jesus. Furthermore, if it can be demonstrated that these first-century events were not the primary focus of Jesus's words, then the fundamental basis for such a late dating of the Synoptic Gospels has been effectively removed. (*Reinventing Jesus*, 28–29). For additional information on the dating of the Synoptic Gospels see D.A. Carson and Douglas J. Moo, *An Introduction to the New Testament,* 2nd ed (Grand Rapids: Zondervan, 2005).

[9] Timothy Paul Jones, *Misquoting Truth* (Downers Grove, IL: IVP Books, 2007), 69.

[10] Komoszewski, Sawyer and Wallace, 86.

[11] Wallace, Daniel B. "A Brief Introduction to New Testament Textual Criticism," class notes from Greek Exegesis and Sermonic Structure (Dallas Theological Seminary, Dallas, TX, 1980), 5.

[12] Ibid.

[13] Komoszewski, Sawyer and Wallace, 77.

[14] Norman L. Geisler and William E. Nix, *A General Introduction to the* Bible (Chicago: Moody Press, 1986), 390.

[15] It may be of interest to note the extent of Constantine's order to Eusebius:

"I have thought it expedient to instruct your Prudence to order fifty copies of the sacred Scriptures, the provision and use of which you know to be most needful for the instruction of the Church, to be written on prepared parchment in a legible manner, and in a convenient, portable form, by professional transcribers thoroughly practices in their art. The catholicus of the diocese has also received instructions from our Clemency to be careful to furnish all things necessary for the preparation of such copies; and it will be for you to take special care that they are completed with as little delay as possible." (Philip Schaff, ed., *The Nicene and Post-Nicene Fathers* [Grand Rapids, MI: Wm. B. Eerdmans Publishing Company, 1956], 1: 549.)

Constantine's order assumes a recognized body of Scripture. If there was some attempt on his or Eusebius' part to add or detract from that body history fails to record it.

[16] Geisler and Nix, 388–408.

[17] Jeffrey adds that "the evidence is overwhelming that the Greek originals of the Gospels and New Testament Epistles were widely copied, distributed, and translated immediately into Hebrew, Syriac, Latin, Coptic, and other languages. These New Testament documents were treasured by the churches and read in their Sunday services within the first century. If anyone had wanted to introduce a false miracle, an imaginary event, or theologically deviant doctrine into the Gospels, they would have faced an almost impossible task. In order to successfully introduce a false statement, the forger would have to simultaneously forge and insert this counterfeit passage into every single manuscript copy of the Gospels in every country and language without being detected or challenged by any Christian." (*Jesus: The Great Debate*, 51–52). [Jeffrey may have overstated the case a bit. One might suggest that a forger would

only have needed to insert the counterfeit passage into the better manuscripts, thus perhaps aiding the story's acceptance. Still, however, the odds are seemingly insurmountable for the same reasons given by Jeffrey.]

[18] Geisler and Nix, 420.

[19] Ibid.

[20] Craig L. Blomberg, *The Historical Reliability of the Gospels* (Downers Grove, IL: IVP Academic, 1987), 203. Geisler and Nix also note:

"It is advisable to mention again that quotation technique has changed throughout the course of history, as has the work of translation. That, along with the fact that modern scholars employ different criteria in distinguishing a citation from an allusion, may provide a basis for disagreement on just *what* is a quotation." (*A General Introduction to the Bible*, 423)

[21] Bruce M. Metzger, *New Testament Studies: Philological, Versional & Patristic* (Leiden: E.J. Brill, 1980), 171.

[22] Ibid.

[23] Metzger, *The Text of the New Testament*, 86.

[24] Geisler and Nix, 348.

[25] Frederic Kenyon, *Our Bible and the Ancient Manuscripts*, 4th ed (London: Eyre and Spottsiswoode, 1951), 42 – 43.

[26] Gleason L. Archer, *A Survey of Old Testament Introduction* (Chicago: Moody Press, 1974), 61.

[27] Geisler and Nix, 348–349, 380.

[28] Ibid., 361.

[29] Archer, 25.

[30] You may wish to refer to the following works as a beginning point for an overview of the Old Testament and the issues related to its authorship and accuracy:

1) Archer Jr., Gleason L. *A Survey of Old Testament Introduction*, 3rd ed (Chicago: Moody Press, 2007).

2) Geisler, Norman L. *A Popular Survey of the Old Testament* (Grand Rapids, MI: Baker Books, 1977).

For an in-depth discussion pertaining to Old Testament introduction, you may wish to consider:

1) Harrison, Kenneth. *Introduction to the Old Testament* (Grand Rapids, MI: Eerdmans, 1969).

2) Kitchen, Kenneth A. *On the Reliability of the Old Testament* (Grand Rapids, MI: Eerdmans, 2003).

[31] Geisler and Nix, 195.

[32] Nelson Glueck, *Rivers in the Desert: A History of the Negev* (New York: Farrar, Straus and Cudahy, 1959), 31.

[33] Robert Dick Wilson, *A Scientific Investigation of the Old Testament,* Reprint (Homewood, AL: Solid Ground Christian Books, 2007), 71.

[34] You can view pictures of ancient Hattusha at: http: //www.hattuscha.de.

[35] Patrick Zukeran, "Archaeology and the Old Testament," Probe Ministries, http: //www.probe.org/theology-and-philosophy/theology---bible/archaeology-and-the-old-testament.html (accessed June 21, 2007).

[36] Walter Rast and R. Thomas Schaub "Bar edh-Dhra ," Expedition to the Dead Sea Plain, http: //www.nd.edu/~edsp/babedhdrah.html (accessed June 22, 2007).

[37] Bryant G. Wood, "The Discovery of the Sin Cities of Sodom and Gomorrah, Part 1 of 2," Ankerberg Theological Research Institute, http: //www.johnankerberg.org/Articles/_PDFArchives/science/SC3W0903.pdf (accessed June 21, 2007).

[38] Rast and Schaub, "Bar edh-Dhra ."

[39] Ibid.

[40] Ibid.

[41] Wood, "The Discovery of the Sin Cities of Sodom and Gomorrah, Part 1 and 2."

[42] Ibid.

[43] Zukeran, "Archaeology and the Old Testament."

[44] Information for this section summarized from the following issues of *Biblical Archaeological Review*: *BAR* 20.2 (Mar/Apr, 1994) 26; *BAR* 20.4 (Jul/Aug, 1994) 54; BAR 20.5 (Sep/Oct, 1994) 22; BAR 20.6 (Nov/Dec, 1994) 47.

[45] Eliat Mazar, "Did I Find King David's Palace?" *Biblical Archaeological Review* 32.1 (Jan/Feb 2006): 17–27, 70.

[46] Ibid, 18.

[47] Helen Bond, "Pontius Pilate," The Ecole Initiative, http: //ecole.evansville.edu/articles/pilate.html (accessed March 10, 2008.

[48] Pat Zukeran, "Archaeology and the New Testament" Probe Ministries, http: //www.probe.org/site/apps/nlnet/content2.aspx?c=fdKEIMNsEoG&b=4245331&ct=55188 15 (accessed March 10, 2008).

[49] John McRay, *Archaeology and the New Testament* (Grand Rapids: Baker Academic, 1991), 203–204.

[50] Ibid., 204.

[51] Walter Bauer, "πολιταρχης," *A Greek-English Lexicon of the New Testament,* 2nd ed, trans. William F. Arndt and F. Wilbur Gingrich (Chicago: University of Chicago Press, 1979), 686.

[52] Kyle Butt, "Archaeology and the New Testament," Apologetics Press, http: //www.apologeticspress.org/articles/2591 (accessed March 12, 2008).

[53] John McRay, 295. See also: Jack Finegan, *Light from the Ancient Past,* 2nd ed (Princeton: Princeton University Press, 1959), 352.

[54] C. Schuler, "The Macedonian Politarchs," *Classical Philology* 55 (April, 1960): 90-100. John McRay suggests an additional three inscriptions in his article "Archaeology and the Book of Acts," *Criswell Theological Review* 5.1 (1990): 74-75.

[55] John McRay, 295.

[56] Butt, "Archaeology and the New Testament."

[57] Jeffrey, 82.

[58] Ibid., 81.

[59] Clermont-Ganneau's published report can be accessed via the following link: http: //dqhall59.com/Charles_Clermont_Ganneau/index.htm.

[60] Jeffrey, 82–83.

[61] Ibid., 83.

[62] Jack Finnegan. *The Archaeology of the New Testament* (Princeton: Princeton University Press, 1992), 366–371.

[63] Jeffrey, 89–90.

[64] An excellent digital image of the Caiaphas Ossuary can be accessed on the World Wide Web.

[65] Charles C. Ryrie, footnote on Ezekiel 38: 2, *The Ryrie Study Bible* (Chicago: Moody Press, 1995), 1323.

[66] Komoszewski, Sawyer and Wallace, 54.

[67] Ibid.

[68] Ibid., 57–58

[69] Strobel, 65.

For an excellent discussion on the types of variants and their significance see Chapter 4 in *Reinventing Jesus* by Komoszewski, Sawyer and Wallace.

[70] Ibid., 65.

[71] Komoszewski, Sawyer and Wallace, 84-89.

[72] Komoszewski, Sawyer and Wallace note:

"The more direct pipeline a manuscript has to the original, the better are its chances of getting the wording right. Also, the manuscripts that elsewhere prove to be the most reliable are given preference. Thus, a meticulous scribe working on a fifth-century manuscript may produce a more reliable text than a third-century scribe who is more interested in getting the job done quickly" (84).

[73] See Metzger, 209-211.

[74] Komoszewski, Sawyer and Wallace, 61.

[75] Strobel, 64.

[76] Komoszewski, Sawyer and Wallace, 95.

[77] Ibid., 95.

[78] Ibid., 95.

[79] Wallace, Daniel B. "A Brief Introduction to New Testament Textual Criticism," 7. Material supplemented from Komoszewski, Sawyer and Wallace, 89–95.

[80] Komoszewski, Sawyer and Wallace note:

"The text [of the New Testament] tended to grow over time rather than shrink, although, it grew only 2 percent over fourteen hundred years. Scribes almost never *intentionally* omitted anything" (92).

[81] Ibid., 107.

[82] Craig Blomberg notes, however:

"The standard scholarly dating, even in very liberal circles, is Mark in the 70s ... that's still within the lifetimes of various eyewitnesses of the life of Jesus, including hostile eyewitnesses who would have served as a corrective if false teachings about Jesus were going around."

He goes on to point out there is good evidence to suggest that the book of Acts (written by Luke) was written no later than AD 62 (This assumes a date for Paul's martyrdom by Nero of AD 64. At the end of Acts Paul is still under house arrest in Rome, his case still not having come to trial). If Luke precedes Acts (as the introduction to Acts would indicate; see Acts 1: 1, 2) and, at the latest was written a year earlier, this would mean a date of AD 61 for Luke's Gospel. Furthermore, a majority of scholars also believe from the similarity of some of the material between Mark's

Gospel and Luke's that it is likely that Mark's Gospel was one of the sources he used (Mark was an associate of the Apostle Peter/Luke states he researched other material in the first few verses of his Gospel).

This would mean, then, that the Gospel of Mark should be dated no later than AD 60 (Strobel, 33–34). For a scholarly treatment on the dating of the Synoptic Gospels, based on the dating of Acts, see Roman historian Colin Hemer's book, *The Book of Acts in the Setting of Hellenistic History* (Winona Lake: Eisenbrauns, 1990).

[83] J.P. Moreland, "The Case for Christianity" (compact disc series available through the Christian Apologetics Department of Biola University, La Mirada, CA).

See also: Komoszewski, Sawyer and Wallace, 33–38. Also see Strobel, 42–44.

[84] Komoszewski, Sawyer and Wallace, 33–34.

[85] Birger Gerhardsson, *Memory and Manuscript: Oral Tradition and Written Transmission in Rabbinic Judaism and Early Christianity* (Grand Rapids, MI: Wm. B. Eerdmans Publishing Company, 1998), 134–135.

[86] Komoszewski, Sawyer and Wallace note:

"The interval between Jesus and the written Gospels was not dormant. The apostles and other eyewitnesses were proclaiming good news about Jesus Christ wherever they went. This, of course, would have happened both in public settings and private meetings … The stories about Jesus and the sayings of Jesus would have been repeated hundreds, perhaps thousands, of times by dozens of eyewitnesses before the Gospel was ever penned." (Ibid., 29)

[87] Strobel, 35.

Timothy Paul Jones provides an excellent summation concerning this statement in his book *Misquoting Truth* (Downers Grove: InterVarsity Press, 2007. See pages 89–92). He notes that the two Greek words which Paul used in the first sentence of verse 3 (translated by the active and passive forms of the verb "to pass on" in the New Living Translation I've provided) were commonly used by an author to signal a message intended for oral tradition. Furthermore, he also notes that Paul uses the Hebrew equivalent of Peter's name (Cephas) in his Greek translation as well as a grammatical construction employed in connecting clauses commonly used within Hebrew and Aramaic. Jones concludes that, given the fact that Aramaic was the language primarily spoken by the people of Judea and Galilee, this was an early formulation of oral history passed on to him when he (according to Galatians 1: 8) traveled to Jerusalem to meet with the Apostle Peter—an oral tradition that likely had developed within 36 months of the events themselves.

[88] Ibid., 35.

[89] Material for this section, including the chart, comes from Komoszewski, Sawyer and

Wallace, 116–117. A more extensive discussion is included in Part 4 of *Reinventing Jesus*, 169–215, and is well worth the read.

[90] "About the Nag Hammadi Library Section," The Gnostic Society Library: The Nag Hammadi Library, www.gnosis.org/naghamm/nhl.html (accessed June 18, 2007).

[91] Strobel, 67–68.

[92] Paul Copan, *True for You, but Not for Me* (Minneapolis: Bethany House Publishers, 1998), 97.

[93] Ibid.

[94] Milton Fisher, "The Canon of the New Testament," in *The Origin of the Bible*, Philip Wesley Comfort, ed. (Wheaton, IL: Tyndale House Publishers, 1992), 65 – 78.

[95] Geisler and Nix, 283.

[96] Fisher, 71–72.

[97] Geisler and Nix note that "the destruction of biblical manuscripts during the pre-Constantine persecutions, especially under Decius (249–251) and Diocletian (302/3–305), was widespread throughout the Roman Empire. Even after Diocletian abdicated (305), the persecution begun in his reign continued until the Edict of Toleration (311) and the Edict of Milan (313). Diocletian's Edict in 302 was followed by the systematic destruction of the Scriptures and other church books, which resulted in the loss of untold numbers of biblical manuscripts. Only the library at Caesarea (in the East) was spared … Later, even this great library was destroyed by the Moslems (AD 638) as they took control of much of the territory of the ancient Roman Empire." (281)

[98] Geisler and Nix, 277–282.

[99] Ibid., 282.

[100] Fisher, 74.

[101] Geisler and Nix, 293.

[102] Komoszewski, Sawyer and Wallace note that "A book that was perceived to have been written after the time of the apostles was categorically rejected" (128; see also 145).

[103] Komoszewski, Sawyer and Wallace, 132.

[104] Jones, 136.

[105] This would seem to be so in relation to the work of the Jesus Seminar. For a good explanation of the process applied to the sayings of Jesus in the Gospels see Komoszewski, Sawyer, and Wallace, 33–50.

Dating of the Gospels can also be affected by those who presuppose Jesus was *unable* to supernaturally predict future events as New Testament scholar Donald Guthrie notes:

"This predictive power of Jesus is so generally denied by Synoptic investigators that it is no wonder that the dates of Mark, Matthew and Luke are all bound up together in the dating of Mark The argument runs as follows: First, since the predictive power of Christ is denied, it is assumed that Mark was produced only a few years before the fall of Jerusalem (cf. Mk. xiii, 14, and Mt. xxiv, 15). Secondly, Matthew used Mark and therefore must be dated after the fall of Jerusalem. Thirdly, both Ignatius and the *Didache* appear to have cited Matthew's Gospel and so the latter must have attained authority some time before the writings of the former. Fourthly, therefore the probable date of Matthew is AD 80–100." (*New Testament Introduction* [Downers Grove, IL: InterVarsity Press, 1976], 45–46) [It should be noted that many scholars— including conservative ones—believe that Matthew and Luke used Mark's Gospel as a source for theirs. One can ascribe to the source hypothesis and still hold to an early dating (i.e., no later than AD 60) of Mark's Gospel which, of course, would allow Matthew's to be written earlier as well.]

[106] Fisher, 65–78.

[107] Fisher, 70.

[108] McDowell, *The New Evidence That Demands a Verdict* (Nashville: Thomas Nelson, 1999), 103.

[109] After Justin's death in Rome, Tatian became involved with Gnosticism, was excommunicated for aberrant doctrine (c. 172) and returned to the East during which time his *Diatessaron* was spread and became popular in Syrian churches. Eventually all 200 copies of the *Diatessaron* were destroyed because of Tatian's involvement in the heretical sect of the Encratites (Geisler and Nix, 513–514).

[110] Donald Guthrie, *New Testament Introduction* (Downers Grove: InterVarsity Press, 1976), 33.

[111] Ibid., see 33–44.

[112] Guthrie cogently remarks:

"It is true that neither the Gospel itself nor Papias tells us which Mark was the author, but it is difficult to believe that the Roman community would have published a Gospel attributed to an unknown Christian named Mark, if it were known already that Barnabas' nephew with the same name had been a companion of both Paul and Peter." (69 / f.n. 1)

[113] Ibid., 99–100.

[114] Guthrie, 258–260. Guthrie also notes:

"Our confidence in Irenaeus' testimony is supported by the recognition that all subsequent to him assume apostolic authorship of the Gospel without question (Tertullian,

Clement of Alexandria, Origen). If they were merely repeating Irenaeus' opinion, they must have considered that opinion of sufficient value to repeat without suspicion." (260)

[115] Ibid., 246. See also Daniel B. Wallace, "The Gospel of John: Introduction, Argument, Outline," Bible.org, http: //www.bible.org/page.php?page_id=1328.

# CHAPTER 20

# How God Engaged Humanity Through Creation (Or, Why Belief in God may be Considered Rational)

The thought that one who thinks spiritually can also think rationally is a foreign concept to most living in the Western world. In my experience, presenting rational reasons for belief in God's existence is often met by wonder in the one who has yet to know and believe. I can virtually see the wheels turning in a person's head as I venture into this new, uncharted territory.

Previously, I have presented the basic elements that I often share with someone who is skeptical. As with Jorge, my purpose is to challenge disbelief with substantive reasoning, suggesting belief in God as rational—the logical outcome of considering the evidence.

It is misdirected to think that reason or logic will bring a person to salvation. Apart from the divine working of God the Holy Spirit, whose job it is to bring conviction and faith sufficient leading to belief (see John 16: 7–11), salvation will never occur.

I do think, however, that God's Spirit uses rationality and evidence as part of the process of conviction that leads to salvation. If we are to love God with our minds following salvation, it seems reasonable to suggest that we must accept Him with our minds on the path to salvation. How else can we explain Paul's rational yet impassioned speeches before Festus (Acts 25) and Herod Agrippa (Acts 26), not to mention his point-by-point presentation of the Gospel to the philosophers in Athens (Acts 17)?

I sometimes use currently accepted thinking as the beginning point for a discussion, as long as it does not contradict where I am headed. For example, though the Big Bang theory is debated within the Christian community, it is not of great debate in secular society. Among most students, the Big Bang is accepted virtually a priori. Therefore, I will use current thinking in the realm of cosmology to demonstrate rational evidence for believing in God's existence. Obviously, one must evaluate carefully where to draw the line on this approach. In my thinking, there is a difference between using something accepted as fact (i.e.—by the one with I'm conversing) for the sake of argument and affirming that "something" with the intention of validating its factuality.

I keep the big picture in mind—I want to initially persuade the unbeliever to at least consider belief in God by presenting reasons that help demonstrate the merit of such. For the one who is unsure, my ultimate desire is to lay a *rational* foundation for the Christian worldview ultimately allowing me the opportunity to share the Good News of Jesus Christ. Let me now, briefly, point to five particular areas of study which, I believe, may help you challenge your friends consider the rationality of belief in God.

## Cosmology

Cosmology is defined as the "branch of science dealing with the large-scale structure, origins, and development of the universe."[1] Though from the time of the ancient Greeks it was believed that the universe was eternally caused (i.e.— Plato affirmed an uncaused First Cause and Aristotle taught the existence of a Prime Mover), it was largely through the influence of Christianity that Western civilization, by-in-large, affirmed the belief that the universe had been created by an all-powerful God. In the late eighteenth century, however, this perspective began to be challenged when Immanuel Kant argued for the infinite nature of the universe. That which Kant postulated only seemed to be confirmed by the observations of astronomers, as telescopes became more powerful and the universe's vastness apparent. By the end of the nineteenth century the infinity of the universe was virtually regarded as scientific fact.[2]

### The Big Bang

As the science of astronomy continued its development in the late nineteenth and early twentieth centuries, astronomers began to take note of the radial speed and velocity of stars and gaseous and planetary nebulae. In 1910, for example, Vesto Slipher measured the velocity of the Andromeda Nebula and discovered it to be 30 times greater than previously documented. By

1917 Albert Einstein had developed his Theory of Relativity. Using this theory, Dutch astronomer Willem de Sitter used Einstein's equations to develop his own model of the universe, a model in which the universe was expanding.[3]

It was, however, the renowned astronomer Edwin Hubble (after whom the Hubble space telescope is named) who solidified the expanding universe model as being the preeminent model within the scientific community. Beginning in 1924 and using the 100-inch Hooker telescope at the Mount Wilson Observatory near Los Angeles, he identified and studied the distance of our universe's galaxies. By 1929 he had determined that the wavelength of electromagnetic radiation emitted by these galaxies would lengthen in proportion to their distance from the earth (or, the point of observation). This correlation between a galaxy and its radial velocity has become known as "Hubble's Law."[4]

Therefore, according to Hubble's Law, the velocity of a galaxy is proportional to its distance. The further a galaxy was away from the earth, for example, the faster it was "moving away" (i.e., the distance between us and it was increasing).[5] This confirmed de Sitter's model. And it also seemed to confirm a similar model postulated by a Belgian priest Father Georges Lemaitre, who suggested in a paper written in 1927 that the universe had begun as a single atom, multiplying innumerable times into the universe we see today. In essence, the universe was expanding.

The Big Bang theory (unwittingly so named by astronomer Fred Hoyle—one of the model's opponents—in a comment he made in a radio interview in 1950) had found the support it needed.[6] (Later discoveries—such as the discovery by Arno Penzias and Robert Wilson in 1965 of the universe's background radiation, as well as the findings of the Cosmic Background Explorer [COBE] satellite in the early 1990s—led to virtually a complete dismissal of either the steady state or oscillating-universe models of the universe by the scientific community.[7]) The theory asserts that the universe came into existence as a "singularity" around 13.7 billion years ago. All that exists today—time, space, matter, and energy—was contained in this infinitesimally small "singularity." For some unknown reason, that "singularity" exploded (or expanded) with incomprehensible density and heat (the "explosion" occurring everywhere simultaneously).

It is important to remember that *nothing*, including space, existed prior to the Big Bang. As the universe continued to expand and cool, the single force which existed at the beginning separated into the four fundamental forces we recognize today (the strong nuclear force, weak nuclear force, electromagnetic force, and gravitational force), atomic particles bonded, elements formed, and eventually, the planets and galaxies came into existence.[8]

I admit I am not a scientist. I have, however, always been fascinated by science and respect the intellect of those who study the field so arduously. I freely admit that there are serious questions that must be addressed as to whether or not Big Bang cosmology can be aligned with the Bible's model of creation.[9] Where this and other cosmological theories conflict with God's revealed Word, His Word must remain preeminent, for it will be proven accurate with the passage of time.

**Please Note:** My purpose here is *not* to necessarily affirm Big Bang cosmology but simply to acquaint you with the current thinking of the majority of students with whom you will interact. This will help you ask the right questions of the one you have chosen to engage.

The Big Bang is the one model of secular cosmology (i.e., as opposed to the steady-state or oscillating-universe models) that has virtually eliminated discussion of an infinite universe, thus allowing for the possibility of a Creator. Logically speaking, if something has a beginning, then it must also have a cause sufficient to explain that beginning.[10] Since the universe is now assumed to have a beginning, it is only logical to suggest it has been caused. Simply to suggest that our universe has come from another universe or from quantum inflation only moves the reality of cause-and-effect back one degree. From my perspective, such theories do not fundamentally change the equation but only add additional and unknown variables to the equation thus necessarily increasing the equation's complexity making the solution all the more difficult.

So when I ask someone if he or she thinks it is possible that something can come from nothing, most will concur that it's quite unreasonable, for none of us can cite an instance where something has come from nothing.

Both logically and actually, most will affirm that something that is must come from something—or Someone.[11]

Sometimes I then ask the following: "Given the fact that something must have a cause, why is it that I choose to opt in the direction of a personal God as opposed to a personality-less force as the origin of all that we know?" I then briefly suggest the grand themes of beauty and suitability for life of the world. It is as though both the universe and world in which we live have been designed, not simply for our survival, but for discovery and enjoyment!

## The cosmos' suitability for life

But first, let me ask, have you ever stopped to consider how are our universe and world are so amazingly tuned to sustain life as we know it? Scientists say it's because of the *anthropic principle*: that "everything about the universe tends toward man, toward making life possible and sustaining it."[12] Physicist/philosopher Robin Collins notes:

> Over the past 30 years or so, scientists have discovered that just about everything about the basic structure of the universe is balanced on a razor's edge for life to exist. The coincidences are far too fantastic to attribute this to mere chance or to claim that it needs no explanation. The dials are set too precisely to have been a random accident.[13]

As scientists have continued to explore the depths of our universe and our world, they have begun to recognize a connection between the constants and parameters of the universe and our earth and the requirements for life as we know it. If those thirty-odd constants[14] were adjusted even slightly, life would not be possible.

Consider just *three* of those constants:

1.  **Strong nuclear force**. The strong nuclear force constant is what binds together the protons and neutrons in an atom (otherwise, for example, two positively charged protons could not remain together in the nucleus of an atom). Therefore, even if only slightly weaker, nuclei with multiple protons would not bond and hydrogen would be the only element in the universe. If

slightly stronger, there would be an insufficient supply of many life-essential elements. Life would not be possible either way.[15]

2.   **Gravitational force**. Of all the forces in the universe gravity is the weakest (with the strong nuclear force being billions upon billions time stronger than gravity). Given the wide range of force strengths in the universe, it is conceivable that gravity could be much stronger. If the gravitational force was increased ever so minutely, humans and other large animals would be crushed.[16] If slightly weaker, no heavy elements essential to life would exist.[17]

3.   **Electromagnetic coupling constant**. This is the force that binds electrons to protons in the atom. If this constant were slightly smaller, an electron would not maintain its orbit around the nucleus; if larger, an atom would not share an electron orbit with other atoms. Molecules would not form, and life would be impossible.[18]

Scientists have searched for a "Theory of Everything" or "Grand Unified Theory" that would explain exactly why the constants are as they are. Even with such a discovery, however, the complexity of the universe would only be amplified, not reduced, and the plausibility of a Grand Designer even more apparent.[19]

If this is your field of study or an area of interest, I would challenge you to study further the unique characteristics of our world, alone, and its suitability for life. Consider, for example:

- the force of surface gravity
- thickness of the earth's crust
- tilt of the earth's axis
- the oxygen-to-nitrogen ratio in our atmosphere
- the earth's rotation[20]

Virtually any changes in the established parameters would have significant effect on the suitability of earth as a habitat for life. In evaluating the significance of just 19 of these parameters, astrophysicist Hugh Ross states that they "in themselves lead safely to the conclusion that much fewer than a trillionth of a trillionth of a percent of all stars will have a planet capable of sustaining life."[21]

# Biology

The mystery and magnitude of biology, as well as in cosmology, provide compelling evidence for the existence of a Grand Designer. In cosmology, science attests to the beginning of the universe and the suitability-for-life environment sustained by the very laws and constants of the cosmos. In biology, the dual concepts of complexity and information suggest it is unreasonable to think that all has come about simply by the equation of chance + mutation + natural selection + time.

With scientific understanding having increased exponentially during the 20th century, the complexities of animal and human biological systems have become better understood. It is the increasingly evident complexity that has begun to challenge the very premise of Darwinian evolution.

### Integrative complexity

The complexity evidenced in the design and development of particular biological systems seems to suggest the need for a Designer or intelligence. Perhaps one could call this an integrative or functional complexity. For particular animals to survive or for particular organs to function, the simultaneous coordination of various elements is required—thereby making natural selection an unlikely candidate to ensure their survival and replication.22

As a scientist, Darwin realized that he had to anticipate objections and answer those objections if his theory were to survive. The eye was an organ that Darwin addressed in *Origin of the Species* in Section VI, "Difficulties of the Theory." Given the fact that little was known about how an eye functioned, Darwin attempted a solution, "not by actually describing a real pathway that evolution might have used in constructing the eye, but rather pointing to a variety of animals that were known to have eyes of various constructions … and suggesting that the evolution of the human eye might have involved similar organs as intermediates."[23]

But this is no longer the nineteenth century and a great deal has been discovered about the eye, as well as our other organs. By virtue of the scientific understanding we now possess, one must seriously question how such complex and coordinated organs and organ systems could have developed apart from information and intelligence.

I have chosen to include a description of the biochemical processes essential for sight as a way to highlight the incredible complexity of the process and to illustrate the concept of integrative complexity. Biochemist Michael Behe writes:

> When light strikes the retina a photon is absorbed by an organic molecule called 11-*cis*-retinal, causing it to rearrange within picoseconds to *trans*-retinal. The change in shape of [the] retinal [molecule] forces a corresponding change in shape of the protein, rhodopsin, to which it is tightly bound. As a consequence of the protein's metamorphosis, the behavior of the protein changes in a very specific way. The altered protein can now interact with another protein called transducin. Before associating with rhodopsin, transducin is tightly bound to a small organic molecule called GDP, but when it binds to rhodopsin the GDP dissociates itself from transducin and a molecule called GTP, which is closely related to, but critically different from, GDP, binds to transducin.
>
> The exchange of GTP for GDP in the transducinrhodopsin complex alters its behavior. GTP-transducinrhodopsin binds to a protein called phosphodiesterase, located in the inner membrane of the cell. When bound by rhodopsin and its entourage, the phosphodiesterase acquires the ability to chemically cleave a molecule called cGMP. Initially there are a lot of cGMP molecules in the cell, but the action of the phosphodiesterase lowers the concentration of cGMP. Activating the phosphodiesterase can be likened to pulling the plug in a bathtub, lowering the level of water.
>
> A second membrane protein which binds cGMP, called an ion channel, can be thought of as a special gateway regulating the

number of sodium ions in the cell. The ion channel normally allows sodium ions to flow into the cell, while a separate protein actively pumps them out again. The dual action of the ion channel and pump proteins keeps the level of sodium ions in the cell within a narrow range. When the concentration of cGMP is reduced from its normal value through cleavage by the phosphodiesterase, many channels close, resulting in a reduced cellular concentration of positively charged sodium ions. This causes an imbalance of charges across the cell membrane which, finally, causes a current to be transmitted down the optic nerve to the brain: the result, when interpreted by the brain, is vision.

If the biochemistry of vision were limited to the reactions listed above, the cell would quickly deplete its supply of 11-*cis*-retinal and cGMP while also becoming depleted of sodium ions. Thus a system is required to limit the signal that is generated and restore the cell to its original state; there are several mechanisms which do this. Normally, in the dark, the ion channel, in addition to sodium ions, also allows calcium ions to enter the cell; calcium is pumped back out by a different protein in order to maintain a constant intracellular calcium concentration. However, when cGMP levels fall, shutting down the ion channel and decreasing the sodium ion concentration, calcium ion concentration is also decreased. The phosphodiesterase enzyme, which destroys cGMP, is greatly slowed down at lower calcium concentration. Additionally, a protein called guanylate cyclase begins to resynthesize cGMP when calcium levels start to fall. Meanwhile, while all of this is going on, metarhodopsin II is chemically modified by an enzyme called rhodopsin kinase, which places a phosphate group on its substrate. The modified rhodopsin is then bound by a protein dubbed arrestin, which prevents the rhodopsin from further activating transducin. Thus the cell contains mechanisms to limit the amplified signal started by a single photon.

*Trans*-retinal eventually falls off of the rhodopsin molecule and must be reconverted to 11-*cis*-retinal and again bound by opsin to regenerate rhodopsin for another visual cycle. To accomplish this *trans*-retinal is first chemically modified by an enzyme to transretinol, a form containing two more hydrogen atoms. A second enzyme then isomerizes the molecule to 11-*cis*-retinol. Finally, a third enzyme removes the previously added hydrogen atoms to form 11-*cis*-retinal, and the cycle is complete.[24]

Frankly, in that biochemistry is not my forte, I find the description above quite overwhelming. Regardless, I am amazed as to just how the *elements* of the eye (the cornea, lens, pupil, rods, cones, macula, retina)—not to mention the interworking of the various proteins and chemical transactions cited above—came to be selected and then coordinated. Furthermore—and here's the *big* question: Why, in the first place, would natural selection have chosen some of the proteins, enzymes, processes and the like cited above when, apart from their interrelationship and inter-working, they have little or no significance to the function of sight? And all that has just been detailed relates to the eye alone. What about the optic nerve? And what about the brain and its ability to transmit and translate signals sent via the optic nerve so that what we see is a fair semblance of reality? Indeed, it is almost as though natural selection had the *idea* of seeing before sight ever existed.

## Irreducible complexity

The example of the eye sufficiently illustrates the concept of complexity to most of us, but there are those who still suggest that complex organs could have developed over a period of time via natural selection. And that is where it is important to understand the concept of irreducible complexity, as introduced by Michael Behe in his book *Darwin's Black Box: The Biochemical Challenge to Evolution* (1996). Behe takes the concept of complexity to the molecular level and suggests that if Darwinian evolution is sufficient to explain the development of life as we know it, then it must successfully deal with what we observe at the microscopic level as well.[25]

Behe describes irreducible complexity as "a single system which is composed of several interacting parts that contribute to the basic function, and where the removal of any one of the parts causes the system to effectively cease functioning."[26] In other words, irreducible complexity can be compared to the lowest common denominator in math; any further reduction of one of the fractions in the equation renders the equation unsolvable.

Darwin himself recognized that "if it could be demonstrated that any complex organ existed which could not possibly have been formed by numerous, successive, slight modifications my theory would absolutely break down."[27] Behe, in turn, focuses attention on the molecular realm, virtually unknown in Darwin's day, and posits that evolution could not produce these irreducibly complex biological "machines" not simply because they are too complicated, but due to the fact that the very means Darwin suggested—natural selection—only selects systems that are functional.[28]

Thus in the case of an irreducibly complex biological system, it stands to reason that for the process of natural selection to take effect *the system would have had to exist as an integrated whole from the very start.* Though someone might think of, or even observe, a less complicated system (perhaps suggesting a precursor to the current and more complex one), the key question is still, "given the complex system at hand, how could that particular system have arisen when there is no meaningful functionality, apart from the totality of those parts working together?" Even if the individual parts (e.g., particular proteins in the molecular world) do serve a purpose in other ways, it is their *purposeful integration within the particular complex system* that defies evolutionary explanation via natural selection.[29]

What is Behe suggesting? Quite simply, irreducible complexity suggests intelligence in the design process. Consider just one of Behe's examples: cilium.

Cilia (Latin for "eyelash") are the "whiplike hairs" on the surface of cells that serve to move fluid across the cell's surface and, if the cell is stationary, to help propel it through fluid. An example of the former function is found in the epithelial cells of the respiratory tract (each cell containing about 200 cilia each), where the cilium move synchronously to move the mucus toward the throat for elimination. An example of the latter function would be the role they play in propelling single-celled organisms (eukaryotes) through a fluid.[30]

According to Behe, though cilia were once considered simple in construction, scientists now consider them to be complex molecular machines. Each cilium consists of about 200 protein parts and "of at least a half dozen proteins: alpha-tubulin, beta-tubulin, dynein, nexin, spoke protein, and a central bridge protein. These combine to perform one task—ciliary motion—and all of these proteins must be present for the cilium to function."[31]

Behe concludes that "since the complexity of the cilium in irreducible, then it can not have functional precursors. Since the irreducibly complex cilium can not have functional precursors it can not be produced by natural selection, which requires a continuum of function to work. Natural selection is powerless where there is not function to select."[32]

Thus the very existence of irreducible complexity at the molecular level suggests the role of a Designer. Otherwise, how could have mutation, plus natural selection, plus time alone been able to produce, modify, and select those particular mechanisms that do not exist with meaningful, coordinated purpose without all parts being present and functioning?

**Specified complexity**

Is it integrative and irreducible complexities alone that point to the role of a Designer in the realm of biology? Not at all. It is the presence of specified complexity, found in the structure of the cell, that profoundly suggests the necessity for an intelligence that transcends naturalistic means of development.

The cell, once thought to be a blob of protoplasmic substance, led to a variety of chemical evolutionary theories in an attempt to explain the origin of life. Graduate student Stanley Miller's experiment at the University of Chicago (1952), wherein he electrically charged a gaseous mixture of methane, ammonia, water vapor, and hydrogen to produce a small yield of amino acids (the "building blocks" of life) gave added impetus to such theories.[33]

As we now know, the cell is not simply a dense accumulation of some substance. It is, according to geneticist Michael Denton, "a veritable microminiaturized factory containing thousands of exquisitely designed pieces of intricate molecular machinery made up altogether of

100 thousand million atoms, far more complicated than any machine built by man and absolutely without parallel in the non-living world."[34] Denton continues by noting that from the cell of the tiniest bacteria to that of the human being, "the basic design of the cell system is essentially the same" so that "no living system can be thought of as being primitive or ancestral with respect to any other system, nor is there the slightest empirical hint of an evolutionary sequence among all the incredibly diverse cells on earth."[35]

Let's focus, for a moment, on just the development of proteins within the cell—each human cell containing upwards of 100 million proteins. Proteins are large molecules composed of chains of specifically ordered amino acids and are an essential component for life. A typical protein consists of 200 to 300 amino acids; the largest protein found in the human body is *titin*, which is found in the skeletal and cardiac muscles and consists of a single chain of 29,000 amino acids!

One might infer from Stanley Miller's experiment that an arbitrary mix of particular amino acids would be all that is necessary for a particular protein's development, but this is far from the case. Oxford philosopher of science John Lennox notes, "Proteins are immensely specialized and intricate constructions … and cannot be produced simply by injecting energy into the raw materials for their construction."[36] As noted previously, each protein has a particular function within the cell and works in combination with other proteins to accomplish very specific tasks, much like the arrangement of machines in factory assembly lines.

Though all proteins are developed by the linkage of amino acids it is the *specific sequencing* of the amino acids comprising the protein that determines the function of the particular protein molecule. Because of this specific arrangement related to function, one protein can seldom be substituted for another protein with a different arrangement. It is the origin of such specified complexity that has challenged current materialistic evolutionary thought.[37]

The term "specified complexity" introduces a concept of vital importance. Though the term can be applied elsewhere (e.g., in any situation which requires purposeful cause to be ascertained), in the world of biology it is applied to the study of particular sub-cellular components which exhibit amazing intricacy and function related to a specific purpose within the cell. It is this combination of intricacy and purposeful function that beg the question pertaining to the origin of the information assumed to be necessary for the production of such a component.

But before proceeding further, let's take a look at the term and break it apart so that the concept therein is clearly understood. First, the word *specified* is critical; it refers to something as having *meaningful function*. In other words, does there seem to be a special purpose for an event's occurrence or (as in our discussion) particular biological components' existence?[38]

Complexity, on the other hand, considers the unpredict-ability—hence, the improbability—of a chance happening. Can it be reasonably assumed that, given sufficient opportunity, chance is the most reasonable explanation? Of course, it naturally follows that the more complex something is, the less likely its occurrence will be deemed the result of mere chance.[39]

Therefore, the term "specified complexity" describes a resultant action as having a sufficiently high level of improbability, combined with a sufficiently explicit purpose (i.e., corresponding to an independently occurring function), thus suggesting the probability to be too high for chance to be considered the cause.[40] Christian philosopher J.P Moreland notes it is this dual concept of *purpose* plus *improbability* to which various fields of science consistently appeal in order to demonstrate the role of an intelligent agent. Whether in the field of forensic science, archaeology, psychology, or even neurology, scientists have developed a grid for deter-mining whether or not an event or result finds its cause in the laws of nature or in the purposeful action(s) of an intelligent agent.[41]

Moreland outlines the three levels of this grid while illustrating its importance in helping to evaluate the origin of an event or existence of a particular object or component—whether its existence should be attributed to chance or design. The grid develops around the following evaluative questions:

1.   Is the event or component **necessary** (had to happen that way) or **contingent** (did not have to happen that way)?

2.   If contingent, is the outcome **complex** (thus suggesting a low probability of a chance occurrence due to the complexity involved) or **simple** (the possibility of a chance occurrence cannot be ruled out due to a lack of complexity)?

3.   If complex, does it possess **specification** (i.e.—is it important for some other reason beyond the fact that it simply happened or that it exists; does there appear to be alignment with a particular end or function)? *It is the combination of complexity and specification which give rise to intelligent agency.* [42]

Exhibit "A": Chance or Intelligence?

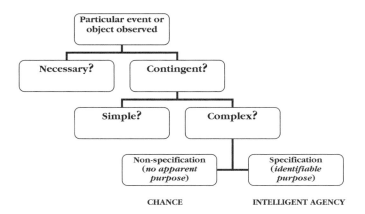

Perhaps the following illustration will add dimension to the explanation above. Let's say we are taking a hike atop one of the mesas of New Mexico, and you happen to discover a rather small, flat piece of rock, part of which is triangular in shape, with a smaller square base at the middle of the bottom of the triangle. You might ask, "Is there something about rocks that require them to be small and triangular in shape, with smaller square bases?" Obviously not. The presence of other rocks, larger rocks with a myriad of various shapes, would suggest no. Thus, this particular shape of rock is not *necessary*, but *contingent*.

Given this shape is contingent, then, is it a *simple* or *complex* shape? Given the fact that we can find flat rocks, a flatly-shaped rock is simple. And given that we can even find triangular-shaped rocks, the triangle shape does not necessarily indicate complexity. However, given this particular rock's flat, thin, triangle shape—along with the smaller square piece located midway at the base of the triangle—as well as the unique sculpting on the flat portion of the rock and sharpened edges, this rock must be viewed as complex, if for no other reason than to find such a rock is very unusual.

But complexity, in and of itself, does not necessarily indicate design. Complexity must be associated with *purpose* in order for an appeal to intelligence to be made. The flat, triangular-shaped rock has a purpose that transcends its existence as that kind of a rock. It is associated with a particular function—that of hunting animals. And we would call that "rock" an arrowhead.

Therefore, we have designated these seldom-occurring patterns of small, flat, triangular-shaped rocks as arrowheads because their configuration is not necessary but contingent, but it is also complex—its arrangement with the perfectly shaped triangle, sharpened edges, textured sides, and the square sitting midway at the base of the triangle, suggests complexity. And it is not meaningless but specific—that is, its design is associated with a corresponding, meaningful function or purpose (i.e., it has meaning apart from its existence as a rock shaped in such a manner). Such a design would, therefore, be sufficient to prompt an inquiry as to intelligence behind the design.

Interestingly, our understanding of specified complexity has come from the mathematical science of information theory, which was developed most notably by Claude Shannon of Bell Telephone Laboratories (*A Mathematical Theory of Communication*, 1948). Shannon provided a mathematical means of measuring information and hypothesized that the order of particular symbols records information.[43] It can be deduced further that the particular symbols, themselves, do not possess information; it is their ordering (within a predetermined framework) that conveys information. The information conveyed is external to the medium or symbol by which it is transmitted.

Consider the example of the arrowhead. Its usefulness has not so much to do with the fact that it is made *of* rock as with *how* it is fashioned from the rock and *how* the design fits with its usefulness for hunting animals.

In the case of the protein molecule, the usefulness of the particular protein molecule does not have as much to do with the fact that it is formed by a combination of amino acids as it does with the complex and special combination of amino acids relative to a particular function. Thus one is able to say the protein molecule possesses both complexity and specification, traits most often associated with intelligent causation.

Even as scientists came to understand the specified complexity of the protein molecule, the source of the information directing the sequencing was a mystery. Thus, the question arose, "How did these specifically complex structures come to be?" The probability of chance being a sufficient cause seemed remote.

You may be aware that a revolution began in molecular biology with the discovery of the double helix of deoxyribonucleic acid (DNA) in 1953 by Francis Crick and James D. Watson. With the discovery of DNA, it was determined that the cell itself contained the design and manufacturing center essential to the development of protein molecules.

With the ensuing inquiry into the DNA, molecular biologists soon discovered that DNA not only served as the "design center" for protein molecules, but they also saw how DNA stored the required information. It was Crick who, in 1955, "first proposed the 'sequence hypothesis' suggesting that the specificity of amino acids in proteins derives from the specific arrangement of chemical constituents in the DNA molecule."[44] In other words "the complex but precise sequencing of four nucleotide bases (A[denine], T[hymine], G[uanine], and C[ytosine]) stores and transmits the information necessary to build proteins. Thus, the sequence specificity of proteins derives from *prior sequence specificity*—from the information—encoded in DNA [emphases mine]."[45]

It is the presence of information—evidenced in the particular ordering of the amino acid chains in protein molecules, as well as in the nucleotide chains in the DNA—that defies simply naturalistic explanation. In every other realm, information is the result of intelligence. So one is surely compelled to ask, why should we not assume the same here as well?

Some origin-of-life scientists continue to propose models of self-organization based on their observation of other natural occurrences (e.g., vortices formed as water drains from a bathtub, crystalline structure that develops as water freezes and a snowflake is formed, etc.). Could it be that, though far more complex, such self-ordering tendencies account for the sequencing of the amino acids in the protein or the ordering of the nucleotide bases in DNA? Upon closer examination, most scientists find such self-ordering models less than plausible.[46]

At the root of this discussion is the question, what exactly is meant by "order"?

It is agreed that *two* types of order exist: Order of the first kind is derived from the material of which something is made and is, therefore, *inherent* to the object (e.g., the structure of water molecules causes them to crystallize when frozen). The second, however, does not arise from the structure of the material or within matter itself and is, therefore, *external* to the object.[47] For example, there is nothing inherent to the particular amino acids or nucleotide bases that causes them to organize as they do and as randomly as they do, yet with such complexity and specificity.

It is also important to observe that the first kind of order can be rather simple in that it is recurring and predictable, whereas the second kind of order is not. And it is the degree of apparent "randomness" that allows the second kind of order to be rich in information content—content required to accomplish very specific and defined purposes. Meyer concisely explains:

> Whereas information requires variability, irregularity, and unpredictability—which is what information theorists call complexity—self-organization gives you repetitive, redundant structure, which is known as simple order. And complexity and order are categorical opposites.[48]

Thus, I would suggest that the specified complexity, exhibited in the development of protein molecules and, even more fundamentally, in the coding of the DNA molecule, is that which defies ascribing mere chance as the cause of either. Moreover, as one considers the various levels of complexity demonstrated in the realm of biology (integrative, irreducible, and specified), the plausibility of the causal activity of an intelligent agent seems all the more rational.

## Psychology

In psychology, it is the sense of self that seems to set apart humans so dramatically from the other species of the animal kingdom. Humans are just different—and vastly so. Though countless attempts have been made since Darwin to bridge the gap between the higher orders of the animal kingdom and the human species, those attempts have had relatively disappointing results.[49]

When it comes to human consciousness, it seems evident that something lies beyond simply the physical description of the person. In fact, one could suggest that it is this very element of conscious existence (its source being that which the Bible calls the soul[50]) that results in our measuring a person more by the "who" than the "what." Even though research suggests that 98 percent of the atoms in the human body today will be replaced by other atoms within the next six months, nobody would suggest that you are not you six months from now! You transcend the simple quantification of your body's physical attributes.

From the viewpoint of the philosophical position of physicalism, however, only the material part of the person exits. The immaterial, spiritual part of the person does not exist; indeed, everything—even feelings and emotions—are chemically induced and simply products of the environment in which we live. Francis Crick (who proposed the structure for DNA) summed up this position succinctly when he stated: "You, your joys and your sorrows, your memories and ambitions, your sense of personal identity and free will, are in fact no more than the behavior of a vast assembly of nerve cells and their associated molecules."[51]

In fact, physicalism is the logical outcome of the naturalistic worldview—the worldview that holds that our existence can be owed, solely, to the forces and interaction of nature. And naturalism is likely the predominant view of the majority of your friends.

I have discovered that one very effective way of helping someone consider the possibility of a God is to help guide the individual to the ultimate conclusions of his/her belief system. Though a majority of those with whom I interact hold to a naturalistic worldview, most believe that there is more to the person than simply the physical aspect.

The worldview to which many ascribe will not allow them the option of holding to a chance existence by naturalistic means *and* a life of purpose and meaning as an independent and volitional individual. It is when one is confronted with the ultimate conclusions of his or her belief system—conclusions one often does not ascribe to or live by—that a gateway is opened to continuing dialogue.

Christian apologist and philosopher J.P. Moreland points out that human consciousness cannot be described in purely material terms. He suggests that a simple definition of human consciousness is "what you are aware of when you introspect. When you pay attention to what's going on inside of you, that's consciousness. … In short, consciousness consists of sensations, thoughts, emotions, desires, beliefs, and free choices that make us alive and aware."[52]

In my thinking, the implications of this are profound. *The fact that I can know something about myself that no doctor, neurologist or scientist can know suggests that there is a part of me that is not physically determined.*

Moreland continues by asserting that human consciousness is a product of the mind, often considered in Western society as one and the same with the brain. He points out, however, that though the mind and the brain closely interface, they possess properties that are very different and are, therefore, separate entities.

For example, our thoughts are not properties of the brain but of the mind. Thoughts are not of material substance; they do not have any weight; they are not spatial and are not composed of chemicals, as is our brain. Though the brain and mind have a "causal dependency" on one another, they are not the same, for their effects are very different. Indeed, our mental states are not the same as our brain states.[53] A neurosurgeon may have the ability to determine when we are thinking and to evaluate the part of the brain that is used in that process, but he or she does not have the ability to tell us what we are thinking, strictly by examining the brain's activity.

To demonstrate this point, Moreland points to the pioneering work of neurosurgeon and founder of the Montreal Neurological Institute, Wilder Penfield (1891–1976). During his professional career, Dr. Penfield pursued the treatment of epilepsy, developing what became known as the "Montreal procedure."

Given that many patients who suffer from epilepsy receive some kind of warning, or aura[54], Penfield theorized that if he could identify the exact area of the brain associated with the sensation experienced during the aura, perhaps that particular brain tissue could be removed or destroyed, thus eliminating the area of seizure activity. How did he accomplish this? Penfield would remove the skull cap of an anesthetized, yet still lucid patient, stimulate various parts of the brain's cerebral cortex with a mild electrical current, and then question the patient as to what he or she was experiencing.

It was during Penfield's pioneering work in the treatment of epilepsy that a remarkable discovery was made:

> Stimulation anywhere on the cerebral cortex could bring responses of one kind or another, but he found that only by stimulating the temporal lobes (the lower parts of the brain on each side) could he elicit meaningful, integrated responses such as memory, including sound,

movement, and color. These memories were much more distinct than usual memory, and were often about things unremembered under ordinary circumstances. Yet if Penfield stimulated the same area again, the exact same memory popped up—a certain song, the view from a childhood window—each time. It seemed he had found a physical basis for memory, an "engram."[55]

Penfield recalls in his book *The Mystery of the Mind* that as he would touch his electrode to the motor cortex of one hemisphere of the patient's brain, causing the patient to, for example, move his or her hand, he would ask the partially anesthetized patient about the sensation. "Invariably his response was 'I didn't do that. You did.' When I caused him to vocalize, he said, 'I didn't make that sound. You pulled it out of me.'"[56] The patient was able to distinguish between his body's response to an external physical stimuli and volitional mental activity that he might exercise in producing a similar effect.

Even when the electrode's stimulation caused the patient to vividly recall past experiences, to move various parts of the body, and to give the patient the impression that objects were growing larger and moving in their direction, Penfield noted of the patient:

He remains aloof. He passes judgment on it all. He says "things *seem* familiar," not "I have been through this before." He says, "Things are growing larger," but he does not move for fear of being run over. If the electrode moves his right hand, he does not say, "I wanted to move it." He may, however, reach over with the left hand and oppose his action.[57]

One of the compelling evidences for this "otherness" of the human species seems to be the ever-present reality of volition or free will. Penfield also noted that, from all he observed, "There is no place in the cerebral cortex where electrical stimulation will cause a patient to believe or decide."[58]

Yes, it is *I* who choose to do certain things when *I* choose to do them. And the awareness of the decision process surely indicates that I am not a creature who acts simply in response to particular stimuli. Moreover, sometimes I even find myself choosing to do those things that seem less beneficial for my well-being than the other potential options.

This "conflict of interest" is perhaps most often apparent in matters involving natural or moral law—those fundamental guidelines for moral behavior that seem to occur naturally.[59] Though some of us may object by suggesting that our responses are simply instinctive—either to help another member of the species or to save ourselves from potential calamity and protect our progeny—there seems little explanation for why we often give a "second thought," considering the course of action we ought to take.

C.S. Lewis observes that when we hear a man's cry for help, for example, we are torn between two impulses: one, to help; and two, self-preservation. But Lewis goes on to observe that there is another impulse—a *third* impulse—that challenges us to put aside the drive of self-preservation and, rather, to follow the inclination to answer the man's cry for help. Obviously, this mediating influence cannot be considered the same as either of the other two impulses in that it compels us to follow one and not the other. Lewis considers this "third thing" the natural or Moral Law which resides in each of us. In using the analogy of a piece of music's relationship to the piano, he suggests that "The Moral Law tells us the tune we have to play; our instincts are merely the keys."[60]

The 2003 movie *Radio* tells the true story of a young, intellectually disabled black man (called Radio because of his love for music on the radio), growing up in 1970s South Carolina, and the white football coach, Harold Jones, who both defended and befriended him. It is a timeless movie that focuses on the value of life, even for one who is unable to fit into the mainstream of society.

Why would a white football coach go to such extraordinary lengths to befriend a young black man, particularly one who did not possess the intellectual capabilities to attend school, much less play football? This question is answered during a discussion between Coach Jones and Radio's mom.

Radio's mother is somewhat skeptical of the coach's involvement. As they drink coffee at the kitchen table, she looks at the coach and asks, "So why are you doing all this for my son?"

The coach replies, "Because I think it is the right thing to do."

And the mother responds, "But there are many times we know the right thing to do and choose not to do it."

That is the "oughtness" that C.S. Lewis addresses. Helping Radio benefited neither the coach nor his team. In fact, more often than not, his close association with Radio was opposed by his associates, team, and at times, even the black high-school principal.

But Coach Jones knew it was "the right thing to do." There likely would be other needy people in Coach Jones' life. Yet he chose to help this particular needy person (Radio) at this particular time and to an extent that would ultimately jeopardize his coaching career. One must look elsewhere for a solution to the seeming randomness of "oughtness," rather than to the descriptive remedy provided in physicalism, which assumes a biological reason behind every human activity.[61]

The question that emanates, then, from the field of psychology is: "Why do I possess this sense of self?" If all that I am is physical and, therefore, able to be quantified in natural terms, why am I so important to myself, in a manner that extends far beyond self-preservation and my role in the continuance of the species? Why is there a compelling sense that *I* am far more than just my physical makeup? And why is it that I can be physically fit, yet emotionally distraught?

Why is it that I think thoughts about my thoughts—debating and evaluating decisions that may have little to do with the "necessities" of life? And what of the seeming randomness to my thoughts? I will often move from thoughts of a serious nature to thoughts of pleasure, and I find that moments of enjoyment are interrupted by thoughts of serious consideration. My explanation is that I wanted to do so, which is the very reason why we hold people responsible for their actions.

My life experience suggests that I am far more complicated than a creature who simply responds to certain chemical stimulus. And if that is all I am, having been designed to respond accordingly, why do I even think about the "why" and then question or debate it? Why?

From where does this strong sense of "oughtness" come? If I am a determined being, should I not simply move from one stimulus to another, seamlessly navigating the pathway of life in response to the stronger force that attracts, while moving away from that which repels? And why the seeming inconsistency? Sometimes this "oughtness" helps me (I feel good about doing this or that), and at other times it helps others more than myself (either putting me in harm's way or removing time, energy, or resources from me).

If there is no God, then I must wonder, "Why *me*?"

# Sociology

If the intriguing question in the realm of psychology has to do with the sense of self, then I suppose the penetrating question in sociology is "Why do we have a sense of the selfhood of others?" Sociology is the field of study that examines human behavior, particularly as it relates to the development of society. Fundamentally, it studies the various expressions of human relationships within the context of family, culture, and/or subculture and, ultimately, civilization.

My interest in this particular area was recently piqued again when I read an article in *Smithsonian* magazine that summarized the assessment of two well-known researchers of primate behavior, the husband-and-wife team of Robert Seyfarth and Dorothy Cheney. Seyfarth and Cheyney spend their summers in the Okavango Delta of Botswana, where they study vervet monkeys (a type of African monkey) and baboons, among those animals studied for many years for their near "humanlike" communication and social skills.

Though this team of researchers previously has touted the social development of baboons in particular, their assessment has been somewhat moderated. The article's author notes:

> Cheney and Seyfarth have gradually come to the conclusion that monkeys don't actually recognize that other monkeys have minds. They feel grief themselves, for instance, but almost never comfort other monkeys who happen to be grieving. They do not seem to be able to put themselves in another monkey's place. Sylvia [one of the baboons observed], for instance, once made a long water crossing with her baby clinging to her belly. Since Sylvia herself could breathe, it did not dawn on her that her submerged baby couldn't, and as a result it drowned at her breast.[62]

Seyfarth goes so far as to say, "They [baboons] aren't furry little humans. They're just monkeys."[63] On the other hand, given the recent pronouncements that "98 percent of the DNA, or the code of life, is exactly the same between humans and chimpanzees,"[64] I find it intriguing how very different we are and how vastly different are the families, cultures, and societal structures we develop in conjunction with the other members of *our* species. From my perspective, Seyfarth seems more the realist.

The ability to recognize the selfhood of another and to engage at that level seems a uniquely human ability. Thus, I would like to suggest that it is at the level of relationship among mutually identified selves that human family and cultural and societal organizations set themselves far and away from the seemingly similar groupings participated in by other members of the animal kingdom.

Surely it is at the level of human relationship where we discover at least two great differences between human interaction and those of other members of the animal kingdom: *personality* and *morality*. Indeed, it is the very nature of *human* relationship that suggests there is something far deeper. Let me give an example:

My mother contracted dementia several years before she died. Her doctor confirmed that her particular form of dementia was due to multiple mini-strokes, which deprived the brain of blood, thus resulting in brain-tissue death. I remember the doctor showing me the digital image of my mother's brain (generated by the MRI) and pointing out the particular area of the brain where the tissue was no longer living.

During a nine-year period, my family and I watched my mom steadily deteriorate mentally. During this time, she eventually lost her ability to recall past events and names, and, eventually, she could not identify the specific members of my family.

Yet, amazingly, though there were occasions when mom thought I was my dad, there was still an unexplainable bond of relationship that existed until the day she died. Whenever a family member would walk into her room, there was an immediate connection on a level beyond her ability to quantify exactly who that person was.

Here's my point: If all we are is simply a compilation of atoms and molecules given to electro-chemical stimulation, then why did my mom not simply stop being my mom when her ability to process and store information was severely inhibited? Why was it, even toward the end of her life—when she could no longer construct a sentence—that her face would light up whenever her children would enter her room and she would reach to give us a hug?

And why did *I* not feel the freedom to jettison the relationship…period? Mentally and physically, my mother had become a very different person as a result of the dementia and old age. Yet, all I can say is that, even though the relationship changed in a way that is difficult to describe, the day my mom died was the day I lost someone to whom I related differently than to anyone else in the world. Why? *Because she was my mom.* And because she was my mom, we shared a very special relationship—one that transcended her deteriorating condition.

I would suggest, too, that it is the differing levels of relationship within human experience that defy physical explanation. Why is it that we relate to some people more positively than others? Why shouldn't each gender relate to the same and opposite gender in a somewhat consistent fashion? Are we really to believe that both attraction and conflict have something to do with the fundamental urge to mate, thus ensuring the continuance of the species? If so, then why are those same emotions evidenced between members of the same sex? Why is it that I like some guys better than other guys; some becoming friends, others simply acquaintances and others to be avoided?

Relationships among humans are different from other members of the animal kingdom. There is the seemingly intrinsic need for substantive and long-lasting relationship that goes beyond the need to mate and bear children. Furthermore, humans possess the ability to relate to each other in a manner that is even stronger than the physical, for it can remain even when the physical diminishes.

Let's consider another aspect that affects the human relationship: the problem of evil. If God does not exist, then it seems unclear why the problem of evil is a problem. Why have humans, for countless centuries in countless discussions and through countless writings, even bothered with it? Why shouldn't we just accept the fact that when someone does something that hurts us, that it is just the flexing of their proverbial muscle? Isn't it just survival of the fittest being played out?

Yet no one lives this way. When offended or hurt by another, our response of "that's not fair!" suggests that we all appeal to a fundamental and commonly understood standard of justice and fairness in the context of human relationship.

Every highly-developed culture since the beginning of the recording of modern history has codified responses to deal with the abuses that occur in human relationship. It is one thing to say *I* possess an understanding of what is right and what is wrong; it is quite another (perhaps more significant) to say that my *community* or my *culture* agrees on this matter.

With all the discussion today on tolerance and multiculturalism, it seems we have lost sight of the forest for the trees. Because the focus has been on our differences from other cultures, we have failed to observe the commonalities. To some, the diverseness of cultural mores is sufficient proof to dismiss the concept of natural or moral law. To those, C.S. Lewis responds accordingly:

> There have been differences between their moralities, but these have never amounted to anything like a total difference. If anyone will take the trouble to compare the moral teaching of, say, the ancient Egyptians, Babylonians, Hindus, Chinese, Greeks and Romans, what will really strike him will be how very like they are to each other and to our own ... Men have differed as regards what people you ought to be unselfish to—whether it was only your own family, or your fellow countrymen, or every one. But they have always agreed that you ought not to put yourself first. Selfishness has never been admired. Men have differed as to whether you should have one wife or four. But they have always agreed that you must not simply have any woman you liked.[65]

Obviously, it is this moral law that provides a framework for society. Our society, at the community, state, and national levels, supports law enforcement because the majority agrees that stealing and killing and child abuse are wrong.

World War II was fought because the vast majority of people and nations recognized that Hitler did not have the right to suppress a nation through murder or to force himself on the sovereign states of others. Society—at *every* level—would disintegrate if there were not some kind of moral code to serve as a framework for justice within that society. And to simply suggest that this occurred after the formation of a society misses the point completely; a society could not form if there was no common agreement *first* on essential issues such as fairness and justice.

Of what does "relationship" truly consist, and why does it continue, despite the physiological and mental decay of those involved? Should there not be some connection between the two, if all we are is a chance collection of atoms and molecules?

Given the tremendous diversity of the world's cultures, why has there been such commonality when it comes to understanding what is right and fair in relationships between the people of those cultures? And why does one person or one culture have the right to project its own understanding of fairness and justice on others, if there is not an inherent belief that the person or culture is not somehow aware of a kind of transcultural, commonly understood standard?

All that we as humans know suggests that the compelling experiences of relationship and an understanding of good and evil point to the activity of a Divine Agent who possesses personality and transcendent qualities of justice and fairness. In our experience, only minds with personalities set standards and build relationships. To suggest differently seems not only illogical, but it also militates against the very philosophy of naturalism posited by those who suggest otherwise. If, indeed, we cannot reason from that which we know to inform us of reality, then a greater force than nature has blinded our eyes and clouded our minds.

## Philosophy

Her name was Jamie, and she had recently started working at one of my favorite restaurants. On another occasion, we had spoken previously, and her interest in spiritual things seemed minimal at best. This day, however, would be different.

As Jamie began to wait on me, her countenance seemed to indicate that she was burdened. Rather than delve too quickly into a heavy conversation, I thought it best to wait. A few minutes later, however, Jamie returned and sat down across from me.

"So," I began, "how's Jamie today?"

"Life's a grind. I'm going nowhere. Eat, work, sleep—it's the same every day." Jamie's response was telling—and a mirror-like reflection of so many others in our culture.

Why is that Jamie, like so many, expect more from life than simply attending to the activities of life essential for survival? Indeed, how is it that the primary tasks of the animal kingdom have become, in our thinking, the secondary tasks of life, to be subjugated to personal fulfillment and meaningful existence? Why has this search for a meta-narrative of life engulfed the thoughts and imaginations of men and women throughout the centuries?

If we are here by chance, then from where does this search for purpose find its source? If we are really here for primarily one purpose—to ensure the continuance of the species—why do we even *think* about any other?

Whatever the assessment of particular philosophers concerning life, their very investigation into the meaning of life suggests they have considered that something more should be expected of life than simply sheer existence.

To this point, I find intriguing the words of the ancient Jewish philosopher and king, Solomon (ca. 1000 BC), written 3000 years ago:

> For everything there is a season,
>     a time for every activity under heaven.
> At time to be born and a time to die.
>     A time to plant and a time to harvest.
> A time to kill and a time to heal.
>     A time to tear down and a time to build up.
> A time to cry and a time to laugh.
>     A time to grieve and a time to dance.
> A time to scatter stones and a time to gather stones.
>     A time to embrace and a time to turn away.
> A time to search and a time to quit searching.
>     A time to keep and a time to throw away.
> A time to tear and a time to mend.
>     A time to be quiet and a time to speak.
> A time to love and a time to hate.
>     A time for war and a time for peace.
>
>     (Ecclesiastes 3: 1–8 NLT)

As he completes his list of human endeavors and desires which, through the poetic tool of merism[66], covers the spectrum of virtually every activity imaginable, he questions what value, if any, is to be found in such an array of seemingly endless and conflicting tasks when he asks: "What do people really get for all their hard work?" (Ecclesiastes 3: 9 NLT) Indeed, Solomon could easily be understood here to resonate with Jamie's frustration. Surely there must be more to life than just the "daily grind."

Rather than retreat to despair, however, Solomon makes this poignant remark: "Yet God has made everything beautiful for its own time. He has planted eternity in the human heart, but even so, people cannot see the whole scope of God's work from beginning to end" (Ecclesiastes 3: 11 NLT). Herein Solomon seems to be suggesting a connection between the activities of humanity and the grand purposes of God. The latter is not fully disclosed but still the prospect is indelibly imprinted on the human soul.

From a positive perspective, individuals like Jamie, who strive to discover greater purpose in and meaning from the activities of life, affirm such an inherent desire. Conversely, the anxiety and depression that so many experience when the monotony of life's activities seemingly smothers any hope of something more also are suggestive of this desire.

And so it was with Jamie. I attempted a response that I hoped would help her think through the root of her frustration. "Jamie, let me tell you what I think is going on. You are searching for a greater purpose in life, sort of a meta-narrative of what life is all about. You want to know why you are here. Am I right?"

"Yes," she replied.

There is a fundamental longing in the hearts of men and women that calls them to desire more. It is a desire that, if not properly addressed, will lead to an assortment of diversion tactics and vices, ultimately resulting in boredom and a sense of meaninglessness and loneliness. The call of that greater purpose— of that extra-temporal significance—will never be satisfied by appeasing the desires of the temporal self.

Jamie's comments revealed the despair of one who had searched for substance in life by pursuing that which is temporal. Such a person will one day wake up, look in the mirror, and admit, "I have traveled a long road only to discover the end has become the beginning." Consider the words of the French philosopher Blaise Pascal (1623–1662):

> We desire truth and find in ourselves nothing but uncertainty. We seek happiness and find only wretchedness and death. We are incapable of not desiring truth and happiness and incapable of either certainty or happiness. We have been left with this desire as much as a punishment as to make us feel how far we have fallen.[67]

Perhaps, however, a ray of hope can be discovered through the hurting.

If Solomon was correct, and if there is a God who has created us for His purposes, then one's meaning and significance in life lies beyond that which is immediately apparent. Indeed, there is a connection between the human and the divine; a point of contact between the seemingly meaningless details of life and the prospect of being a part of something more grand. C.S. Lewis would suggest that for one to live life *as* it is while thinking that such is *all* there is would be to settle for something far less than one should.

> We are half-hearted creatures fooling about with drink and sex and ambition when infinite joy is offered us, like an ignorant child who wants to go on making mud pies in a slum because he cannot imagine what is meant by the offer of a holiday at sea. We are far too easily pleased.[68]

I am confident that the daily grind is repugnant to us not so much because the activities are so horrible, but because the lives we live here—consisting of a variety of seemingly endless activities and desires—call us to anticipate an "end" or purpose (the Greeks used the word *telos*) for our existence. It is in the absence of knowing that greater purpose (which Solomon directly associates with God and His plan) that the daily grind of life becomes exactly that; when all the achievements of life, no matter how great, seem to fall short of bringing the ultimate satisfaction for which we all strive.

It is Lewis who would even go so far as to suggest that the nagging sense of a desire that no temporal activity seems to satisfy, as well as that longing for what he would call one's "own far-off country," hint at the reality of an eternity. He writes:

> Do what they will, then, we remain conscious of a desire which no natural happiness will satisfy. But is there any reason to suppose that reality offers any satisfaction to it? "Nor does the being hungry prove that we have bread." But I think it may be urged that this misses the point. A man's physical hunger does not prove that that man will get any bread; he may die of starvation on a raft in the Atlantic. But surely a man's hunger does prove that he comes of a race which repairs its body by eating and inhabits a world where eatable substances exist. In the same way, though I do not believe (I wish I did) that my desire for Paradise proves that I shall enjoy it, I think it is a pretty good indica-tion that such a thing exits and that some men will. A man may love a woman and not win her; but it would be very odd if the phenomenon called 'falling in love' occurred in a sexless world.[69]

Few other themes resonate so consistently with those with whom I speak than the appeal to greater purpose in life. Everyone wants to believe he or she is here for something larger than simple existence. If the naturalistic, we-are-here-by-chance worldview is true, then the human race has chosen to reject its mandate to be content with survival and procreation. Our desire to know and be happy in the process testifies accordingly. We are creatures who desire to leave a legacy.

As we continued to talk, I assured Jamie that our lives *do* have meaning because we have been created for purpose by a God of purpose. That purpose, however, has become blurred because contact and communication with God has been broken; we have turned our backs on God. And it is that broken contact and communication with God that leads to the brokenness in life that confronts us.

The fact that humans throughout the millennia have engaged in discussion on the meaning and merit of life suggests that we are compelled to think more highly of our existence than the naturalistic worldview would allow. Apart from the consideration of a personal, Creator God, there seems to be little explanation for the human dilemma over despair and temporality, as well as the counterparts, the quest for inner happiness and eternality. Pascal poignantly observes:

All men seek happiness. There are no exceptions. However different the means they may employ, they all strive towards this goal. The reason why some go to war and some do not is the same desire in both, but interpreted in two different ways. The will never takes the least step except to that end. This is the motive of every act of man, including those who go and hang themselves.

Yet for very many years no one without faith has ever reached the goal at which everyone is continually aiming. All men complain: princes, subjects, nobles, commoners, old, young, strong, weak, learned, ignorant, healthy, sick, in every country, at every time, of all ages, and all conditions.

A test which has gone on so long, without pause or change, really ought to convince us that we are incapable of attaining the good by our own efforts. But example teaches us very little. No two examples are so exactly alike that there is not some subtle difference, and that is what makes us expect that our expectations will not be disappointed this time as they were last time. So, while the present never satisfies us, experience deceives us, and leads us on from one misfortune to another until death comes as the ultimate and eternal climax.

What else does this craving, and this helplessness, proclaim but that there was once in man a true happiness, of which all that now remains is the empty paint and trace? This he tries in vain to fill with everything around him, seeking in things that are not there the help that he cannot find in those that are, though none can help, since this infinite abyss can be filled only with an infinite and immutable object; in other words by God himself. [70]

Let's summarize the big questions:

- In cosmology, from where did that infinitesimally small amount of time, space, energy, and matter originate? Is it really rational to think that something came from nothing?

- In biology, how does one explain such complexity and information in the coordination of organs and systems, all the way down to the molecules, cells, and DNA? Is it rational to think that such creative information comes from a mindless cause when, in every other realm, information always has as its source intelligence?

- In psychology, why do we think about whom we are and what we do? Is it rational to think that the depths of human personality and morality have been generated by a personality-less and amoral cause?"

- In sociology, how do we explain the intricacy of human relationship and the laws of fairness and justice that govern that realm? Is it rational to think that we can have relationships (that even transcend physical deterioration), and moral codes (that transcend cultural divides), if there is no Divine Agent who possesses personality and who is just?"

- In philosophy, why spend so much talking about this if we are creatures here by chance. Is it rational to think that we could even identify some kind of consistent approach to a philosophy of life, much less purpose for life, if chance is our author?

My aim with the above questions is to gain a hearing to present the claims of Christ. Most people hold the position of agnosticism or even atheism because belief in God, as they understand it, is based on erroneous understanding of faith (e.g., "believing in something that cannot be proven").

Therefore, my desire is to demonstrate that although you cannot prove God scientifically, there is abundant evidence in other realms that provide observable data that allows one to conclude that belief in God may provide the most consistent explanation for some of life's very important questions—in all fields of study.

Often, at the conclusion of my brief presentation of the evidence, I ask, "Have you ever investigated Jesus's claims as to how He said He factored into the equation of knowing God?" My prayer is that God's Spirit has used my often inadequate presentation of rational evidence as a first step in removing the barriers to belief, so that my friend may discover the answer to life's purpose through a relationship with the divine Son of God.

# Notes

1 cosmology. Dictionary.com. Unabridged (v 1.1). Random House, Inc., http: // dictionary.reference.com/browse/cosmology (accessed July 24, 2007).

2 Kenneth D. Boa and Robert M. Bowman, Jr., *Twenty Compelling Evidences that God Exists* (Tulsa: RiverOak Publishing, 2002), 52 – 53.

Consider also the remarks of John C. Lennox:

"For much of the modern scientific era following Copernicus, Galileo and Newton, belief in general reverted to the idea of a universe infinite in both age and extent. Thereafter, from the middle of the nineteenth century, this view began to come under increasing pressure, to the point that it has completely lost its domination. For belief in a beginning is once again the majority view of contemporary scientists" (*God's Undertaker: Has Science Buried God?* [Oxford: Lion Hudson plc, 2007], 65).

3 William Tucker, "Big Bang: Simon Singh Takes on the Cosmos," The New York Academy of Sciences, http: //www.nyas.org/publications/readersReport. asp?articleID=25&page=1 (accessed July 24, 2007).

4 C.R. Nave, "Hubble's Law," The HyperPhysics Web site of the Department of Physics and Astronomy of Georgia State University, http: //hyperphysics.phy-astr.gsu. edu/hbase/astro/hubble.html#c1 (accessed September 13, 2007).

5 Charles Lineweaver and Tamara M. Davis, "Misconceptions about the Big Bang," Scientific American.com (March 2005 issue), http: // www.sciam.com/article.cfm?articleID=0009F0CA-C523-1213- 852383414B7F0147&pageNumber=1&catID=2 (accessed July 26, 2007).

Lineweaver and Davis explain further: "The expansion of our universe is much like the inflation of a balloon. The distances to remote galaxies are increasing. Astronomers casually say that distant galaxies are "receding" or "moving away" from us, but the galaxies are not traveling through space away from us. They are not fragments of a Big Bang bomb. Instead, the space between the galaxies and us is expanding. Individual galaxies move around at random within clusters, but the clusters of galaxies are essentially at rest."

6 Tucker, "Big Bang: Simon Singh Takes on the Cosmos" (accessed July 24, 2007).

7 Boa, 55–56.

8 Jay M. Pasachoff, "Big Bang Theory," MSN Encarta Encyclopedia, http: //encarta. msn.com/encyclopedia_761570694_2/Big_Bang_Theory.html (accessed September 8, 2008).

9 See Chapter 5 in *Refuting Compromise: A Biblical and Scientific Refutation of "Progressive Creationism" (Billions of Years) As Popularized by Astronomer Hugh Ross* by Jonathan Sarfati (Green Forest, AR: Master Books, 2004).

Additionally, John Lennox notes that "not all scientists are convinced that the Big Bang model is correct. For example, there are difficulties created by possible alternative interpretations of the red-shift, and the recently discovered evidence that the expansion of the universe seems to be accelerating—a circumstance which raises the question of the existence of a hitherto unknown force that acts in the opposite direction to gravity" (*God's Undertaker: Has Science Buried God?*, 65).

[10] The *Kalam Cosmological Argument* states three propositions: #1) Whatever begins to exist has a cause, #2) The universe had a beginning, therefore, #3) The universe has a cause. See interview with William Lane Craig in *The Case for a Creator* by Lee Strobel (Grand Rapids, MI: Zondervan, 2004), 97–109.

[11] Undoubtedly, you will eventually run into the person who makes the following statement: "Well, if everything that exists must be caused, then God, too, must have a cause." Logically, only those things that have a beginning must also have a cause. From a Christian perspective, God is timeless and uncaused. He has always existed. If one thinks this is illogical, then simply ask, "Well, what is the difference between suggesting the existence of a timeless/uncaused God and a timeless/uncaused universe? At some point you must accept an uncaused cause. Otherwise, you are forced to accept an infinite regression of causes which may be possible in theory but can never be possible in actuality." From that point I would consider exploring with the individual the suitability for life in the cosmos in seeking to determine whether or not it makes more sense to posit a mindless/personality-less force or a personal God as the origin of all that we know. Furthermore, the existence of "selfness" and personality within the human experience would also seem to beg for a cause greater than an impersonal and mindless one.

[12] Hugh Ross, "Design and the Anthropic Principle," Reasons to Believe, http: //www.reasons.org/resources/apologetics/design.shtml (accessed August 2, 2007).

Note: American physicist John Wheeler was the one who first popularized this principle. It is important to understand (as Ross makes clear in his article) that just because someone accepts the underlying observations giving foundation to this principle he may *not* necessarily conclude that such is the evidence of divine design. Wheeler himself, for example, suggests that *human observation* has influenced this thus leading, really, to the deification of man.

[13] Lee Strobel, *The Case for a Creator* (Grand Rapids, MI: Zondervan, 2004), 161.

[14] Stephen C. Meyer, "Evidence for Design in Physics and Biology" in *Science and Evidence for Design in the Universe*, ed. Michael J. Behe, William A. Dembski, and Stephen C. Meyer (San Francisco: Ignatius, 2000), 60.

[15] Ross, "Design and the Anthropic Principle" (accessed August 2, 2007).

[16] Strobel, 131–132.

[17] Ross, "Design and the Anthropic Principle".

[18] Ibid.

[19] Strobel, 137.

[20] John Lennox notes:

"When we think of the specific conditions that are needed nearer home in our solar system and on our earth, we find that there are a host of other parameters that must be just right in order for life to be possible ... The distance from the earth to the sun must be just right. Too near and water would evaporate, too far and the earth would be too cold for life. A change of only 2 percent or so and all life would cease. Surface gravity and temperature are also critical to within a few per cent for the earth to have a life-sustaining atmosphere—retaining the right mix of gases necessary for life. The planet must rotate at the right speed: too slow and temperature differences between day and night would be too extreme, too fast and wind speeds would be disastrous" (*God's Undertaker: Has Science Buried God?* [Oxford: Lion Hudson plc, 2007], 71).

[21] Ross, "Design and the Anthropic Principle".

[22] Dr. Jobe Martin has demonstrated this using a variety of animals whose very survival requires such coordination. See his book, *The Evolution of a Creationist* (Rockwall, TX: Biblical Discipleship Ministries, 2004).

[23] Michael Behe, "Molecular Machines: Experimental Support for the Design Inference," Access Research Network (Michael Behe Files), http: //www.arn.org/docs/behe/mb_mm92496.htm (accessed August 3, 2007).

[24] Ibid.

Lennox points out that even Richard Dawkins recognizes the incredible complexity of the eye and the odds against it simply evolving by *chance* (see *Climbing Mount Improbable* [New York: Norton, 1996], 67). Of course, this does not dissuade Dawkins in his allegiance to evolution for he emphasizes the role of natural selection as the primary means by which the eye would have developed. Rather than being simply a selection process (as its term suggests), however, Lennox explains that Dawkins must posit that "natural selection is a law-like process that sifts the random mutations so that evolution is a combination of necessity and chance ... [that it will] find a faster pathway through the space of possibilities. The idea here is, therefore, that the law-like process of natural selection increases the probabilities to acceptable levels over geological time" (*God's Undertaker*, 103). Lennox continues by evaluating the merits of making natural *selection* something more than simply that: a *selection* process that works best when resources are limited (i.e., by favoring strong progeny over weak). In the case where resources are *not* so limited, however, natural selection would be of less and less value in that most progeny would survive. This would result in tremendously multiplied variation with the end result that chance, alone, would be the primary agent in evolutionary development, something which neo-Darwinists (such as Dawkins) would not accept (see chapter 6 in *God's Undertaker*).

[25] Strobel, 194.

[26] Behe, "Molecular Machines: Experimental Support for the Design Inference".

[27] Charles Darwin, *Origin of the Species,* 6th ed (New York: New York University Press, 1988),151.

[28] Ibid, 154.

[29] Behe, "Molecular Machines: Experimental Support for the Design Inference".

[30] Strobel, 200–201.

[31] See extended discussion by Behe in both Strobel (201–204) and in "Molecular Machines: Experimental Support for the Design Inference."

[32] Behe, "Molecular Machines: Experimental Support for the Design Inference".

[33] Stephen C. Meyer, "DNA and Other Designs," First Things 102 (April 2000), First Things web site, http: //www.firstthings.com/article.php3?id_article=2598.

The Urey/Miller experiment, however, assumed an early atmosphere consisting largely of "reducing gases" which is a view not given much credence today. Rather, many scientists suggest (from the vantage point of Big Bang cosmology) that the early earth consisted of an atmosphere that was chemically neutral. Also, even if we assume the same kind of atmosphere as Urey/Miller, Meyer points out that human intervention was necessary to prevent "cross reactions" which would have served to break down and degrade the amino acids that formed.

In addition, John Lennox notes that the prevailing opinion among geochemists today is that the earth's early atmosphere "did not contain significant amounts of ammonia, methane or hydrogen that were needed to produce a strongly reducing atmosphere as required by the Oparin hypothesis [suggested by A.I. Oparin in the 1920s, who posited that life had arisen as a result of chemical reactions between the atmosphere—composed primarily of methane, ammonia, hydrogen and water vapor—and chemicals found in the earth as they were exposed to ultraviolet radiation from the sun and other naturally-occurring sources of energy], but was much more likely to have consisted of nitrogen, carbon dioxide and water vapor. There is also evidence of significant amounts of free oxygen … In short then, the evidence suggests that the atmosphere of the early earth would actually have been hostile to the formation of amino acids" (*God's Undertaker*, 120).

[34] Michael Denton, *Evolution: A Theory in Crisis* (Chevy Chase, MD: Adler & Adler, 1986), 250.

[35] Ibid.

[36] Lennox, 122.

[37] Meyer, "DNA and Other Designs."

38 William A. Dembski. "The Chance of the Gaps," International Society for Complexity, Information and Design, http: //www.iscid.org/boards/ubb-get_topic-f-10-t-000013.html (accessed August 13, 2007).

Dembski notes: "Given an independently given pattern, or specification, what level of improbability must be attained before chance can legitimately be precluded? ... To answer this question we need the concept of a probabilistic resource. A probability is never small in isolation but only in relation to a set of probabilistic resources that describe the number of relevant ways an event might occur or be specified. There are thus two types of probabilistic resources, *replicational* and *specificational* ... Probabilities can never be considered in isolation, but must always be referred to a relevant reference class of possible replications and specifications. A seemingly improbable event can become quite probable when placed within the appropriate reference class of probabilistic resources. On the other hand, it may remain improbable even after all the relevant probabilistic resources have been factored in. If it remains improbable and if the event is also specified, then it exhibits specified complexity (complexity here being used in the sense of improbability)."

39 William A. Dembski, "Intelligent Design," Design Inference Website: The Writings of William A. Dembski, http: //www.designinference.com/documents/2003.08. Encyc_of_Relig.htm (accessed August 13, 2007).

40 Lennox explores the concept of specified complexity from the vantage point of mathematics when he explains that the complexity of a string of symbols (i.e., binary digits, letters, words, etc.) can be determined by the degree to which that string can be reduced to an algorithmic function. Algorithmic information theory (that which is fundamental to computer programming) ascertains the degree of information content or complexity of a string by the complexity of the algorithm required to generate the sequence.

It is important to recognize that just because something is complex (i.e., algorithmically incompressible) does not mean it possesses high information content (as the random symbols produced by a toddler playing on the keyboard of a computer). On the other hand, an author working on the same computer and using the same symbols will produce a high degree of complexity (i.e., algorithmically incompressible randomness) yet with high information content. The difference between the former and the latter examples is that the work of the author corresponds to the rules of the language in which the author is writing. It is this correspondence between the symbols so assembled by the author in conjunction with the laws of language, thus having meaning beyond the symbols themselves, that gives rise to the concept of specified complexity. Though both strings of symbols (by the child and the author) are random, and therefore complex, the former is random yet arbitrary while the latter is random yet specified (144–145).

41 J.P. Moreland, "Intelligent Design: Explaining the Controversy" (compact disc available through the Department of Christian Apologetics, Biola University, La Mirada, CA 90639).

Note also Dembski: "Intelligence leaves behind a characteristic trademark or signature—what within the intelligent design community is now called specified complexity. An event exhibits specified complexity if it is contingent and therefore not necessary; if it is complex and therefore not readily repeatable by chance; and if it is specified in the sense of exhibiting an independently given pattern. Note that a merely improbable event is not sufficient to eliminate chance—by flipping a coin long enough, one will witness a highly complex or improbable event. Even so, one will have no reason to attribute it to anything other than chance." ("Intelligent Design")

[42] Ibid.

[43] Charles B. Thaxton, "DNA, Design and the Origin of Life," Origins, http: //www. origins.org/articles/thaxton_dnadesign.html (accessed August 8, 2007).

[44] Meyer, "DNA and Other Designs."

NOTE: Crick's "sequence hypothesis," founded in his belief that the DNA gene is solely responsible for all inherited traits, posited that there should be a one-to-one correspondence between the total number of genes and the total number of proteins. (A *gene* is a segment of the DNA that encodes specific proteins foundational to inherited traits. Though it is often thought that the entirety of the DNA codes for such proteins vis-à-vis inheritable traits, only about *one* to *five percent* of the DNA is directly related to genetic coding or comprises what is referred to as the *genome*, that is, the complete set of genetically-relevant segments of the DNA.) The hypothesis suggested that the *sequencing* of the four nucleotides (A, C, G & T) in the DNA directly determine the sequencing of the 20 amino acids found in living organisms thus distinguishing one from the other. Thus all inherited traits would find their source solely and only in the DNA.

Results from the Human Genome Project (1990–2001), however, severely challenged this thesis by discovering that, of the 100,000+ (some estimates exceed 500,000) proteins found in the human body, the human genome is comprised of only around 30,000–40,000 genes. These results (which essentially undermined the very theory on which the Human Genome Project was founded) suggest at least two important conclusions: 1) the difference between life as a human and some other form of life (i.e.—plant life or a lower form of animal) cannot be quantified simply by the extent of the genome (corn, for example, has 40,000 genes) and, 2) the number of inherited traits, exceedingly greater than the human genome can account for, must result from other factors as well (such as "alternative splicing" whereby the DNA gene's nucleotide sequence is "cut and spliced" into new combinations resulting in redesigned messenger RNAs resulting in the production of proteins that differ in their amino acid sequence from sequence that originated in the DNA).

For an excellent summary of current research in this area see *God's Undertaker* (Chapter 8) as well as the article "Unraveling The DNA Myth: The Spurious

Foundation of Genetic Engineering" by Barry Commoner (Harper's Magazine, February 2002 and able to be accessed at http: //www.mindfully.org).

[45] Ibid.

Additionally, Lennox notes that "the smallest proteins possessing biological function that we know of involve at least 100 amino acids and so the DNA molecules corresponding to them have as many as 10130 sequence alternatives, only a minute portion of which will have biological significance. The set of all possible sequences is therefore unimaginably large. Moreover, under equilibrium conditions, since there are no chemical affinities between the bases, it follows that all sequences of a given length exist with essentially the same probability. This fact, incidentally, entails the probability of a purely random origin for a specified sequence of biological significance so small as to be negligible" (Lennox, 147).

[46] Meyer notes at least two problems facing the self-organizational models. First, the structure of DNA depends on several chemical bonds. Yet, there are *no* chemical bonds between the nucleotide bases that run along the spine of the helix—where the genetic instructions within the DNA are encoded. Second, the four bases of A, C, G and T can attach just as readily to *any* site on the DNA backbone (thus making all sequences just as probable or improbable). Furthermore, the same type of chemical bond occurs between the bases and background regardless of whether A, C, G, or T attaches. Thus "differential bonding affinities do not account for the sequencing of the bases." (The same reasoning applies to the sequencing of the RNA molecule, thus presenting a similar challenge to those who would suggest that life began in an "RNA world"—indeed, causing one to wonder how information appeared in functioning RNA molecules in the first place.) ("DNA and Other Designs").

Paul Davies states bluntly:

"Life is actually *not* an example of *self*-organization. Living things are instructed by the genetic software encoded in their DNA (or RNA) ... The theory of self-organization as yet gives no clue how the transition is to be made between spontaneous, or self-induced organization [i.e., such as that observed in convection cells]—which in even the most elaborate non-biological examples still involves relatively simple structures—and the highly complex, information based, genetic organization of living things" (*The Fifth Miracle* [New York: Simon & Schuster Paperbacks, 1999], 141).

[47] Thaxton, "DNA, Design and Origin of Life" (accessed August 8, 2008).

[48] Strobel, 234.

[49] Carl Wieland citing the article by Richard Conniff in *Smithsonian* magazine (October 2001, 102–104) in which Conniff summarizes the research of Robert Seyfarth and Dorothy Cheney suggesting that there are "severe limitations on intelligence and communication in monkeys." ("Furry Little Humans?," *Creation Archive* 24: 3, Answers in Genesis, www.answersingenesis.org/creation/v24/i3/humans.asp [accessed August 9, 2007]).

[50] J.P. Moreland suggests: "The soul is the ego, the 'I,' or the self, and it contains our consciousness. It also animates our body. That's why when the soul leaves the body, the body becomes a corpse. The soul is immaterial and distinct from the body." (Strobel, 254.)

[51] Francis Crick, *The Astonishing Hypothesis—The Scientific Search for the Soul* (London: Simon and Schuster, 1994), 3.

[52] Strobel, 254.

[53] J.P. Moreland, "Why I Should Believe in Life after Death," *Evangelism and the Case for Christianity* (compact disc series available through the Christian Apologetics Department, Biola University, La Mirada, CA 90639).

[54] auras. Epilepsy.com, http: //www.epilepsy.com/epilepsy/auras.html (accessed August 22, 2007).

[55] Wilder Penfield. "A Science Odyssey: People and Discoveries," Public Broadcasting Service, http: //www.pbs.org/wgbh/aso/databank/entries/bhpenf.html (accessed August 22, 2007).

[56] Wilder Penfield, *The Mystery of the Mind* (Princeton: Princeton University Press, 1975), 76.

[57] Ibid., 77.

[58] Ibid.

[59] See discussion by C.S. Lewis on this in his first chapter of *Mere Christianity* (San Francisco: Harper Collins, 2001).

In his *Critique of Practical Reason*, Immanuel Kant had previously identified this sense of "oughtness" referring to it as the "categorical imperative;" it is "categorical" in that everyone possesses a category of understanding pertaining to morality and it is "imperative" in that drives one to act upon it (see chapter 17 in *Defending Your Faith* by R.C. Sproul [Wheaton, IL: Crossway Books, 2003]).

[60] Lewis, 10.

[61] Lennox, 53.

In his discussion on the philosophy of scientific reductionism (i.e., reducing scientific problems into smaller and simpler components in order to make investigation simpler) and, in particular, epistemological reductionism (which essentially asserts that "higher level phenomena can be explained by processes at a lower level") Lennox states that "the ultimate goal of such reductionism is evidently to reduce all human behavior—our likes and dislikes, the entire mental landscape of our lives—to physics. This view is called 'physicalism,' a particularly strong form of materialism."

[62] Richard Conniff, "Monkey Wrench," *Smithsonian* 32, no. 7 (2001): 102.

[63] Ibid.

[64] *Astrobiology Magazine*, "Ape vs. Man: Volatile DNA?," http: //www.astrobio.net/ news/article1173.html (accessed August 23, 2007).

[65] Lewis, 6.

[66] Donald R. Glenn, *Ecclesiastes*, in *The Bible Knowledge Commentary* (Old Testament), ed. John F.Walvoord and Roy B. Zuck (Wheaton, IL: Victor Books, 1985), 983.

Glenn notes: "The fact that Solomon utilized polar opposites in a multiple of seven and began his list with birth and death is highly significant. The number seven suggests the idea of completeness and the use of polar opposites—a well-known poetical device called merism—suggests totality (cf. Psalm 139: 2–3)."

[67] Blaise Pascal, *Penses* (New York: Penguin Books, 1983), 146.

[68] C. S. Lewis, *The Weight of Glory* (New York: Harper Collins, 2001), 26.

[79] Ibid., 31–32.

[70] Pascal, 74.

# Section IV

# Alan's Story: The Spiritual Journey of a Friend

It was a little over eight years ago when he first came to work in the financial planning firm where my office is located. He was a twenty-seven-year-old Jewish man, born and raised in Long Island, New York.

Having lived in South Florida for 15 years, I had become quite accustomed to the Jewish culture and the fact that few were Orthodox (devout followers of the Torah), many were conservative (holding firmly to Jewish tradition), and the majority likely were reformed (uniting chiefly in their Jewish ethnicity). Essentially, I had learned that I would never really know where a Jewish individual stands, spiritually, unless I asked!

Alan had not been in our office long before my good friend and principal of the firm, Rob, ended up in a discussion with him about political matters, which in turn ended up in a discussion concerning spiritual matters and, for some reason, ended up with me in the picture. It's not the approach I prefer, so I knew I had to make the best of whatever opportunity could be salvaged from a poor introduction to a discussion about the relevance of God.

What I do remember about that initial interchange, however, is that Alan knew relatively little about his Jewish heritage. Later, I would discover he had not attended synagogue since his bar mitzvah at age 13, something which is not all that unusual among those less than Orthodox. Yet, interestingly, now Alan was beginning to develop an interest in the heritage of his people. It would be at this point that I would attempt to build a bridge of relationship.

I still remember our first lunch together. It was at a new restaurant on the intracoastal waterway across the street from our office. I had made the purpose of our lunch clear to Alan—it was to share with him the background of his people from the perspective of the Jewish Scriptures (our Old Testament). And so I did, setting the backdrop of God's choice for a nation, their significance in history as a vehicle through which God would provide redemption, and, ultimately, the fact that God would culminate world history in the land of Israel.

And it was then that I said something that I had never said to anyone, Jew or Gentile. I looked at Alan and announced, "I have an agenda in our relationship."

If nothing else caught his attention on that particular day, it was evident this statement did! Being a young Jewish guy from New York, he was intuitively programmed to watch for others' agendas. I was pretty sure of this and thought it best to lay it on the line.

I continued. "My desire is for you to someday come to know that Jesus is the Messiah, God's redeemer, of the Jewish people." Ironically, during the years that would follow, Alan would occasionally tell others that I had made my agenda clear. I guess the up front approach was the way to go with a New Yorker; God surely knew!

I am always amazed how God will take the things I say at times—things I've never really even thought about or said before—and use them uniquely in the life of an individual. And so it was in the case of telling Alan my agenda.

That first lunch led to many others, and I came to learn much about Alan and his background. The more I learned, the more I realized how very different our backgrounds were. From a human perspective, the chances of our developing any kind of friendship would have been slim at best. He grew up in New York; I in California. He was Jewish; I was a Gentile. His political persuasion was more liberal; mine more conservative.

Years ago, one of my college professors made a statement that has served me well as I work to develop relationships with those who do not know Christ. Dr. Cook would say: "Christians all too often become relatively related to the absolutes and absolutely related to the relatives." Though the context was different, the principle reflects great wisdom and has broad application. Dr.

Cook was encouraging his students to keep the major issues major—and the minor issues minor. Indeed, when a person does not know Jesus Christ, there is only *one thing* that truly matters and it is what that person does with God's Son. Everything else is secondary.

I do not expect a non-Christian to act or think like a Christian. Accepting that person as he or she is allows me the freedom to build the friendship in order reach that person with the life-transforming message of the Gospel.

Thus, in my relationship with Alan, I never discussed politics and often listened to him convey thoughts about such matters that were a far cry from the way I viewed matters. My focus was on one objective: allowing God to use me as witness to His grace and truth.

As our relationship developed, it became evident that God was using my input to at least some degree. Alan seemed to be thinking more about spiritual things, even though that involved a wide range of considerations. For example, there was a period when he was intrigued by the writings of Deepak Chopra. Yet even at such times, I felt the better policy was to ask pertinent questions than to offer a summary statement of my opinion; my questions, of course, were designed to cause him to consider the inconsistencies of his particular system or worldview.

You may respond, "Deepak Chopra? I don't know anything about the guy, nor would I be able to ask poignant questions relative to the inconsistencies of his religion! So where would that leave me?"

Well, I had never read any of Deepak Chopra's writings, nor did I suggest to Alan that I had. But I was somewhat familiar with Eastern religion and its pantheistic worldview. Given the fact that Alan's introduction to Chopra's philosophy was recent, my understanding of Eastern religion was sufficient to the task, allowing me to ask sufficiently pertinent questions.

My recommendation to you is to learn the fundamental premises of the major worldviews to which you are exposed. Though a worldview may take on various forms in various cultures, the premises generally remain the same, regardless of the messenger.

As a person begins to explore the viability of the existence of God, there can be some interesting twists and turns. Sometimes, it is important for us to allow the person the opportunity to explore the territory, rather than dictate the path. My purpose in asking good questions is to help the individual evaluate the path he or she is traveling and, by God's grace, also allow me the opportunity to present the perspective of God's Word. As you engage in this process, you will be amazed at the clarity of the Christian worldview. No other worldview faces the realities of life with such clarity and explanatory power.

As my relationship with Alan developed, I also had the privilege of getting to know his son, Zach, who had been born to a young woman with whom Alan had a relationship during his years in college. Though he and this woman never married, Alan cared deeply for Zach, never viewing him as an inconvenience but as a son whom he sincerely loved. And it would ultimately be because of Zach that my relationship with Alan would reach another level.

I will never forget that morning when I arrived at the office. It was a typical November day in South Florida—mid-70s, billowy clouds marching across a sea of blue, and rays of sunshine illuminating the palms that lined the street leading to our office building.

As I began to walk up to the doorway of the building, Alan seemed to appear from nowhere. As soon as our eyes met, he hurriedly approached me. "Carmen, I've been trying to reach you. I didn't have your cell number, so I have been attempting to reach Rob to get it. I need your help."

The tone in his voice suggested an urgency I had never heard from Alan. It was clear that he needed to talk, so I suggested we return to my car to give us a private meeting place.

Almost as soon as the doors to the car were closed, Alan broke down and cried. He shared with me that he was deeply concerned about Zach; that there were some issues going on in his life that needed to be addressed, and he wasn't quite sure how to handle them.

As we talked, it became clear that Alan's concerns required someone more knowledgeable than I. It was then that I thought of a very good family friend, Sarah, whose background as a psychologist had allowed her a great deal of wisdom in dealing with similar situations involving kids. Before Alan left my car, I prayed with him and told him I would call my friend immediately.

By the end of the day, Alan and Sarah had connected and an appointment had been set up. And in the weeks that followed, Sarah proved herself an invaluable asset in handling the issues Zach was facing. Clearly, God provided another member of His family to bring assistance. Providentially, Sarah's assistance and Alan's gratitude for that assistance resulted in the creation of a stronger bond in the relationship between Alan and me.

One morning near the end of that year, Alan was talking to me about some of the reading he was doing on spiritual matters. It was all a bit discouraging to me; he definitely didn't seem to be moving in a direction I'd hoped he would. Then, it happened again. I made a recommendation that until that moment I cannot ever recall making to anyone else.

Alan had unresolved questions about who God was, if Jesus was really God's Son, and—at least from my perspective—seemingly innumerable others. Frankly, it felt to me that if Alan was to explore all the questions he was considering while following the path he was pursuing, he would need more than a typical lifetime. So I blurted out, "Alan, why don't you just ask God to help you to know who He is? If you are sincere in this search, He is big enough to defend Himself."

Alan stood still and looked at me. It was as though I had made a profound recommendation. He then smiled and responded, "I think I will! Instead of praying to my brother, I'm going to start praying to God." (Alan's brother had died several years earlier and had been, I supposed, Alan's connection to the supernatural.)

That was the last substantive conversation we had about spiritual things until after the holidays. We did have other conversations about spiritual things, but that one was the most significant. I'm quite convinced you cannot plan it that way; you simply need to be available for God to use you at the time and in the way He chooses. Only God knows of the work *He* is accomplishing in the life of the individual. Sometimes it's obvious to those of us who observe, sometimes absolutely not.

And so it was with Alan. About two months into the new year, a movie was released that featured the story of the five missionaries who had been martyred in Ecuador in the 1950s. From the reviews I'd read, it seemed like the kind of opportunity I needed to help move my discussions with Alan to the next level.

The memory of inviting Alan to see the movie will remain with me for a long time. It was a workday morning, not unlike most others, when Alan walked into my office. But on this particular morning, I knew it was my day to take the lead by inviting him to the movie.

"Alan," I said, "there is a new movie coming out that I would like for us to see. The gist of the movie addresses the question of whether there is something bigger to live for in this life than simply ourselves. It's a true story of five missionaries who went to the jungle of Ecuador to convey a message of God's love, and they were killed for doing so."

Alan immediately responded, "I can't believe you are mentioning this. You cannot imagine all that has been going on in my life. As I've been praying to God, I have seen all these changes, not just on *one* front but on *multiple* fronts! And I've only prayed to Him a couple of times."

Two weeks later, Alan and I went to see the movie. Afterward, as we'd prearranged, we went out to dinner so we could talk about the impact of the movie. That dinner will always remain one of the more memorable dinners of my life, primarily because of Alan's friendship coupled with the realization that God was giving me the awesome privilege of being used by Him in the life of a friend.

Almost as soon as the dinner began, Alan looked across the table and said simply, "Carmen, I now believe there is a God. Too much has happened in my life over the past several months; things that have no other explanation." He went on to convey how he was quite confident God had answered his prayers— specific requests to which he had seen specific answers.

With those remarks, I decided to dig a bit deeper. "So does that mean you want to establish a relationship with God through His Son, Jesus?" I queried.

"God has done so much for me already. I think I'm OK with my relationship with God as it is," Alan replied honestly.

Somehow, I needed to help him see the connection between the two; a relationship with Jesus was not simply an "add on" but an essential part of the package.

"Let me ask you, Alan … who was your favorite president, the one from whose national and economic policies you felt you benefited most?"

"Bill Clinton, I suppose," Alan responded.

I continued with my illustration. "Let's suppose President Clinton was to call you: 'Hey, Alan, this is Bill Clinton. I was wondering if you would be available for dinner some evening.' I suppose you could respond in a couple of ways. You *could* say, 'Well, thanks so much, Mr. President, for the call, but that really won't be necessary. I really did appreciate your terms in office, and I surely liked your policies, but there is no need to get together.' Or you might say, 'Oh, Mr. President! It is such an honor that you have called. It would be my privilege to meet you in person. I benefited so much from your policies during your terms in office; to get to know you *personally* would mean a great deal to me.' Your interest in developing a more personal relationship with President

Clinton would be due to the fact that, even from a distance, you had come to appreciate his work.

"My point is this, Alan: God has accomplished some things in your life that you believe confirm His existence. And now, He wants to invite you to know Him, not just at a distance but *personally*. That is why He provided a way for you to know Him through His Son, Jesus Christ. Alan, if the day comes when you desire to take God up on His offer, what would that look like? In other words, what would you do in order to solidify that relationship?" I knew it was very important at this point to make sure Alan understood what it "looked like" to place trust in Jesus for the work He had accomplished in his place.

Not unexpectedly, Alan responded, "I don't know."

So, not for the first time, I reviewed with Alan the Gospel message—that God created humanity for relationship with Him, yet humans were separated from God and every day confirmed that separation by acts of indifference to and rebellion against God; how God had chosen to place the penalty for our attitudes and actions on His own Son, Jesus; and finally that through placing trust in Jesus for the forgiveness He had paid for by dying in our place (the penalty God had prescribed), we could have acceptance before God.

Though Alan listened intently, I knew this was a decision he needed to make in his own time, as God continued to accomplish His work in Alan's life. I decided to simply leave the door open.

"Alan," I said quietly, "I just want you to promise me one thing. When the day comes that you decide to place your trust, your confidence, in Jesus as God's Son and the work He has accomplished for you, I want you to call me, whether night or day. Or, if it is during the day and at the office, I want you to walk into my office and simply say, 'I'm ready.'"

He agreed, and we both decided it was time to wrap up—one of the more significant dinner conversations of my life had come to an end.

But that conversation would prove to be only the beginning.

Two weeks later, Alan walked into my office.

On Friday, February 17, 2006, Alan placed his trust in Jesus as the Messiah of his people, receiving both perfect forgiveness and acceptance. As the Apostle Paul proclaimed, Alan was now a "new creation in Christ Jesus; the old is gone, the new has come!"

In the months that followed, Alan and I would meet to study God's Word (initially, reviewing the lessons for new Christians, which are provided for your use at the end of this book). His growing commitment to Christ was a privilege to observe; his openness with his friends about his new faith was a joy to behold. A little more than a year later, Alan married a lovely woman who also was a follower of the Messiah (though as a Gentile).

Even as I write, I am reflecting on the passage of Scripture that Alan and I discussed this morning in our study of God's Word. The Apostle Paul writes:

> As we pray to our God and Father about you, we think of your faithful work, your loving deeds, and the enduring hope you have because of our Lord Jesus Christ (I Thessalonians 1: 3 NLT).

In the work of spreading the Gospel throughout the Mediterranean world, God had given Paul associates, like Silas and Timothy, to help him in his mission. But the majority of those associates were those whose lives had been transformed by the Gospel and who, like the apostle, had taken up the torch and carried that message of life and hope to members of their families, as well as those within their culture.

The Thessalonians were like that. Their work for Christ resulted from their faith in God. It was not simply a task; it was a work, effort, or initiative that found its root in love—both for God and for those they cared for so deeply. And even in the toughest of times, either due to familial or political or religious persecution, they stayed the course. Their endurance was noteworthy, for it was founded on the confident expectation that Christ was theirs, and they were Christ's.

And so I commend you to consider the great responsibility that God has placed in your trust. May your faith cause you to take seriously your primary responsibility of representing God and the Gospel of Christ before your family, friends, and all who cross your path. And may you do so out of love—for God and for others—as you, with great confidence, keep your eyes focused on the author of our salvation who will, Himself, one day return to take us to be in His presence.

By God's grace, through the power of His Spirit, be willing to take the initiative to *engage* people for Christ!

# SECTION V

# Appendices

# Engage! Group Study Guide Outline

Using the material in this book to help students *engage!*

[Note: The *Conversation among Two Friends* has been designed to complement the study guide and vice versa. You may choose to use the various conversations as both an introduction to and/or illustration of the material and its use.]

## Objectives

To develop the faith of Christian students by helping them:

- understand foundational truths that set Christianity apart from other worldviews, cults, and religions

- engage their friends in significant conversations about God using the three key questions:

  1. "Is there a God?"

  2. "If so, is He knowable? (Can you have contact and communication with Him?)"

  3. "Have you ever investigated the claims of Jesus Christ and what He said about the role He played in knowing God?"

- lead a friend to understand why belief in God is rational, and faith in Christ is essential.

# Week #1

Focus: Learning to *engage* rather than *react*.
[Dramatic vignette based on Lisa and Ryan conversation in Chapter 12)

Content explored:

1.  Introduce two major questions of Christian students:

    a.  "Can I share my faith without offending my friends?"

    b.  "Is the Christian faith both credible and defensible?"

    (By the end of the course, students will conclude that the answer to both questions in an unequivocal yes!)

2.  Offer overview of three major worldviews: atheism, theism, pantheism.

3.  Address key question: "Can one know, with equal certainty, that which is true in the spiritual realm, even as we know it in the physical realm?" (Use illustration contrasting our society's perception of truth in the spiritual realm versus truth in the physical, as presented in Chapter 5/Melissa's story.)

4.  Challenge students to consider the role God has given them to be His representatives (see 2 Corinthians 5: 20).

5.  Introduce the three questions:

    a.  "Is there a God?"

    b.  "Is He knowable?"

    c.  "Have you ever investigated the claims of Jesus Christ and what He said about the role He played in knowing God?"

    Assignment: Ask three non-Christian peers if they think it is rational to believe in God and why. E-mail responses and questions to group leader. Read chapters 1–3.

# Week #2

Focus: Engaging those who do not believe or are not sure if God exists. [Dramatic vignette based on Ryan and Lisa conversation in Chapter 13)

Discussion: Ask students to share the responses they received when asking the question of their friends, "Is there a God?"

Content explored:

1. How to engage an atheist/agnostic. (Have students give recommendations based on that which they learned through the reading assignment.)

2. Summarize first two sections (cosmology and biology) in chapter 18. (If you have students who have an interest in science, allow them to help you in your presentation.)

3. Make a list of some of the key questions you may wish to ask an atheist/ agnostic in order to engage him or her. Help students think through a couple of questions to ask, initially, in order to determine whether or not the person they have chosen to engage has an interest in conversing about spiritual matters (for example, see the recommendation I make near the end of Jorge's story in chapter 4).

4. Have students role–play, illustrating how they may choose to engage the atheist/agnostic.

Assignment: Have students consider returning to one of the students they "interviewed" previously (e.g., for their first assignment), who claimed either to be an atheist or an agnostic. Have them attempt to continue that conversation in view of what they have just learned. Otherwise, have them find someone new. Students should read chapters 4 and 5.

# Week #3

Focus: Moving those who may not believe (or are not sure) if God exists to a position of openness to explore the possibility that He may.

[Dramatic vignette based on Ryan and Lisa conversation in Chapter 14]

Discussion: Have several students share the conversations they had the previous week.

Content explored:

1.  Discuss how to move an atheist to the position of agnostic and both atheist and agnostic to a position of at least being willing to consider the evidence pertaining to the rationality of belief in a God. (Have students give their input, based on the reading assignment.)

2.  Summarize final three sections (psychology, sociology, philosophy) of Chapter 18. (If you have students who have particular interest in any of the particular subject areas, you may wish to involve them in your presentation.)

3.  Review some of the key questions from these areas. For example:

    a.  "If there is no God, then from where do we have this concept of good and evil? And how can we assess—even on a global basis— the goodness or badness of the actions of others, if there is not some kind of mutually understood standard?" (For example, Lewis' Moral Law Giver discussion.)

    b.  "Is it possible that this sense of purpose all humans seem to possess suggests that we have been designed for something other than mere survival and reproduction of the species?"

    c.  "Why do you and I feel we are someone special and deserve something bigger and better?"

    d.  "Why has humanity, throughout the ages, debated the meaning of life? Shouldn't we be satisfied with having a mate and bearing children if we are simply complex biological organisms?"

4.  Have students work together in groups to list the key points from

each of the areas covered during weeks 2 and 3. Have the groups report and list all responses on a white board.

Assignment: Have students continue their conversation with one of the friends they previously interviewed (e.g., "Hey, that class I've been attending about my faith has caused me to think about some interesting questions. Mind if I get your opinion?"). Students should read chapters 6, 7, and 18.

# Week #4

Focus: Helping students understand how the unique aspects of Christ's life and influence can help even a skeptic more clearly understand the merits of His claims.

[Dramatic vignette based on Ryan & Lisa conversation in Chapter 15]

Discussion: Have students share what they experienced in conversations the preceding week.

Content explored:

1.  Summarize material from chapter 19.

2.  Introduce third key question: "Have you ever investigated the claims of Jesus Christ and what He said about the role He played in knowing God?"

3.  Have students meet in groups and consider how they might move a conversation from the general to specific; how they could move from discussing simple belief in God to considering the evidence of Jesus as potentially being God's revelation of Himself to humanity. List ideas on white board.

4.  Conclude by giving "Lord, Liar, or Lunatic?" illustration found in Jose's story (chapter 11).

5.  Introduce Gospel tract (e.g., *Connecting with God*) or other presentation of the Gospel message that students can use.

Assignment: Have students begin a new conversation or continue an old one, and e-mail results to group leader. Have them read chapters 8, 9, and 19.

# Week #5

Focus: Explore evidence from chapter 20 that demonstrates why the New Testament is a reliable source of information and an accurate record of the life and claims of Jesus.

[Dramatic vignette based on Ryan & Lisa conversation in Chapter 16)

Content explored:

1.  The manuscripts:

    a.  first-century documents (as opposed to Gnostic gospels, etc.)

    b.  pervasive distribution

    c.  explanation concerning variants

2.  The evidence:

    a.  historical

    b.  prophetical

    c.  archaeological

3.  The message

    a.  early manuscripts containing key passages concerning Christ's divinity

    b.  pervasive proclamation of Gospel message (oral culture)

    c.  memory-in-community concept (would prevent apostles from changing message)

4.  Review Gospel presentation (role-play with student would be excellent here. Then have students break into pairs and practice the same).

Assignment: Have students continue conversations. As a matter of information, have students share with their friends new information they learned about the Bible. E-mail responses and questions to instructor. Students should read chapters 10, 11, and 20.

# Week #6

Focus: Present an overview of key insights and illustrations presented during the past five weeks and help students construct a meaningful presentation of the Gospel.

[Dramatic vignette based on Ryan & Lisa conversation in Chapter 17]

Content explored:

1.  Three key questions (students should know these by heart!)

    a.  "Is there a God?"

    b.  "If so, is He knowable?"

    c.  "Have you ever investigated the claims of Jesus Christ and what He said about the role He played in knowing God?"

2.  Broad overview of material covered. (Assign each area to a group of students and have groups present summary.)

    a.  Rational reasons for believing in God

    b.  The uniqueness of the life and claims of Jesus

        i.   His life and words

        ii.  His unique influence

        iii. His resurrection

    c.  The Bible as a reliable source of information

        i.   the authors

        ii.  the manuscripts

        iii. the message

3.  Have students make a list of three friends with whom they have yet to share Christ. Have them commit to praying for these friends on a daily basis.


Assignment: Have students ask God to give them the confidence to engage one of the friends on their list in a spiritual conversation sometime during the next week. Plan one "debrief" session in a month, during which students can report on new conversations as well as surface questions they have found difficult to answer.

# Follow-up Guidelines for New Christians

(Note: The publisher grants permission for the following lessons to be reproduced for individual and non-commercial, ministry purposes)

# CONVERSATIONS WITH NEW CHRISTIANS #1
# REVIEWING YOUR DECISION TO BELIEVE IN JESUS

- ✔ Open with prayer

- ✔ "Let's first review several important ingredients about your decision to believe in Jesus. Then we can answer some of the important questions you may have."

- ✔ Four important ingredients:

**#1**—*Everyone* is sinful (i.e., imperfect in our very nature). Only God is holy (i.e., infinitely perfect in every way). The Bible says: "For all have sinned and have fallen short of God's glory [God's perfect nature]." Mankind's sinfulness is shown by the sins we all commit—lying, cheating, bitterness, hatred, jealousy, unkindness, etc.

**#2**—In the beginning, God created man to have contact and fellowship with Him. Yet because of man's sin, God could not continue having fellowship with mankind as He originally had enjoyed. In fact, man's sinfulness required a penalty. That penalty was death (eternal separation from God). If God had chosen to ignore man's sin, He would have had to reject His own nature. Yet in His great mercy and love, God provided a way to both satisfy His holy (perfect) nature and show His love toward you and me.

**#3**—God's solution is found in the person of Jesus Christ. Jesus was God's Son—the perfect demonstration of God's character. God determined to judge Him in *our* place. Because Jesus lived a perfect life, He could be the perfect payment for our sin! God's prophet Isaiah (who lived 700 years before Jesus's birth) wrote the following:

> "But it was the Lord's good plan to crush him and cause him grief…And because of his experience, my righteous servant will make it possible for many to be counted righteous, for he will bear all their sins" (Isaiah 53: 10a and 12b NLT).

**#4**—Jesus did not remain in His tomb. He came back to life (was "resurrected") to demonstrate that He had obtained victory over the very thing that had caused His death—sin. God now requires all people to believe in His Son, Jesus, as the perfect payment for their sin. Jesus is God's only provision for a present and all-eternity relationship with Him. Those believing in Jesus have been given the privilege of becoming a part of God's family. Let's look at something written by Jesus's follower, John:

> "But to all who believed him and accepted him, he gave the right to become children of God" (John 1: 12 NLT).

✔ **Key Questions:** What does God say in the Bible about your relationship with Him now? Do you think you can trust God to keep His Word? Why don't we pray (talk to God) right now and thank Him for your new relationship with Him?


Next meeting: _____

             Date           Time           Location

# CONVERSATIONS WITH NEW CHRISTIANS #2
# YOUR NEW LIFE IN CHRIST

✔ Pray

✔ **A Key Question:** "Now that I am a part of God's family, what does Jesus do for me?"

Though we will talk about many things that Jesus does for you, one very important thing He does is to give you eternal life. Eternal life is a life lived in relationship with the God who created you. (The Bible calls this relationship a gift from God!) Let's read what Jesus's follower John wrote about this gift of eternal life:

> "My sheep listen to my voice; I know them, and they follow me. I give them eternal life, and they will never perish. No one can snatch them away from me, for my Father has given them to me, and he is more powerful than anyone else. No one can snatch them from the Father's hand. The Father and I are one" (John 10: 27–30 NLT).

Jesus used the example of a shepherd (a common occupation in His day) to illustrate a spiritual truth—the relationship between Him and those who believe in Him.

✔ **Key Questions:** What does Jesus say about those who are His sheep? What does Jesus say He gives His sheep? Can anyone threaten and steal you (one of His sheep)? Who is protecting Jesus's sheep? How does this make you feel?

It was the responsibility of the shepherd to both care for and protect the sheep. In Jesus's case, He gave His life for His sheep to make sure that they would be safe and secure forever! Jesus also said that His Father (God) protects the sheep, too.

(*Notice this*: By saying "I and the Father are one," Jesus claimed equality with God. There are a number of other places in John's writings where Jesus made this same claim, either directly or indirectly.)

✔ **Key Question:** If both Jesus and God the Father are protecting us, is there anyone or anything that can separate us from their love and care?

Why not take just a moment to thank God for His care and protection of you!

Next meeting: _____

                Date            Time           Location

# CONVERSATIONS WITH NEW CHRISTIANS #3
# GROWING IN YOUR NEW RELATIONSHIP / PRAYER

✔ Pray

✔ **A Key Question:** "If it is true that God has given me a new life in Christ, what do I need to do in order to experience all that He has given me?"

As with any friendship, it is important to make sure that you do your part to develop your new relationship with God. One of the most important ingredients of any relationship is communication. We must have contact with the other person if we are going to get anywhere in our relationship with him.

God has made it possible through *prayer* (talking with God) and *the Bible* (hearing from God) to develop our new relationship with Him. God truly desires for us to get to know Him better so that He can help us become all He created us to be.

Let's look at what Jesus taught His followers about *prayer*. Two of Jesus's followers, Matthew and Luke, recorded Jesus's answer to His 12 disciples (close followers) when they asked Him how to pray. Let's look at Matthew's account of the incident, found in his book in the Bible (Matthew 6: 9–13). Why not see if you can find this in your Bible? (Matthew is the first book in the second major division of the Bible called the New Testament—we will learn more about this next time.)

✔ **Key Questions:** In looking back at what you read, what do you think were some of the key ingredients in Jesus's model prayer? Does it encourage you to pray when you think of God as a loving and caring Father?

Perhaps the following summary of some of the important ingredients in Jesus's sample prayer will help you:

**Praise**: praise God for who He is. Give thanks for what He has done for you. (verse 9)

**Affirm**: affirm your desire to see God's work done on this earth and for you to cooperate by choosing to please Him in all that you do. (verse 10)

**Two Requests**: request that God provide life's basic needs for you, your family and friends. Request also that God keep you from sin. (verses 11 and 13)

**Confess**: confess when you have sinned. And be willing to forgive others for what they have done against you. Thank Him, too, for His forgiveness. (verse 12)

Why not take a moment, right now, to pray using the "ingredients" of Jesus's prayer?

Next meeting: _____

              Date           Time          Location

# CONVERSATIONS WITH NEW CHRISTIANS #4
# GROWING IN YOUR NEW RELATIONSHIP / THE BIBLE

✔ Pray

✔ **A Key Question:** "I know that I can talk to God, but how do I hear *from* God? Isn't that an important part of my relationship with Him too?"

Absolutely! That is why God has given us His book, the Bible. Over 40 different individuals wrote the 66 books found in the Bible. And although these men lived over a period of 1,500 years, they wrote with complete agreement. How could this be? The Bible claims to be *inspired* by God, as though God spoke every word Himself. Yes, God directed the thoughts of the human authors so that they accurately recorded, without error, all that God desired to convey to us.

(*Note: It seems incredible that a book like the Bible could truly exist, yet if God is truly God, is there any reason He could not have accomplished such a task?*)

It may be helpful for you to know that the 66 books of the Bible are divided into two major sections: the Old Testament and the New Testament. The Old Testament was originally written in the Hebrew language. It records the history of the nation of Israel and how God prepared that nation for the coming of His Messiah (or Deliverer). There are 39 books in the Old Testament.

The New Testament was originally written in the Greek language. It records the story of the coming of Jesus, the Christ (*Christ* is the Greek word meaning *Messiah;* the Jewish people in Jesus's time were looking for their *Messiah* to deliver them from Roman oppression). It also includes a history of the spread of the Good News about Christ throughout the Mediterranean world during the first century, as well as letters written to groups of Christians during that same time.

✔ **A Key Question:** "Why is it so important for me to read the Bible?"

The Apostle Paul (the word "apostle" means "one sent" by Jesus to spread His Good News) spoke of the importance of the Bible when he wrote:

> "All Scripture ["the writings" given by God] is breathed out by God and profitable for teaching, reproof, for correction and for training in righteousness, that the man of God may be competent, equipped for every good work." (2 Timothy 3: 16,17)

In other words, the Bible is important for the Christian because it is God's "owner's manual" for life. It tells us about God and His truth (*teaching*), when we've done wrong (*reproof*), how to get back on the right track (*correction*), and how to live in a way that is pleasing to God (*training in righteousness*). As a result of reading and applying God's Word to your life, God will be able to use you to accomplish great things for Him.

✔ **A Key Question:** Can you think of any greater privilege and responsibility in life than that of serving the awesome Creator God? Why not take a moment right now to consider setting aside a specific time each day for the next week when you can read the Bible and talk to God?

## Suggested Reading Guide

**Day #1** John 2: 1–11-Jesus turns water into wine.

**Day #2** John 4: 46–54-Jesus cures a government official's son.

**Day #3** John 5: 1–18-Jesus cures a paralytic.

**Day #4** John 6: 6–13-Jesus feeds thousands of people.

**Day #5** John 6: 16–21-Jesus walks on water.

**Day #6** John 9: 1–7-Jesus heals a blind man.

**Day #7** John 11: 1–45-Jesus restores life to a man named Lazarus.

Set aside just 15 minutes each day to read the part of the Bible listed and to pray. (Remember Jesus's model prayer from last time?) As you read, keep the following in questions in mind:

- What is going on? What is being said? Who is involved?
  (This is the art of <u>observation.</u>)

- Why is this important? Why did the writer choose to include *this* story or conversation? What is the *main* point of this passage?
  (This is the art of <u>interpretation.</u>)

- How can I apply what I have learned? Have I learned something new about God, about Jesus, or about my relationship with Him?
  (This is the art of <u>application.</u>)

## When I'd like to read and pray:

_____

When?                              Where?

Next meeting: _____

            Date          Time         Location

# CONVERSATIONS WITH NEW CHRISTIANS #5
# GOD'S INDWELLING SPIRIT

✔ Pray

✔ **Key Question:** "I know that I now have a relationship with God, but sometimes I don't feel much different from before. What do I need to do?"

It may surprise you, but it is not just difficult but impossible for you to live the Christian life. You must depend on God's help! In fact, on the night before He was crucified, Jesus told His disciples, "apart from me you can do *nothing*" (John 15: 5).

✔ **Key Question:** If Jesus was leaving this earth and *knew it* (don't forget—Jesus's death for us was part of God's plan), how could He help His disciples? Was He planning to leave them helpless?

Absolutely not! In fact, Jesus told His disciples that He was going to ask His Father to send God's personal representative (the Holy Spirit) to be with them in His absence. Knowing that He would not be with them much longer, He wanted them to understand that although He would not be with them physically, God's Spirit would be with them spiritually. Read the following words of Jesus as recorded by John:

> "And I will ask the Father, and he will give you another Advocate, who will never leave you. He is the Holy Spirit, who leads into all truth. The world cannot receive him, because it isn't looking for him and doesn't recognize him. But you know him, because he lives with you now and later will be in you" (John 14: 16–18 NLT).

Even as Jesus, God's Son, possesses all the qualities of God, so does the Holy Spirit. The Bible teaches us there is one God. Yet God has chosen to reveal Himself as three Persons—God the Father, God the Son, and God the Holy Spirit. Each divine "Person" possesses all the qualities of God, though each is often shown to accomplish special responsibilities in the fulfillment of God's great plan.

One of the unique responsibilities of the Holy Sprit is to accomplish God's desired work within the life of the Christian. This does not mean that Christ or the Father does not share in that presence, only that it is the Holy Spirit who has been determined to help the Christian live a life pleasing to God and to experience the qualities of a "God-filled" life.

> [**Note:** Even in the paragraph cited above from John 14, Jesus ends by saying "I will not leave you as orphans; *I will come to you.*" During the same conversation with His disciples (verse 23), Jesus said that both He *and His Father* would make their home in the life of the believer. The relationship shared between the Father, the Son, and the Spirit is such that the presence of one assumes the presence of the others.]

✓   **Key Question:** How does it make you feel, knowing that God is living within you right now? Does it challenge you, encourage you, or make you a bit nervous? Consider this: The God who loved you enough to send His own Son to give His life for you has placed His Spirit to live within you so that you can be all that God designed you to be! Now, how do you feel about that?

Why not take the next few days to learn more about the Holy Spirit's work from what Jesus said? As you read, ask yourself three questions:

- What does Jesus say about the Spirit? To whom or about whom is He speaking? (Observation)

- What did Jesus mean by what He said? (Interpretation)

- What do Jesus's words mean to me? (Application)

Once again, your daily Bible reading will be from John's Gospel (*Gospel* means "good news").

# Suggested Reading Schedule

**Day #1**  John 3: 5–8

**Day #2**  John 7: 37–39

**Day #3**  John 14: 25–26

**Day #4**  John 15: 26–27

**Day #5**  John 16: 7–11

**Day #6**  John 16: 12–15

If you didn't set aside a specific time last week to read God's Word and pray, why not do so this week? Hearing from God and talking with Him is such an important part of your relationship with God. It is a great privilege not to be taken for granted.

When I'd like to read and pray:

_____

When?                              Where?

Next meeting: _____

Date             Time             Location

# CONVERSATIONS WITH NEW CHRISTIANS #6
# THE IMPORTANCE OF OBEDIENCE

✓  Pray

✓  **Key Question:** "I now know that God's Spirit lives within me and that it is His job to help me become all God desires. But shouldn't I be doing something as well?"

Absolutely! Your responsibility as a Christian is to follow all that Jesus modeled and taught. During the same discussion Christ had with His followers about the Holy Spirit (see last lesson), He also added an important caveat that would influence one's relationship with Him:

> "All who love me will do what I say. My Father will love them, and we will come and make our home with each of them. Anyone who doesn't love me will not obey me. And remember, my words are not my own. What I am telling you is from the Father who sent me" (John 14: 23–24 NLT).

One of the most important responsibilities you now have is to consistently follow and obey Christ's teachings. It is our obedience to Christ that demonstrates our love for Christ! And it is obedience to the teachings of Christ that pleases God as well.

In fact, Jesus taught that the Christian who obeys all He taught is one within whom both the Father and Son feel perfectly at home. It is the obedient Christian who experiences the fullness of a life lived in friendship with God.

After Jesus's resurrection, He spent many days with His disciples, teaching them. As a result, Christ's teachings are reflected in the Gospels (Matthew, Mark, Luke, and John) as well as the many other books of the New Testament. For our Bible reading this week, we will focus on some of Jesus's teachings reflected in a letter written by the Apostle John (one of Jesus's closest friends).

Even as it was the Holy Spirit's job to help bring these teachings back to the disciples' memory so that they could write them down (see John 14: 26), so it is His job to help us understand the Bible today. Yes, the Bible is the world's only book that comes with its own Instructor!

✓ **Key Question:** "So what happens when I sin? As much as I would like to obey Christ always, I have to admit that even since becoming a Christian I have done things that are wrong. What do I do?"

Later in his life, the Apostle John, wrote about this very important issue to the Christians of his day (first century AD) when he said:

"If we confess our sins, He is faithful and just to forgive us our sins and to cleanse us from all unrighteousness" (I John 1: 9). This first letter of John's is located near the end of the Bible.

When we disobey God, it is important to do three things:

#1—**Admit** to God you've sinned ("confess" means "to say the same thing" about your sin as God does).

#2—**Accept** God's forgiveness. Jesus paid God's price for *all* our sins. Because of this, God is *faithful* (consistent) and *just* (right) to forgive us.

#3—**Affirm** to God your desire to follow Christ's example and teachings in all you do. Ask Him to give you the strength to live in a way pleasing to Him. Remember: the Holy Spirit is there to help.

**Idea:** If you have never confessed your sins to God, you may wish to write all your known sins on a piece of paper. When finished, write the words of I John 1: 9 across the page. As you look at each sin you've written, admit to God you've sinned. *Thank Him* that He has forgiven you for *all* that you have done wrong. Ask Him to give you the strength to live a Christian life in growing obedience. Then tear up the paper and throw the pieces away.

✓ **Key Question:** Can you think of anywhere else you can receive forgiveness such as this? How does this make you feel about God? Does it want to make you serve God more or less? Why?

Since you have already become acquainted with John's first letter (I John), let's focus our reading for the week on this very important book. Do you remember some of the important questions to ask as you read? If not, go back and review the questions at the end of Lesson #4.

## Suggested Reading Schedule

**Day #1**   I John 1: 1–7

**Day #2**   I John 1: 8–2: 2

**Day #3**   I John 2: 3–17

**Day #4**   I John 2: 28–3: 3

**Day #5**   I John 3: 16–18

**Day #6**   I John 4: 11–21

**Day #7**   I John 5: 11–15

When I'd like to read and pray:

_____

When?                                    Where?

Next meeting: _____
                    Date            Time            Location

# CONVERSATIONS WITH NEW CHRISTIANS #7
# BEING A MEMBER OF THE FAMILY

✔ Pray

✔ **Key Question:** "I am beginning to understand more about the importance of my relationship with God. But from reading I John, it also
seems as though my relationship with *other Christians* is also important. What, exactly, is my relationship now to others who also believe
in Jesus?"

Simply stated, you are now a part of *God's* family! In the Gospel of John
we read:

> "But to all who believed him and accepted him, he gave the
> right to become children of God. They are reborn—not with
> a physical birth resulting from human passion or plan, but a
> birth that comes from God" (John 1: 12,13 NLT).

That means that other Christians are now your brothers and sisters.
Just imagine—if you were not from a large family, you are now! But
more importantly, you are part of a family that is designed to help you
become all God desires.

It is for this reason that *love* is such an important factor in God's family,
as it is in any family. While on this earth, Jesus told His disciples:

> "So now I am giving you a new commandment: Love each
> other. Just as I have loved you, you should love each other.
> Your love for one another will prove to the world that you are
> my disciples" (John 13: 34–35 NLT).

Love is the rule that is to govern God's family. In fact, Jesus felt so
strongly about this that He considered Christians' love for one another
as a visible indicator of whether they were truly His followers.

Yes, it is to be in a family environment, where love is the rule, that you
and I, as Christians, are encouraged to experience all God has created
for us. In God's family, we all need each other!

It is for this reason that God gives each and every family member (you're
included) particular gifts and abilities that help him or her build up

and encourage the *spiritual growth* of other Christians. The Bible tells us that God gives special gifts to each of us so that we can have a meaningful role in His family. Some family members teach the Bible, others show mercy, some always seem meet the needs of others, while others help provide correction when needed.

> **Idea:** Why not begin to ask God to show you what gift(s) He has given you? During the next few months, begin to seriously think about abilities you have and how they can be used to help build the members of God's family.

> **Key Question:** "I have known some Christians who don't show God's love at all. Where do *they* fit in with this picture?"

There are surely many people who say they are Christians but who are not. Remember: a Christian is not someone who just attends a church or who is raised in a Christian family (that's a common misconception). The word Christian refers to a person who is a follower of Jesus Christ and accepts His teachings as from God. According to the Bible, for one to be a Christian he or she must place personal trust in Jesus as God's Son and accept His death as the only means of payment for sin resulting in separation from God.

But you are right! There are Christians who do not always act like Christians.

Even as in a biological family (where the parents and children are related physically), so it is in God's family (where everyone is related spiritually through faith in Christ). Some members are "older" or more mature than others. That means that some are going to act like Christians more than others do.

Yet it is out of love (a commitment to the well-being of the other person) that you and I are to encourage our brothers and sisters in Christ, even as they are to do the same for us. True, sometimes encouragement involves criticism. Yet even a word of criticism can be offered out of love, if done with the proper attitude. Above all, our goal is to help each and every one of our brothers and sisters show by how they live that Jesus is God's Son!

✔ **Key Question:** "I don't really have many Christian friends. How do I begin to develop relationships with the members of my new family?"

Begin by asking the Christian friend who helped you come to know Jesus or even with the friend who is helping guide you through this study. Have that person introduce you to some of his or her Christian friends. Some may even meet on a regular basis at the school you attend.

Also, ask them to take you to the church they attend. The word "Church" (when spelled with a capital "C") is really another word for "God's family." We use it most often today, however, to refer to the particular places where Christians meet for the purposes of worshipping God, studying the Bible, and getting to know other followers of Jesus. A good church is a great place to begin developing the kind of relationship with the members of God's family as described above.

**Idea:** For your next meeting, why not plan to go with your Christian friends to the church they attend?

Next meeting: _____
                        Date              Time              Location

**Suggested Reading Schedule:** Pick your own! Since you are familiar with the writing of the Apostle John, a good place to begin reading would be the Gospel of John. It will give you an even better understanding of the life of Jesus and all that He did for you and me.

# Recommended Resources

## Books

Bock, Darrell L. *The Missing Gospels: Unearthing the Truth behind Alternative Christianities.*

Nashville: Nelson Books, 2006.

Copan, Paul. *True for You, But Not for Me.* Minneapolis: Bethany House, 1998.

Corduan, Winfried. *Neighboring Faiths.* Downers Grove: Intervarsity Press, 1998.

Lewis, C.S. *Abolition of Man.* San Francisco: Harper San Francisco, 2001.

_____. *Mere Christianity.* San Francisco: Harper San Francisco, 1980.

Lennox, John. *God's Undertaker: Has Science Buried God?* Oxford: Lion Hudson, 2007.

Komoszewski, J. Ed, M. James Sawyer and Daniel B. Wallace. *Reinventing Jesus: How Contemporary Skeptics Miss the Real Jesus and Mislead Popular Culture.* Grand Rapids: Kregal Publications, 2006.

Pearcey, Nancy. *Total Truth.* Wheaton: Crossway Books, 2004.

Pascal, Blaise. *Pensees.* New York: Penguin Books, 1983.

Schaeffer, Francis. *The God Who Is There.* Downers Grove: InterVarsity Press, 1968.

Strobel, Lee. *The Case for Christ*. Grand Rapids: Zondervan, 1998.

_____. *The Case for a Creator*. Grand Rapids: Zondervan, 2004.

Zacharias, Ravi K. *Jesus among Other Gods*. Nashville: W Publishing Group, 2000.

*The Ryrie Study Bible*. Charles Caldwell Ryrie, ed. Chicago: Moody Press, 1995.

# CDs

Moreland, J.P. *The Case for Christianity*. Available through the Christian Apologetics Department, Biola University, La Mirada, CA 90639.

_____. *Intelligent Design: Explaining the Controversy*. Available through the Christian Apologetics Department, Biola University, La Mirada, CA 90639.

Zacharias, Ravi K. *The Ohio State VERITAS Forum*. Available through Ravi Zacharias International Ministries, Norcross, GA 30092. www.rzim.org.

_____. *The Spurious Glitter of Pantheism*. Available through Ravi Zacharias International Ministries, Norcross, GA 30092. www.rzim.org.